CONSCIOUSNESS AND INTENTIONALITY

ADVANCES IN CONSCIOUSNESS RESEARCH

ADVANCES IN CONSCIOUSNESS RESEARCH provides a forum for scholars from different scientific disciplines and fields of knowledge who study consciousness in its multifaceted aspects. Thus the Series will include (but not be limited to) the various areas of cognitive science, including cognitive psychology, linguistics, brain science and philosophy. The orientation of the Series is toward developing new interdisciplinary and integrative approaches for the investigation, description and theory of consciousness, as well as the practical consequences of this research for the individual and society.

Series A: Theory and Method. Contributions on the development of theory and method in the study of consciousness.

Volume 27

Grant R. Gillett and John McMillan

Consciousness and Intentionality

CONSCIOUSNESS AND INTENTIONALITY

GRANT R. GILLETT
Dunedin School of Clinical Medicine
JOHN MCMILLAN
University College Oxford

JOHN BENJAMINS PUBLISHING COMPANY
AMSTERDAM/PHILADELPHIA

TM The paper used in this publication meets the minimum requirements of American National Standard for Information Sciences — Permanence of Paper for Printed Library Materials, ANSI Z39.48–1984.

Library of Congress Cataloging-in-Publication Data

Gillet, Grant, 1950-
Consciousness and intentionality / Grant R. Gillet, John McMillan.
p. cm. -- (Advances in consciousness research, ISSN 1381-589X ; v. 27)
Includes bibliographical references (p.) and index.
1. Consciousness. 2. Intentionality (Philosophy). I. McMillan, John. II. Title. III. Series.
B808.9.G55 2000
126--dc21 00-063052
ISBN 90 272 5147 9 (Eur.) / 1 55619 997 x (US) (alk. paper) CIP

John Benjamins Publishing Co. • P.O.Box 75577 • 1070 AN Amsterdam • The Netherlands
John Benjamins North America • P.O.Box 27519 • Philadelphia PA 19118-0519 • USA

Contents

Introduction

Many recent philosophical discussions of the mind and semantics have attempted to naturalise intentionality. Philosophers such as Millikan and Dretske attempt to show that intentionality involves representational systems and that they have proper functions understandable in biological terms. This implies that we can get some naturalistic purchase upon the problem of misrepresentation and how we might give naturalistic accounts of consciousness. In addition to recent attempts to naturalise intentionality many philosophers have treated the problem of oblique contexts and the failure to carry over truth assignments into oblique contexts as the full extent of the philosophical significance of intentionality.

Consciousness and Intentionality is not an attempt to give a naturalized account of intentionality, at least not in an evolutionary sense, nor is it an investigation of the importance of intentionality for philosophical logic. We take Franz Brentano's suggestion that "intentionality is the mark of the mental" seriously and investigate the implications of intentionality for a phenomenological understanding of the structures of consciousness and its contents. Our ambition throughout this essay is to show that without consciousness we cannot understand our ability to have contentful thoughts and without objects with which we can intentionally engage to form contents for thoughts consciousness is idle or vacuous. This emphasis upon phenomenology and intentionality means that our project has many of the same concerns as the continental tradition.

For many philosophers the topics of consciousness and qualia are closely related to one another but this makes the whole thing very difficult to get a grip on. Qualia are the raw feels that accompany conscious experience. As such they are part of what it is like to be a creature of a given conscious sort. We have approached the contents of consciousness through their intentionality because it is not clear that there is anything more distinctly mental to qualia than there is to the experience of having a brick land on your foot. It is clear that when one is conscious and has some bodily event happen to one then one goes through something in a way that one would not if a similar event happened to somebody else. However it is not clear that this is because of a private inner feel to the experience rather than the fact that it is this body upon which the events impinged. To be conscious is to be subject to (or the subjectivity affected by) what happens to a given body in a way that goes beyond the reactions of the body as a purely physical system but this may reflect no more than the intentional content of events experienced in the first person rather than the third. The fact that one cannot capture and convey the actual event as experienced does not necessarily depend on a feature of the event that is mental any more than the fact that having a brick drop on one's foot is not something that happens to another as a result of a description of that event. This is because one's subjectivity is embodied in a particular body and no other body and is as closely related to the events befalling that body as one's visual perspectives on objects are to one's geometrical relations to objects in the world. We have irreducible perspectives and irreducible feels from the first person perspective but these are perhaps the most easily appreciated aspects of the experiential trajectory of another. One can almost taste the chocolate that another indulgently devours; what one cannot so easily do is see significant and complex experiences as they are seen by another unless one has appreciated the relevant tract of their narrative. Of course, one's narrative goes beyond simple experiences just as one's trajectory through space goes beyond a static or momentary position with respect to some orienting point in the environment. Qualia are what happens when things really happen to you rather than your just thinking about them and arguably that is just like being bruised by the brick hitting your foot rather than watching it hit your friend's foot.

We will begin in Chapter 1 by outlining the problems that are created for an explanation of meaning if the view that consciousness involves the awareness of essentially private states is adopted. These problems prompt us to postulate a publicity requirement for meaning. The publicity requirement must not only provide a means by which mental content can be accessible but must also be consistent with the sophistication typically associated with adult thought and language.

In Chapter 2 we provide an explanation of how fully developed thought and language can be accommodated within an externalised account of meaning. Sophistication of thought and language is accompanied by sophistication of activity. We will draw upon the Wittgenstein's later work, in particular his famous dictum that "meaning is use".

The relationship between consciousness and objects in the world is a fundamental question for epistemology and metaphysics. In Chapter 3 we defend the view that being conscious of objects in the world involves conceptually mediated relationships between a thinker and objects. This position is one that contrasts with both the traditional empiricist view that consciousness involves relationships between a thinker, a representational object, and a state of affairs and the naive realist view that consciousness involves a direct relationship between a thinker and a state of affairs.

In Chapter 4 we apply our earlier claims about the nature of consciousness and mental content to an analysis of action. We defend two central theses: actions have intentional content and actions are purposive. Both of these theses have implications for how those parts of psychology concerned with human action should be understood. Because of the relations holding between action, intentionality and consciousness there is a relationship between the concepts at a person's disposal and what operations they can perform in the world. This means that there is also a relationship between action and a person's social environment. The nature of this relationship is the topic of Chapter 5, where we argue for a number of related theses. Restrictions and constraints that apply to thought and consciousness arise from the relations between human beings in the shared environment and their relation to nature. The environment that we live in is a holistic context for social being. Actions are given sense by the social institutions in which they take place. Important features of self are formed by locating oneself in a discourse where dimensions of self are perceived, responded to, and used as the basis for defining one's position among others and shaping one's conduct in the world.

Those who want to defend the view that social environment is an important determinant of the mind ought to be able to respond to the fact that the mind is the brain and that the brain has evolved in accordance with environmental demands. Any account of consciousness and intentionality that is inconsistent with such a commonly accepted fact will be prima facie implausible. In Chapter 6 we defend the view that the brain is a semantic organ. Because of the relationship between concepts, consciousness and society which we have established in earlier chapters proper brain function requires the active engagement of a mind in a social environment and the understanding of brain function involves an appreciation of that relationship.

In Chapter 7 we will consider what an investigation of intentionality yields for an account of animal consciousness. A phenomenologically informed account of intentionality can further the debate over the consciousness of animals. Animals can be conscious and do exhibit intentionality. The question is in what ways are animal consciousness and intentionality distinct from that which we expect of human beings. We think that a useful distinction can be drawn between thick and thin representations and we argue that animals are best thought of as exhibiting thin conscious states. Thick representations are those that have contents that are both accessible to the subject and are conveyable to other minds.

Chapter 8 investigates a number of apparent anomalies for a general account of consciousness and intentionality. It also includes a discussion of the Freudian unconscious, which is an attempt to show not only how an intentional account of consciousness can do justice to the apparent anomaly of the unconscious but also to show how our view of intentionality can offer a plausible explanation of the unconscious influences on our thinking and behaviour.

Chapter 1

Consciousness and intentionality Foundations

> We understand under Intentionality the unique peculiarity of experiences "to be the consciousness of something" (Husserl 1931 SS 223)

Is there a conceptual, internal, or *a priori* relationship between consciousness and intentionality? Husserl's claim forms part of a tradition that maintains that there is such a relationship and that it is a useful place to begin a philosophical account of consciousness. If one were seeking to explore this relationship one would have to show that the two concepts, when their conceptual structure is analysed, are in some sense co-dependent. Thus, for instance, one might show that the concepts of bachelor and marriage are co-dependent in the requisite way because grasping the content of one immediately makes available to the thinker the content of the other. Another example of the co-dependence that holds in an internal relation might be the idea of morality and the concept of the good; an analysis of one must mention or carry implications for the other. The phenomenological school of philosophy has traditionally claimed that there is an internal relationship between consciousness and intentionality although the relationship is not so obvious or straightforward as the bachelor/marriage case. Despite the fact that it may not be obvious, any orthodox phenomenologist would regard it as an internal or conceptual relationship rather than some looser contingent or genetic association.

In the first section we will lay some foundations by giving an account of consciousness that allows us to attempt to defend and provide a plausible interpretation of the phenomenological claim. We will then spell out some implications of this conceptual relation for a theory of consciousness and a philosophical understanding of the nature of intentionality.

Consciousness

We need first to give in outline some philosophical analysis of consciousness. The one we offer has obvious connections with Wittgenstein's later philosophy and is anti-Cartesian in its major tenets. The outline will be filled in, elaborated, and defended at greater length throughout the rest of the book.

> Acts of consciousness are directed upon objects such that one cannot investigate the acts independently of their objects; and objects are always objects for consciousness such that one cannot investigate objects independently of investigating the conscious acts of which they are objects. (Hammond, Howarth and Keat, 1991: pp. 48–9)

Some initial moves are required to sketch the relation between our view of consciousness and the topics of thought, meaning, and mental content. Our second section will broach the topic of intentionality and its relation to the contents of thought. This allows us to pursue some conceptual underpinnings for the relation between intentionality and concepts and the intimately connected relation between concepts and language — a topic we shall explore in more depth in our second chapter. In our third section we will draw further on the phenomenological tradition in philosophy to say something about the structure of consciousness and the nature of self consciousness.

The "Cartesian" view of consciousness

Wittgenstein makes the following startling claim

> Consciousness is as clear in his face and behaviour as it is in my own case (Wittgenstein 1967)

This view sounds counterintuitive because most of us are closet "Cartesians" in that we believe that consciousness is a private mental state. The term "private" implies that a subject has privileged and direct access to her own conscious experience but others only have indirect access. Indeed an implication of this view is that conscious experience could be more or less intact but inaccessible to others and unassociated with any manifestations in terms of responsiveness to the world. If Wittgenstein is correct his view is not unproblematically true. One plausible reading of it is that it is a pattern of animated and flexible responsiveness to the world that grounds ascriptions of consciousness so that the typical case is one where we can recognize each other as conscious beings unless some disorder disrupts the natural connections between experience and behaviour which underpin our grasp of mental concepts. Given our intuitive leanings toward Cartesianism, we might, however, be more favourably disposed toward this view if the Cartesian conception ran into insurmountable philosophical difficulties.

Cartesian conceptions of the mind accept the premise that my thoughts are in my head and essentially private to me and yours are similarly internal and private to you. I can, however, communicate my thoughts to you by using language. Therefore the theory holds, with Locke and Frege (among many others), that my "inner thought" gives meaning to my words and your inner thought is the basis of your understanding of my words (1977: pp.4–5). But how is it that I know what you mean? I cannot see what thoughts accompany your words and therefore I do not know what they mean. I cannot assume that my understanding bears anything more than a fortuitous relationship to your meaning because there seems to be no essential relationship between my thoughts and yours. On the Cartesian view we have no way of detecting the meanings that lie behind our words and therefore no way of knowing what to make of what another person says.

This, however, is a disturbing conclusion because it implies that we have no justified expectation of achieving a shared conception of truth. To be justified we would need to have some reason to believe that you and I mean the same thing when we say this or that. Consider, for example, a remark such as "That cat is black." On the Cartesian view, what this remark actually means is given by the thought it expresses. Thus, for all you know I might have the thoughts that go with your words "The dog is white" when I say "The cat is black". This implies that what I say or think could be true while what you say (or think) using the same words, is false. Frege argues that this is an intolerable conclusion because scientific knowledge is built on the presumption that what is true is true for anyone who thinks it and that the truth can be communicated and understood by different thinkers. If, however, what a person thinks when she reports a scientific result or writes an essay such as this is possibly opaque to her audience because they cannot ascertain the connection between the words and their meaning-giving inner states, then a foundation for scientific inquiry in clear communication of thoughts is undermined. For this reason, Frege claims that the communication of thoughts and therefore the determination of truth cannot depend on what he calls "men's varying states of consciousness"(1977: p. 17). His objection seems damning if we do think of our thoughts and words as contentful in virtue of acts of consciousness as conceived according to the traditional "inner state" conception. It follows from that theory that the truth as held by you or me depends on inner states and our apparent store of objective knowledge about the world could be based on nothing more than guesswork about the thoughts behind the words of others. The theory seems to imply there may be no essential connection between what I hear and what you mean.

This conclusion is, of course, not meant to be taken seriously; it is as absurd as it is unavoidable on the Cartesian model which informs our common conceptions of consciousness and its mysteries. We therefore need an alternative understanding of consciousness which explains the fact that we can communicate, without systematic ambiguity, about contentful conscious experience. We might be encouraged to seek such an understanding by considering Husserl's worry about inner objects as the objects to which consciousness is directed.

> I perceive the thing, the object of nature, the tree there in the garden; that and nothing else is the real object of the perceiving "intention". A second immanent tree, or even an "inner image" of the real tree that stands out there before me, is nowise given, and to suppose such a thing by way of assumption leads only to absurdity. (Husserl, 1931: p. 243)

It is the need for consciousness to somehow get out into the public world that makes it worth the trouble to visit (albeit briefly) the intellectual bloodbath surrounding the private language argument.

The private language argument

In the section referred to as the private language argument, Wittgenstein draws together strands from the early parts of the *Philosophical Investigations* (PI).[1] These strands concern the argument that meaning is use, the idea of rule following, and the central importance of "agreement in judgements" (PI #241) in any theory of meaning and truth.[2] What Wittgenstein seeks to establish is

---

1. We shall throughout use the initials PI to refer to *Philosophical Investigations* (ed. Anscombe) Oxford: Blackwell, 1989 and use #nn to refer to paragraph numbers within that work. Similarly we will use Z #nn in a parallel way for *Zettel* (ed. Anscombe and von Wright) Oxford: Blackwell, 1967. The relevant section is usually taken to be PI #243–315 (Hacker 1986).

2. The summary nature of the argument as identified by Hacker causes Kripke to locate it in PI #143–242.

that it is not plausible to believe that a person can speak, reason, and have thoughts about objects which are only ever experienced in one person's own private conscious world. This is grist to the phenomenological mill because if mental contents are not private in that way then there is something wrong with the traditional Cartesian picture and one might be able to forge an essential and typical link between consciousness and the public sphere of objects like trees (to recall Husserl's example). The argument centrally concerns language and assumes a certain internal relation between language and thought that we shall examine in more detail in our next chapter.

Meaning is use

Given that Husserl is quite prepared to move quite freely between the meaning of an act of consciousness and its contents, we can help ourselves to the possibility of approaching the idea of mental contents through the apprehension of word meaning (as mooted by Frege's objection above). Wittgenstein's first major claim in PI is that understanding what a word means is a matter of correct use. He remarks:

> For a large class of cases — though not for all — in which we employ the word "meaning" it can be defined thus: the meaning of a word is its use in the language.(PI #43)

Thus, if someone were to say "Get me the book!" and I got the newspaper, there would be some doubt about my understanding of the term "book". If the person asking me wanted to check up on my understanding of the term "book", then she might ask "Do you know what a book is?" or ask me to say whether or not certain things she showed me were books. If I failed to demonstrate any familiarity with the use of "book" in real life situations such as these, then she would be entitled to conclude, from my failure to use the term properly, that I did not understand it. I would, to use Husserl's term, have violated the norm associated with the idea of a book (1931: p. 229). Thus, we could say, with Wittgenstein, that the criterion of understanding is correct use of the concept and that, in the general run of things, correct use is a publicly accessible fact about the thinker.

In fact, when you try to give any other definition of understanding it fails. For instance, an obvious candidate is the Cartesian inner idea or image associated with the word (which we have already criticized on Fregean grounds). A further and more direct criticism of that view emerges if you consider the following scenario. The person whose understanding is in question says "I am trying to understand what you mean by 'book' but I can't concentrate because this image of a thing with two covers and pages inside it keeps distracting me". Obviously the person has an appropriate image in their head and, *ex hypothesi*, the image comes to mind when the term "book" is mentioned but he does not know how to use whatever is occurring to him and therefore he cannot be said to understand the meaning of "book". By contrast, he would be said to understand if, in the relevant circumstances, he responded in the right kind of way or exhibited an ability to make correct use of the term "book".

Rules

When we reflect on what is required to latch on to the meaning or sense of a word or phrase (or the idea that is normatively associated with it) it becomes clear that there is a set of informal and perhaps inchoate rules that must be obeyed.[3] The rules, *inter alia*, determine what kinds of things the word should be applied to and what linguistic links fill in its meaning. Obeying a rule, we could argue — with Wittgenstein, is a matter of mastering a practice or technique (PI #202). Such mastery is gained by using the relevant term in such a way that one's mistakes and successes are manifest and can be corrected, usually through communicative interaction with others (Gillett 1995). That mastery also involves, as Husserl persistently reminds us in relation to what he calls noetic content, a perceived object in the actual world, and not an immanent, private, or mental entity (1931: p. 242). Indeed if I am to correct you by appeal to something it must be something to which we both have access. Wittgenstein concludes:

> Hence it is not possible to obey a rule 'privately': otherwise thinking one was obeying a rule would be the same thing as obeying it. (PI #202)

In the present context the important claim is that some sufficiency of correct application (not to be understood as logical sufficiency) and discursive knowledge has to be present for a person to count as understanding a concept. Thus

---

3. It is important to stress here that we have in mind the 'rules of use for language' as opposed to 'rules of language'. While we are not always immediately aware of the rules of use for language nor easily able to articulate them they are after thought and reflection articulable. If the Chomskians are correct then there are 'rules of language' that most of us are never aware of that are the foundation for language. We are grateful to Maxim Stamenov for pointing out the importance of this distinction to us.

the cognitive or discursive grasp of any rule is predicated on the actual use that one is able to make of it in practice. This is important because it suggests that a key aspect of thinking — understanding the meanings of words — is something that is tied to the public domain. We should not leap to the conclusion that there is no role for the noetic subject however, because an act of thought or intentional act is relational and includes an implicit reference to the thinker through "the way in which the perceived object with its distinguishing features is presented" (Husserl 1931: p. 236).

And here we should note that Wittgenstein's argument also implies that the meaning of any word at all, including mental predicates such as "conscious" is determined by something public. The public nature of meaning brings us to our third point in setting up the private language argument.

Agreement in judgements

When does a person count as having mastered the rule-governed ability to make use of a term? When he has achieved a sufficient level of agreement in judgements with others who have mastered the relevant ability or practice. For instance, Arlo would count as a person who grasped the concept ⟨square⟩ when he is able reliably to judge ⟨that figure is square⟩, ⟨this is not square⟩, ⟨a square is a four-sided plane figure⟩ and so on. Such an ability, evident in Arlo's use of propositions containing the term "square" would both exhibit and, in part, constitute, a grasp of the concept ⟨square⟩. Thus Arlo's understanding of the sense or meaning of the relevant word — or grasp of the related concept — goes hand in hand with exchanges in which his judgements are manifest to others and corrected by them so as to allow him to develop a sense of the difference between right and wrong use. The result of this process is that Arlo gradually converges with the judgements of those who already understand the concept he is trying to learn.

These reflections (tying understanding and meaning to rules and thereby to communicability and corrigibility) have important implications both for our view of what it is to have contentful conscious experience and for our use of mental terms such as "anger", "seeing something red", "being in pain" and "conscious". First, they imply that conscious experience and the categorization or conceptualisation of its contents are tied to participation in a public milieu where a thinker has learnt rules governing the use of concepts. As a corollary of this, it emerges that a thinker's use of concepts to make sense of her experiences is built upon her being with other minds and their interactions with her. We shall see that this, in turn, leads to a fairly strong endorsement of Wittgenstein's anti-Cartesianism and the nature of intentionality.

Wittgenstein and consciousness

Wittgenstein had some very instructive things to say about consciousness and the mind. These things make plausible his anti-Cartesian view of the mind and give us a basis on which we can develop our understanding of the relation between consciousness and intentionality. One or two preliminaries are in order.

First, one can be *conscious simpliciter* or *conscious of* this or that thing. An act of being conscious of something essentially takes an object in the way implicit in the term "intentionality" and that may be an external object, a state of affairs in the world, or one's own state of mind. We will argue that being conscious of something or consciousness as intentionality is the basic type of state and that consciousness (simpliciter) is merely a conglomeration of acts of being conscious of this or that (in this we agree, reservedly, with Hume [1739] when he claims that "with regard to the mind, that we have no notion of it, distinct from the particular perceptions"). Corrigibility and communicability imply that words that denote mental attributes such as consciousness share a certain feature with all meaningful words. That feature is that the meaning of any word depends on more than one person knowing if it is being used correctly on a sufficient number of occasions so that the requisite "agreement in judgments" (PI #241) to establish rule-governed use is achieved. This in turn implies that one cannot learn the meaningful use of a term like "conscious" unless there is some way that correct use of that term can be established intersubjectively. Thus my saying of you that you are conscious (and therefore, if you are learning the concept, your use of "conscious" to describe yourself) must be based on something that can be agreed on by both of us and not merely on my guess about hidden goings on in your mind or head (Gillett 1992). This in turn implies, among other things, that consciousness is a property of beings about which we can make judgments and not a feature of internal processes and states about which we can only conjecture. Wittgenstein emphasizes this point when he remarks,

> Look into someone else's face, and see the consciousness in it, and a particular shade of consciousness. You see on it, in it, joy, indifference, interest, excitement, torpor and so on. (Z #220)

Of course, we may not always be sure about whether a given individual is conscious but we must, in principle, be able to agree on what would count as being in that state for the word "conscious" to have a determinable meaning. Thus an adequate account of consciousness should be able to say how, in general, we are quite competent in judging whether self or others are conscious. At this point there is an interesting convergence between Wittgenstein, the phenomenologists, and clinical neurology (a convergence to which we will return below).

Husserl indicates an interesting basic feature of conscious acts in discussing the phenomenon of directing one's attention towards an object of consciousness.

> The attending ray gives itself out as radiating from the Pure Ego and as terminating in the objective, being directed towards it or deviating from it. (1931: p. 249)

One can almost see, through Husserl's description, Wittgenstein's claim manifest before one's eyes. We do notice other's acts of attention and intuitively connect them to their objects. In fact, this seems to be a sensitivity that we are all endowed with at birth (Butterworth, 1991). Sartre is another who chimes in on the direct apprehension of the conscious presence of the other through her acts of consciousness when he remarks on the look:

> the original relation of myself to the other is not only an absent truth aimed at across the concrete presence of an object in my universe; it is also a concrete, daily relation which at each instant I experience. At each instant the Other is looking at me. (1957: p. 257)

Sartre here recognizes the fundamental, indeed primitive awareness of the other as subject who has me in her sights as object. We all share this primitive experience and therefore we are exquisitely sensitive to the presence of the other as a conditioning ground of experience. This phenomenological recommendation is further reinforced when we turn to the science of clinical neurology.

One crucial indicator of danger in a patient with a head injury or other intracranial catastrophe is deterioration in that patient's level of consciousness. The necessary observations must be made by many different third person attendents and form a coherent record of observations such that the observations of different observers are commensurable. It is therefore central to neurosurgical practice to be able to monitor and record the patient's level of consciousness in some reliable and repeatable way (a topic to which we will return in Chapter 6). If this is true then Wittgenstein's view looks to be on a good footing. In fact he prefigures the idea that it might be possible when he says that we give signs of our mental states (Z #515). A doctor or nurse relies on such signs.

When a doctor or nurse assesses the consciousness of a patient he or she normally uses what we call the Glasgow Coma Scale (Teasdale and Jennett 1974) and scores the level of consciousness. The scoring depends on the patient's levels of responsiveness to things around her. We could call this a state comprised of many different acts involving consciousness of this or that and therefore a state of potentially differentiated intentionality (or object-directedness) and thereby connect these present thoughts to Brentano's claim (1929: p. 58). The cognitive state of the patient entails that he can 'tell' what it is he is perceiving or report on it, because his verbal abilities are just a subset of the range of cognitive abilities he exercises with respect to what is around him.

We might conclude that when we look carefully at the neurological instrument we use to document consciousness we use signs of cognitive engagement with the world and we attend closely to the manifestations of cognitive attunement to the environment. At this point it is worth taking note of Wittgenstein's remark, "An inner process stands in need of outer criteria" (PI #580) because it seems that when we refer to a person as conscious it is the outer criteria that tell us whether the inner state is present (thus it works in exactly the way he suggests). From this we can conclude that when I say "I am conscious", I am, in effect, saying "I am in the state that is generally referred to as consciousness". Therefore Wittgenstein's view is congenial to that which we might adopt on the basis of the clinical fact that we can achieve for inter-observer reliability in assessing levels of consciousness in head injury.

It is because of the externally directed and animated nature of a person's engagement with the world that we can say with confidence that he is conscious in that he fulfils the criteria which underpin our communicable and corrigible use of the term "conscious". It follows that when he says he is conscious he is saying that he is in the state which justifies anybody, including himself, using the term "conscious" (even though he may have different ways of knowing that that is the state he is in from the outer criteria used by the rest of us; Z #472) It also follows from this view that our assessment of conscious level relates closely to the attentive and responsive abilities toward things around us that, we have argued, are central in the grasp of concepts. It therefore looks as if consciousness is indeed manifest as the Wittgenstein would have us believe. However, it is not invariably the case that an observer can tell that someone is conscious and that we might expect that failure of discernment to occur whenever some internal abnormality in the body disconnected cognition from its normal manifestations.

At this point we can regard it as plausible if not proven that consciousness is a matter that is clear to observers in the majority of cases so that we all do use the term "conscious" in a corrigible and hence reliable way. This implies that consciousness is manifest in our reactions and responses to things and leads naturally into the topic of intentionality.

Intentionality

The second term in the relationship that forms the topic of this essay is intentionality or aboutness — the fact that consciousness is at heart consciousness of some object or content. But there are two meanings commonly given to the term "intentionality".

The first is "purposiveness" as in "He intentionally fouled the goalkeeper" or "His omission to warn his wife about the road works was intentional". In this usage the term reflects a degree of sophisticated and rational organization of behaviour such that one pursues a plan or desired outcome by carrying out a series of voluntary actions. (Bratman 1996)

The second sense of intentionality is the feature that we identified at the beginning of the chapter. It is arguably related to the first and is the sense traditionally associated with the discussion of consciousness in the phenomenological tradition. In this sense intentionality is "aboutness" or that feature of states of mind that makes it sensible to talk of them having objects. It carries certain implications that, if the proposed relationship holds good, are going to be part of the understanding of the nature of consciousness

The first implication is that a mental or conscious act has a subject and an object. The subject is the individual whose mental act it is and the object is what it is focused on. This S – O property means that intentionality in the sense of aboutness is typically relational. It is in virtue of its object that any moment of consciousness is contentful, a feature whose central importance was revived for us by Brentano.

> Every mental phenomenon is characterised by what the scholastics of the middle ages called the intentional (or mental) inexistance of an object, and

> what we might call … reference to a content, direction toward an object (which is not to be understood here as meaning a thing)

We may, therefore, consider the intentional in-existence of an object to be a general characteristic of mental phenomena which distinguishes this class of phenomena from physical phenomena.(Brentano [1874]: pp.88–91)

We might note Brentano's leanings toward idealism and the conception of the intentional object as an inner representation. This is made evident by his qualifications and hesitancies in this passage and his use of the term "in-existance" meaning existence in the mind and as an essential component of the mental act. He reasserts this doctrine in relation to acts of consciousness in the same early work as his original claim.

> The term "consciousness" since it refers to an object which consciousness is conscious of, seems to be appropriate to characterise mental phenomena precisely in terms of its distinguishing characteristic, i.e., the property of intentional in-existence of an object (Brentano [1874]: p. 102)

Later he worries about the idealism implicit in these early remarks, worries that Husserl shared about that strand in theories about the object of thought. We develop our own position about the ontology of intentional objects in the third chapter, but for the moment it is worth noting some other phenomenological ideas that will advance our own treatment of the intentionality or aboutness of consciousness.

Brentano, in a later work, extends his discussion of the contents of consciousness by beginning with Descartes' remark about what could be clearly and distinctly conceived: "what is clearly and distinctly contained in the concept of a thing, can be affirmed of it with certainty" (Brentano 1966: p. 17). Here he indicates an implicit distinction between the concept of a thing and the thing that we come to affirm, things which we might interpret in one of two ways. First, it could be the object or referent itself or second it could be a conception of the object produced within the mind. In either case the act of consciousness is the act it is, in part, because of the object (under one of the two construals) with which it is concerned. This gets us close to the kind of essential or internal truth about consciousness that is supposedly captured by his remark about its intentionality and that we have tried to clarify and sharpen through our understanding of the concept of *consciousness*.

In pursuit of the characteristics of clarity and distinctness he elaborates his account of conscious acts and their contents by noting, within what Husserl will later identify as the workings of noesis in a mental act, a distinction between *noticing*, *differentiating*, and *comparing* an object which is the content of a mental act. *Noticing* merely indicates the fact that an object must attract our attention to figure in the contents of consciousness (1966: p. 19). We also, in order to have a distinct idea of the object concerned, need to *differentiate* it from other objects. There is, however a third requirement for us to have a clear discursive or conceptual grasp of what it is that engages our thought. This is best thought of as *comparing* because it entails a linking of one object or feature with others and therefore an implicit comparison or contrast with others so that a categorization can be arrived at. But Brentano is very keen to ensure that we do not assimilate this threefold operation of the mind to mere discrimination or detection of difference.

> The person who differentiates compares, and the person who compares notices the two things that he compares. He must direct his thought towards these two things in particular. (1966: p. 21)

Brentano is here remarking upon our capacity for explicit focusing of consciousness that brings an object into relief and makes it an apt target for judgements as to its nature or the categories that apply to it and therefore its place in the scheme of things. This can be contrasted with an implicit or background consciousness of an object whereby we merely become alerted to the presence of something which could warrant further conscious scrutiny so as to allow it to be characterized (or even just a vague awareness of the presence of something as part of the scene). Thinking and relating to objects therefore involves an active and searching engagement with the object which mobilises our cognitive abilities exactly as we have been led to believe on the basis of the remarks by Wittgenstein, Husserl and Sartre.

> A person who hears a chord and distinguishes every single note that it contains is conscious of the fact that he hears them. But a person who does not distinguish the various notes is only indistinctly conscious of them, since he hears them all together (Brentano, 1966: p. 25)

Brentano's reflections reinforce the view that the contents of acts of consciousness are the result of an active mind exploring experience and therefore evince a multitude of selective acts of focusing and classifying according to similarities and differences between things. Each of these clarifying and illuminating contributions to a thinker's experience of a given situation is a potential target of intentional descriptions in terms of what that moment of consciousness is directed toward. Let us say I see a shape in a heat haze. I am unsure whether it is a camel or two flamingos. I direct my consciousness to the legs, to the head — or is it two heads — to the neck and try and get as clear an apprehension of each of these details and their relative movements as I can. Only thus does the proper or clear and distinct shape of the content of my conscious act become formed. Consciousness and content, if this is a fair characterisation of what goes into a judgement about content, come out, as Brentano and the other phenomenologists maintain, as being coeval with each other in that my act is filled in or made contentful by a relation of information gathering from the world.

At this point we do, it seems, need to step away from the unwitting drift toward the idea that some unmodified appeal to objects in the world will give us a faithful rendition of the contents of mental or conscious states. Objects as contents of mental states and objects in the world (thought of in this extensional sense) are, in an important sense, distinct because of several possibilities inherent in intentional objects, including that of being referentially opaque. In chapter three we will develop our views about the ontology of intentional objects and their properties including referential opacity but it is important at this point to offer a example that illustrates our view.

> I go into my friend's kitchen to find a corkscrew. I see a fish shaped metal object but overlook it as I go on searching for something to open the bottle of wine. I come back out to the dining room and my friend says, "The corkscrew is just on the bench, it looks like a fish."

Here I saw the corkscrew on my first entering the kitchen but I did not see it as a corkscrew (according to that concept or description). By referential opacity we mean the characterizing feature of intentionality whereby thoughts can refer to one object under different descriptions without the thinker being aware that their thoughts are about one object.

This is a *desideratum* of a theory of mental content for a number of reasons. Philosophers now almost universally accept Frege's distinction between sense and reference (Sinn and bedeutung).[4] Assuming that there is something very similar about (indeed a logical connection between) thinking about something and stating something, Frege's important linguistic distinc-

---

4. Fodor is a notable exception to this generalization. He believes that meaning is primarily to do with denotation. "The older I get, the more inclined I am to think that there is nothing at all to meaning except denotation; for example that there is nothing to the meaning of a name except its bearer and nothing to the meaning of a predicate except the property it expresses" (1990: p. 161).

tion should also exist cognitively (Gareth Evans, see Chapter 3). In fact this can be argued for quite simply. Every statement must, in principle, be capable of being thought. To do so, important distinctions that exist in statements must also exist in their thought correlates. Frege's distinction between meaning and reference is such a distinction, therefore must have a correlate in conscious experience. For example, I might well say to a companion "Hesperus has risen". This statement successfully refers to the planet Venus. However, this utterance means *the evening star has risen* (rather than *Venus is in the sky* or *The morning star has risen*). In an entirely parallel way I might think to myself that "Hesperus has risen" and important features of this thought would then be indicated by some analogue of sense and reference (say "way of thinking" and referent).

Woodruff-Smith and McIntyre note that non-intentional relations obey a second principle "conception independence" (1982: p. 13). By this they mean that a relation holding between two non-intentional objects holds irrespective of how they are conceived. Thus if there really is a trout in the riffle then this state of affairs will really exist no matter how the situation is conceived (even if it is not conceived of at all). By non-intentional objects here, We mean those things logically and conceptually prior to our consciousness of them. (In fact it is arguably a misnomer to call these things objects at all, as we have already noted "object" often, particularly to a Kantian, implies conceptualisation.) That an asteroid is falling from the sky is true irrespective of whether we conceive it as a portent of the apocalypse, a shooting star or something romantic to see on a clear warm summer's night. But the principle of conception independence does not hold for intentional relations and is the basis for intentional relations being referentially opaque. Intentional relations are dependent upon the mental act's object being conceived of in a certain way.

Husserl says...

> The matter — to carry clearness a little further — is that peculiar side of an act's phenomenological content that not only determines *that* it grasps the object but also as what it grasps it, the properties, relations, categorical forms, that it itself attributes to it. (*Logical Investigations,* 1970: p. 589)

The claim is that a function of apprehending something determines what that thing is apprehended as. The old woman who lives next door to me and the grey haired woman who works on the same floor as me are the same person. She is the same person, no matter how I think of her. I do not know that the woman who works on the same floor and my neighbour are the same person.

When I hear my neighbour yelling I think ⟨her grandchildren have been misbehaving again⟩ but because I do not know that the woman next door is in fact the woman I have seen at work I do not think that the woman who works on the same floor as me has been having trouble with her grandchildren again. Because I can fail to realize that they are the same person my mental acts in these two cases are distinct and each is dependent upon the particular ways I think of these people. This example does not show that all mental (intentional) acts are dependent upon the concepts employed (although we think this is in fact true). However it does show how they can be referentially opaque.

We will further argue for the general dependence of intentional mental content on concepts in chapter three but, for the moment we ought to reiterate the need for our understanding of the contents of mental acts to take account of the directed consciousness implied by Brentano's distinction between noticing, differentiating, and comparing. Each of these can only be thought of as requiring focused awareness and, immediately that becomes clear, the link between consciousness and intentional content is again staring us in the face. We might say that without consciousness we cannot understand our ability to have contentful thoughts and without objects with which we can intentionally engage to form contents for thoughts consciousness is idle or vacuous (to borrow a form of words from a well known German philosopher).

From this preliminary analysis of consciousness and its contents we ought to emphasize that contents of consciousness are given by acts in which the mind engages with the world as being thus and so. The attributions that categorize things as being thus and so are conceptual and therefore of a kind that one can reason about and link to other experiences. Thus the formation of clear and distinct contents for consciousness implies that there is an internal relationship between consciousness and concepts that are our means of classifying and forging links between different presentations just as Kant (that self-same well known German philosopher) so clearly saw.

The structure of consciousness: Concepts and the self

We have argued that being conscious of something, say a car, is being cognitively engaged with it in some particular way yet to be outlined. In arguing this we have noted that when a person thinks about, or is conscious of something, that act always concerns the thing or object *as a certain kind of thing* — a big noisy moving thing, a car, a 1956 Pontiac saloon, or whatever — and this has implications for the ways in which the conscious subject responds to the thing in question. But distinguishing something as a noisy vehicle, a car, or a 1956 Pontiac is to characterize it according to certain concepts. We have argued that the ability to conceptualise something is essentially linked to articulated rules for the use of signs (typically though not exclusively tied to the meaning and understanding of language). This, in turn, implies that the contents of consciousness, or consciousness as an ongoing stream of instances of being conscious of this or that, involves complex conceptual abilities. We can usefully at this point rehearse some key features of our view at a slightly less breakneck pace and hope thereby to make it convincing. The arguments in this area need to be conducted in the light of certain constraints.

The first constraint on any account of consciousness or mental content is the *principle of economy*. This constraint requires that we do not credit any subject with mental abilities that go beyond those needed to account for the behaviour we see. Thus, for instance, we would not say of a snail that it is trying to hide in the hedge when its behaviour is perfectly well explained by a *taxis* toward dark or shady places (we might, of course, be able to devise a number of experiments which showed us exactly what the movement was aimed at). In order to justify crediting the snail with thoughts about hiding in hedges we would need evidence that it had a concept of hedges as distinct from other shady places such as trees, shrubs, or walls, or hedges as distinct from green leafy masses. Even then we could not possibly get it to show the necessary distinction between artefactual and natural arrangements of shrubbery, boundaries and so on which all would go into thoughts about hedges. We just could not find evidence of this level of differentiation in the snail's behaviour and thus we would be wrong to think of the snail as intending to hide in the hedge. We will argue that we are driven towards a cognitive account of consciousness when we try to make meaningful and defensible distinctions — in the light of the principle of economy — between conscious and mere reflexive or respondent information processing systems.

Wittgenstein remarks,

> I only use the terms the expectation, thought, wish, etc., that p will be the case, for processes having the multiplicity that finds expression in p, and thus only if they are articulated. But in that case they are what I call the interpretation of signs. I only call an articulated process a thought: you could therefore say

> 'Only what has articulated expression'. (Salivation — no matter how precisely measured — is not what I call expecting.) (1975: #32)

Wittgenstein's contrast between salivation and expectation emphasizes the vast difference between a conditioned reflex and the use of a concept in thought. Whereas the former is a fairly narrowly defined response rigidly linked to a stereotyped or specifiable trigger, a concept is an exploratory and unifying tool that can be employed in many diverse situations according to our interests (PI #570). It is useful precisely because it ranges over a wide range of situations and potentially links experiences that may otherwise have no obvious connection with each other. It does this by framing those situations against a conceptual system that is finely crafted to detect and exploit any of the aspects of an experience that may relate to the purposes of the concept-user.

A conscious thought (or indeed anything with the essential and contentful features which warrant calling it a thought) is articulated in terms of the concepts making it up (e.g. that frog is green involves the concepts ⟨frog⟩ and ⟨green⟩) and therefore in terms of the complex patterns of links upon which those concepts draw). What Wittgenstein calls the "multiplicity that finds expression in p" (where p stands for some specification of content in terms of concepts grasped by the thinker), is the richness of the links expressed in the semantic components of p. Thus a conscious mental act such as an "expectation" with its rich and open-ended connections linking it to nuance and conjecture clearly differs from "salivation" with its simple and circumscribed nature.

To fill out this multiplicity or complexity is to spell out what it is to be conscious of some item, *A*, as, for instance, a stoat, a bat, or a matchbox. In any case it emerges that consciousness is complex. The stoat is identified as a stoat only if one also can think of it, for instance, as an enduring object, an animal, as able to perceive and act on what it perceives, and so on.[5] To think of a matchbox is related to thinking of the things that it normally contains, to think that it can be opened, and so on. Abilities to detect these features of an object of consciousness are established over time and the person's mastery of the ways of thinking associated with each of the conceptual terms. We have already argued that the ways of thinking are themselves mastered in interactive human activity. For our present purposes, the interplay of directed gaze,

---

5. We could even say, to echo Brentano, that to think of a stoat one must distinguish it from a weasel which is done on the following basis: *A weasel is weasly distinguished and a stoat is stoatly different.*

investigative activity, and flexible responses to an object underlie the attentional abilities implied by Brentano's dissection of the mental act whereby we individuate of an object of consciouness. This, in turn, is the foundation on which one can begin to appreciate the conceptual complexity of human thought and, as we have seen, mark a being as conscious. In fact, any articulated system of concepts involves just those abilities (to correlate a wide range of experiences and analyse them according to different plans and projects) that characterize conscious rather than reflex activity.

The thrust of these considerations is to reinforce the point that consciousness and conceptually contentful experience go together. We might broaden this in the way that Brentano keeps hinting (and we have suggested) by remarking that any attempt to derive a general conception of consciousness from the rather degenerate variety characteristic of background or undifferentiated consciousness is ill-conceived and that *consciousness simpliciter* (in the philosophically interesting sense in which it relates to judgement and thought) is a state comprising innumerable acts in which one is *conscious of* this or that.

To summarize, we have argued that a philosophical study of consciousness suggests the following theses:

i. consciousness is manifest between subjects;
ii. in its paradigmatic use consciousness is contentful; and
iii. consciousness has an essential link with concept use in that both involve selective, articulated responsiveness to things in the environment.

It is evident that none of these features are exclusive to creatures with language but we shall come to that issue, the question of the correlation between consciousness and brain function, and the idea of unconscious mental content, in due course. We will also come to the issue of the relationship between consciousness and social being, although certain groundwork is already in place for that investigation in that, on our account, concepts imply the rule following that is part of sociality. It is that feature that comes to have a definite significance in the next two foundational topics for the present account.

Brentano raises an issue that is later to be pursued in some detail by Sartre, and concerns the different structural relations between subjects of consciousness and the contents of their conscious acts. One of the most prominent of these is the relation between consciousness and reflection (called by some primary and secondary consciousness) but it will need to be introduced by way of one or two preparatory remarks. Brentano observes,

> the thinking being, in thinking, always relates to more than one object; for example someone who sees, sees something coloured and at the same time perceives himself as the one who sees. The relation to the coloured object is called the relation to the primary object, the relation to himself as the one who sees is called the relation to the secondary object; this does not mean however, that they are primary or secondary in a temporal sense (1966: p. 41)

Brentano's disclaimer about temporality here should probably be extended to make it absolutely clear that he is interested in the logical or internal features of consciousness. If it is taken that way, then it becomes clear that we do not require that a subject actually engages in thinking of herself as thinking of X every time she has an act of consciousness with the contents X, but that it is implicit within the experience of X that she could do so. Thus, reflection on oneself as a secondary object is not always an actual and salient or consciously attended feature of an act of consciousness but is rather a potential, immanent, or *a priori* feature of such acts (suggested, for instance, by the Kantian "I think").

In fact the whole idea of intentionality is often confused with something else that Brentano discusses which concerns what he calls oblique contents of acts of consciousness:

> if we think of a person who denies A, we also think of A in a certain manner; while we think of the person denying A in modo recto, we think of A in modo obliquo. ... A person who thinks, in modo recto, of someone who causes something, will necessarily think, in modo obliquo, of that which is caused and vice versa. (1966: p. 43)

The thought here seems clear although the causal example is problematic in that it seems that when we think of Boris causing a crash *in modo recto* we are also thinking of the crash *in modo recto*. In the case of someone who believes something, say that the earth is flat, we can say that the proposition "The earth is flat" is *in modo obliquo* and therefore deny that proposition in the same true sentence as we report the belief, for instance, "Pierre thinks that the earth is flat but it is not". Some philosophers have limited their discussion of intentionality to this feature in a way that has not advanced the topic. Their problem is evident in the puzzle posed by a non-intentional reading of the sentence "Pierre thinks that the earth is flat" according to which we assimilate it to a conjunction of claims:

(a) Pierre believes proposition (b)
(b) The earth is flat.
(c) The conjunction of (a) and (b) is true.
(d) (a) is true and (b) is false

Clearly the conjunction, in any straightforward sense, of (a) and (b) is not true (thus (c) is false) but it is true that Pierre believes proposition (b) and that proposition (b) is 'The earth is flat'. This has provoked discussions of use-mention distinctions, intentional contexts and so on. Similar problems arise from assertions such as "Dmitri thought about the golden mountain" which does not imply "The golden mountain exists" whereas "Dmitri climbed the golden mountain" does imply "The golden mountain exists". We have already visited this problem in discussing the referential opacity of intentional objects but shall revisit it when we discuss the objects of thought.

We have noted that the problem of oblique contexts and the failure to carry over truth assignments into oblique contexts is taken by some philosophers as an encapsulation of the philosophical significance of the topic. We do not regard it that way. Suffice it to say that most treatments of this issue by analytic philosophers do not get to grips with the internal relation between consciousness and intentionality that was identified by the phenomenologists and that we are exploring. We ought also to note that Brentano's discussion of oblique contexts emphasizes the fact that we are conscious of each other as thinkers who relate to objects in a shared world. We have in fact used this in our arguments but will return to the issue in relation to other topics later.

We can now return to the structure of consciousness as revealed by reflective or secondary consciousness. Sartre talks of the presence of self to self where Brentano has raised the topic of secondary consciousness of self. This possibility of a reflective awareness of self poses a problem for the S–O character of the intentional relation in that it seems that I can occupy two positions in a relationship of unequals, the subject position, S, and the object position, O. This is what leads Sartre to his famous dictum:

> The being of consciousness is a being such that in its being, its being is in question. (1957)

It is worth dwelling on what he means here. He is referring to the fact that a subject or a being-for-itself — a being who can be present and to whom things can be present — is ontologically quite unlike an object or a being-in-itself which can only just be. One is not present to a brick and a brick is not present as a subject of experience sharing my world. Arguably a number of animals share those limitations with a brick (a topic to which we shall return). A person instances what Sartre calls the law of being of the for-itself that "as the ontological foundation of consciousness, is to be itself in the form of presence to itself". (1957: p. 77) Sartre is also fond of pointing out that the very nature of the S–O relation is such that the conscious subject is constantly distinguishing himself from the objects of which he is conscious. Thus the paradox of myself as a secondary content of a conscious act is that the self of whom I can become conscious is by definition not my self as subject (which I essentially am). This leads Sartre to a conclusion that Kant reached some 150 years previously when he demonstrated that the self as rational subject could not be an object in the ordinary sense of the word. In so doing he also prefigured a theme which Sartre finds totally bewitching, the idea of the necessary unity and transparency of consciousness.

Conclusion

Consciousness is comprised, according to the present account, of a multiplicity of acts in which I am conscious of this or that. Each of these acts has certain contents and we have argued that these contents are intentional. We have further argued that the most general and accessible intentional contents are actually conceptual in nature and clothe the world of which we are conscious with certain meanings and significances. The contents of experience are, if we follow Brentano, based on acts in which we notice, distinguish and compare different presentations so as to group the conditions we encounter in principled ways. The implicit activity of conceptualizing our encounters with the world in this way implies, according to Kant, a certain unity underlying conscious experience. In the transcendental deduction of the First Critique he argues that the 'I think' is an essential accompaniment of all experiences. He argues that it is, in fact, an objective condition of all knowledge because it is required to unify representations in such a way as to form a coherent body of conceptually ordered knowledge about the world (B137–8). This is, for Kant, evident in the fact that a rationally ordered set of predicative concepts and categories operating in the dimensions of space and time determines what the contents of experience are. He calls this activity "synthesis", but even without going into the apparatus of categories found in the transcendental deduction we can adduce some support for his idea.

It is evident that if the work of comparison and grouping of presentations is to be done in a principled way certain judgements do need to be made about what is before us. In order for our concepts to have the requisite generality to pick out properties or universals they must be applied in some consistent way on more than one occasion. We can support this with an argument that Kant uses in relation to judgement (which is not part of the Transcendental deduction). For instance, if Eli judges that there is a stoat in front of him then he must exercise in relation to that conscious moment an ability to judge of objects of a certain class that they are stoats. This ability essentially involves having been exposed to a number of different situations in which the judgement ⟨this is a stoat⟩ either was or was not correct and having learned from that training (B172–4). But if the subjectivity, Eli at $T_{1,}$ has to be the same subject who is learning and later uses a given concept, say ⟨stoat⟩, as Eli at T_2, then Eli at any time when the same conceptual ability is in play is the same Eli. One can further support this argument by considering our reasoning in general. Take a syllogism such as the following.

(1) I think this a stoat.
(2) I am prone to mistake weasels for stoats.
(3) This might be a weasel.

Kant notices that unless the contents of (1) and (2) are being brought together in the same rationally ordered domain of thought the inference does not go through because the premises are no more connected with each other than they would be if they were in different minds. He calls this conceptual requirement on our understanding of human beings as rational, concept-using, thinkers the Transcendental Unity of Apperception (B139) and we should regard as no more than a formal condition on the idea of a conscious subject able to have contentful thoughts and experiences.[6]

Kant refused the status of object to the subject who rationally engages with the natural world for the principled reason that he did not believe that self was given as an object at least when we think of self in the mode of being a purely apprehending subject. It is precisely this point that is later developed by Sartre to deny the substantiality of the subject or for-itself. We can therefore note that the unity of consciousness, as embraced by these thinkers is not to be

6. Kant, for instance, explicitly denies that it refers to a Cartesian soul (B406–432).

regarded as any ground for the belief that there exists in each of us a purely mental substance that can be numbered among the objects of the world. We should rather take from Kant and Sartre the view that a subjectivity, interacting with a world of objects and events, has intentional relations to the world around it and on that basis is conscious.

We have argued that this relation is active, manifest, and world involving and therefore that there is, as the phenomenologists claim, an essential relationship between consciousness and intentionality. It remains to investigate in detail the ways in which that claim resonates with arguments about the relation between language and thought, the idea of intentional objects which form the contents of our thoughts, and the nature of relationships between conscious subjects. These topics form the foundations of our intentional theory of consciousness that we will then apply to animals, human actions, the relation between consciousness and the brain and the idea of abnormal states of consciousness and the unconscious mind.

CHAPTER 2

Language and Consciousness

In Chapter 1 we discussed the problems that are created by a Cartesian view of mental content and consciousness. A Cartesian view of meaning suggests that it is my "inner thought" that gives meaning to my words and your corresponding inner thought is the basis of your understanding of those words. The problem for a Cartesian view of consciousness is that it is difficult to see how different individuals can know that we attach the same inner thoughts to the same words. We suggested, following Wittgenstein, that meaning and hence our thoughts must in some way be public or at least constructed in terms that are, in principle, public. Unless mental content is publicly accessible in some way we cannot know that we mean the same things when we use language. Call this *the publicity requirement.* In other words it is a requirement of a theory of meaning and consciousness that it can accommodate the fact that the meanings of our words and the intentional contents of our thoughts are publicly accessible.

Our proposed solution to the publicity requirement is that the rule governed nature of language use shows that competent language or concept users have configured their activity to mutually accessible conditions. For instance, the fact that language users agree in judgements about whether X is a square justifies the idea that they mean the same things by the term "square". The fact that they use the term square in the same conditions evinces the fact that they apply the concept ⟨square⟩ to the same things or that thoughts involving squares have the same intentional contents.

These remarks argue for an important connection between language use and consciousness: a topic much canvassed in the literature. Wittgenstein, Dummett, and Davidson make some strong claims about the internal relation between thought and language. Dummett is particularly forthright,

> (T)he philosophy of thought is to be equated with the philosophy of language: more exactly
> (i) an account of language does not presuppose an account of thought,
> (ii) an account of language yields an account of thought, and
> (iii) there is no other means by which an account of thought may be given. (1981: p. 39)

He is not alone; Donald Davidson remarks "...a creature cannot have thoughts unless it is an interpreter of the speech of another." (1984). However, there may be instances where we want to attribute fairly sophisticated conscious states to animals or prelinguistic children so it behoves us to spell out just what we take this claim to amount to. Instances such as these will show that there is reason to not overemphasise the difference between the intentionality of language users and the intentionality of other creatures and therefore to be cautious about accepting the strong assertions made by Dummett and Davidson. However we might accept, with Wittgenstein, that there are important connections between sophistication in language use and sophistication in mental states and, with Davidson, be somewhat coy about the primacy of one or the other:

> neither language nor thinking can be fully explained in terms of the other, and neither has conceptual priority. (1984: p. 156)

The main objective of this chapter is to outline how understanding concepts and rule following as they operate in the semantics of natural language coheres with contemporary work on the development of articulated intentional content in human thought.

Annette Karmiloff-Smith has looked carefully at the articulation and refinement of thought during cognitive development. Her starting point is that cognitive science should "treat cognitive development as a serious theoretical science contributing to the discussion of how the human mind is organised internally, and not as merely a cute empirical database about when external behaviour can be observed" (Karmiloff-Smith 1992: p. xiii). We also think that cognitive development is important for discussions of intentionality and consciousness and that it provides a good entree into some of the important distinctions and connections that ought to be made when we attempt to relate language and thought. In this chapter our main task is to show how mental content develops in human beings. Our starting point is that human beings become sophisticated in the language that they use as they perform increasingly complex operations in the world. Within the activities that incorporate those operations they use language as a set of markers for significant features of the activity and the world in which it occurs so that charting a person's language also charts their conceptual system.

The major work that inspires this chapter is Lev Vygotsky's analysis pioneered in *Thought and Language.* Although some of the details of Vygotsky's theory do not fare particularly well in the face of contemporary criticism, the idea that conceptual development involves a growing degree of mastery of adult rules and that language and thought develop in mutual relation to one another does survive the criticisms that have been raised. Consciousness we will argue is the domain of experience as marked and pervaded by language. That is the primary thesis of this chapter.

The outline of our argument in this chapter is as follows:

1. Adult human consciousness is intentional (noetic) and this involves ideal mental content (noemata) subject to rules or prescriptive norms.
2. Children's consciousness does not involve the same degree of noetic sophistication as adult consciousness.
3. An examination of the transition from children's consciousness to adult consciousness reveals that adult consciousness relies heavily upon language acquisition and mastery for its noetic sophistication.
4. The normativity and generality of noetic consciousness is a function of the appropriateness of the concept use of one thinker in relation to rules governing the concept use of others.
5. The fact that noetic consciousness involves language satisfies the publicity requirement and allows these rules to be communicated between thinkers.

The development of intentionality in consciousness

Piaget made some important claims about children's consciousness. He speaks of autistic and fully socialised consciousness but does not quite spell out the key distinctions between these different classes of consciousness. However we do begin to see and understand those distinctions through considering some of Vygotsky's ideas.

Piaget considered human consciousness to be, in its origins at least "autistic". By this he meant that "the goals it pursues and the problems it sets itself are not present in consciousness" and "it is not adapted to external reality" and "tends, not to establish truths, but to gratify wishes and remains strictly individual and incommunicable" (Piaget cited by Vygotsky 1962: p.

12). Piaget claims that a six-month-old infant has only autistic consciousness and accepts that such an infant can be conscious although not in the way that maps onto normal attributions of intentional content. Six-month-old infants do pursue goals and set themselves problems, for example the infant that drops a favourite toy will often try to position himself so that he can recover the toy but these problems do not, according to Piaget have built into them the idea of a shared public space of intentionally specifiable objects — objects which have some publicly determinate nature.

To understand what Piaget means it is necessary to introduce a distinction between non-conceptual relations to the environment and intentionally contentful consciousness. There are many levels of relationship to the environment in which the intentional content is problematic, ranging from: the moth attracted to the light-bulb; the dog that hears its owner arriving home; the infant smelling milk on its mother and the introspective philosopher reflecting upon the way she is disposed to act or think on a particular occasion. While all of these cognitive processes may be described as forms of consciousness only the philosopher engaged in thinking about her dispositions can plausibly be described as conscious in a sense that it is plain what the intentional content is. The ability to be able to reflect upon the intentional contents of one's own consciousness is part of what we ordinarily mean by being conscious. This seems to be what Piaget means by being conscious in an adult sense (socialised consciousness), so by autistic consciousness we can understand him to mean that infants are conscious, but do not have the capacity for developing clear conceptions of the contents of their consciousness and do not understand how those conceptions mesh with the public world of objects which are accessible to others. We are also not given a model whereby socialised consciousness and reflective consciousness have any essential relationship to one another.

There are good prima facie reasons for believing that this is true. Adults are capable of doing more with their language and thought than infants. Adults do seem to be able to contemplate the goals and problems they set themselves in a way that infants do not. We will argue that if we understand Vygotsky and Piaget in the light of what we have said about intentionality and the rules governing content this distinction becomes much clearer and the move beyond autistic consciousness and egocentricity becomes available. We are also able to develop an account of self consciousness or reflective consciousness that exhibits the role of socialisation in producing these.

Piaget thought that adult human beings possess fully social consciousness. Social consciousness

> ...pursues aims that are present in the mind of the thinker. It is intelligent, ie., it is adapted to reality and strives to influence it. (ibid. p. 12)

In other words as adult human beings we are capable of reflecting upon the tasks that we are presently pursuing and conscious of them in ways that define them in terms of the content which also informs the consciousness of those we share the world with.

Piaget believes that social consciousness has to be "directed". By this he means that adult thought only becomes directed when the child becomes able to reflect upon her purposes. When her thoughts are amenable to conscious reflection the child can determine the appropriateness of her behaviour in relation to other persons. At this time the child's thought becomes what Piaget calls "socialised". We will argue that socialised consciousness involving attention to one's relation to others is a development that allows the degree of noetic sophistication characteristic of the contents of adult consciousness.

A crucial step toward the development of "socialised thought" is egocentric speech. By this Piaget means the running monologue that children often make when playing or creating. Egocentrism refers to the fact that the child does not perceive the world as a shared world and does not consider the fact that others are looking at him or her until a certain age is reached. On this basis Piaget argues that egocentric speech is directed to no one, therefore is not an attempt at communication. He believes that egocentric speech simply disappears when children's thought becomes "socialised". Although Vygotsky is enthusiastic about Piaget's contributions to developmental psychology, he differs with him at this crucial point. Vygotsky is inspired by a social view of consciousness in which language and practical activity is the key to the intentional contents of consciousness. Whereas Piaget believes that egocentric speech simply disappears, Vygotsky believes that it changes in structure. The child's egocentric speech, according to Vygotsky, becomes "internalised" by which he means the intrapersonal use of what was originally an interpersonal process. What was formerly an accompaniment to a child's activity and a way of publicizing and communicating about that activity becomes "verbal thought" an internal mediation between perception and action (1978: p. 57).

Thus far we have suggested that there seems to be something right about Piaget's distinction between autistic and socialised speech and we have suggested that this seems to have something to do with using language in a way that pays heed to the appropriateness of one's language use for others. In the next section we will outline an experiment of Vygotsky's that aims to investigate the function and fate of egocentric speech.

"Externalisation" and "internalisation"

Vygotsky differs from Piaget on the function of egocentric speech but also has a different view of the relationship between inner or private thought and the resources available in the outer or public world. In *Mind and Society* Vygotsky outlines an experiment that provides a good example of how memory can be "externalised". (Vygotsky 1978: p. 40) The externalisation of memory shows how egocentric speech becomes thought because, like speech, it involves a scaffolding of external activity on which an "internal trick" (or cognitive strategy) can be built.

Children and young adults in four age groups (5–6; 8–9; 10–13; 22–27) were asked to perform three or four tasks. Each of the tasks comprised eighteen questions, seven of which involved a colour. The first task required the participants to answer questions with one word replies. Participants were asked questions such as "Did you ever go in the train?" and "What colour was it?" The second task was the same as the first, except two rules were added. The participants were told two colour words that they were not allowed to use in answering the questions and they were not allowed to repeat a colour name used in a previous answer. So if the two forbidden colour words were red and yellow participants were not allowed to use these colours in their answers. If they were asked "What is your favourite colour?" and they said "blue" and then were asked "What colour was the sky yesterday?" they could not say "blue" in response. The third task required the participants to perform the same task as the second except they were provided with coloured cards to aid them in following the two rules. A participant using the cards might use strategies such as "whenever I have used a colour name I will put the card of that colour into a separate pile" and "forbidden colour cards I will place into a pile of words that I will not use". Participants were only asked to perform a fourth task when they failed to use the colour cards or when they only began to use them late in the third task.

On the third task children in the youngest age group (5–6) were unable to use the cards to help them with the questions. There was no significant difference between the number of errors they made on task two (without the colour cards) and task three (when they had the cards to help them). This is not surprising as they did not use the cards. Children in the 8–13 range showed a significant increase in their success when they were provided with the coloured cards to aid them. Thus far Vygotsky's results are not remarkable, the fact that adolescents and older children are able to use memory aids in this way is not surprising. The most interesting results were from Vygotsky's oldest group. Participants in the 22–27 range did not show any significant difference between their success at task two and three. They made a similarly low number of mistakes on the task without the aid of colour cards and on the task in which they could have used them.

Vygotsky's interpretation of this experiment is particularly relevant in explaining how egocentric speech becomes verbal thought. The children that can use the coloured cards as cues to aid their remembering are using the cards to "externalise" the act of remembering. In other words they use the cards to signify that they ought not use the colour name the card symbolises. Adults performing the second task are just as successful as when they perform the third and the adult's success on the third task is similar to the success rate of the other participant groups that used the cards. To explain the adult's success there must exist a process performing the same function as the cards in the third task for the children. What adults can do in the experiment is make a "mental note" of the colour names that they have used. In such a situation you may use a mnemonic to help you remember and when we do so we use what this experiment suggests, the cognitive trick of "internalising" the sign. Instead of relying upon an environmental cue (the colour cards) the adult is thought capable of organising her thoughts so that when presented with a problematic question she recalls what colours she can use.

This process of internalisation of the sign for memory is the same process by which egocentric speech becomes verbal thought. Egocentric speech is the talk that children make when involved in play. According to Vygotsky, the reason why children often accompany their activities with a running monologue is that it aids them in organising their activity. When watching a four year old play with a toy train and a doll that is supposed to be the driver you might expect to hear the child tell a story about where the driver is taking the train. When a child utters the monologue it gives structure to the play. Vygotsky describes a child whose pencil breaks while drawing a picture of a tram. The child tries to continue drawing the tram with the broken pencil, succeeding only in making grooves in the paper but is eventually frustrated by this, seizes a crayon and continues drawing, saying "the wheel's broken". Saying the wheel is broken is a way of organising the plan that the child is following. Instead of drawing what was an ordinary wheel on the tram the utterance served to make sense of the new structure of the drawing.[7]

The claim is not that adults use verbal thought instead of egocentric speech, rather that the function performed by egocentric speech can be fulfilled by the silent mental operations of an adult. In fact adults do occasionally use egocentric speech; it is called "talking to oneself". Verbal thought and egocentric speech perform the same function, that is they are both means by which human beings organise their activities.

A further series of experiments caused Vygotsky to realise that even egocentric speech has a communicative or at least social function relevant to understanding the development of noetic sophistication in consciousness. In these experiments Vygotsky pursued the observation that egocentric speech tends to occur where there are groups of children and not when a child is alone (1962: p. 136). To investigate the significance of this observation, Vygotsky undermined the presupposition that others could hear and enter into a "collective monologue". He put the child in a situation where either they were surrounded by deaf mutes or foreign language speaking children, or they were relatively isolated from the group, or where the egocentric speech was made inaudible by incidental noise. In each case this "led to the dwindling of egocentric speech" (1962: p. 138). Vygotsky concluded that in egocentric speech "Outwardly, I am talking with myself and for myself, but psychologically my speech is social" (1962: p. 138). If the function of egocentric speech is social what happens to it and how does it function in cognitive development?

Vygotsky is in no doubt that egocentric speech is a phase of internalising the conceptual abilities of the social grouping in which one is learning to think.

The dynamic relation between language and the world

Vygotsky has an interesting objection to the developmental theorist W Stern which further illuminates his theory of the development and relations between

7. The organisation of children's play by egocentric speech is discussed by contemporary psychologists such as Karmiloff-Smith (1992).

word meaning and understanding and thought (1962: p. 27). Stern argues that the fact that words denote objects is a conceptual discovery by the child. He believes that the child establishes a correlation between the word image and a meaning and that there is a specific object image proper to each word or sound image. On this account the sound is a symbol but what it symbolises is an internal image. We have argued that the learning of concepts involves rules and it follows from this that the conditions of application and the symbol must be equally manifest if a regular rule-governed association is to be formed. This implies that Stern is wrong, the learning of language involves linking symbols and conditions in the shared environment.

Vygotsky arrives at the same conclusion and he objects to Stern's picture of the primary link as holding between a sound and an image and argues that no such developmental juncture as the intellectual discovery of denotation actually occurs; rather it dawns on the child that there are word-object pairings. But this arises from the expressive and communicative acts in which the child participates and therefore the candidates for the correspondent to a word are already actual objects in practical and shared communicative space. For a child to have really grasped the relation between language and the correct bit of the world, its use of language must be sufficient for the communication of the relevant content to be conveyed. When you watch small children in such situations they use their whole body to convey their desire in that their verbalisation is accompanied by reaching out with arms, and other gesturing. This is also true when understanding adult speech, in that inflection and body language often play a big role in understanding what someone is saying. Vygotsky's suggestion is that children begin to communicate before they have developed fully the insight that words denote things in the world and they use whatever means they can to individuate the bit of the world about which they want to communicate. This implies that the symbolic function is between objects and words not meanings (intellectual and internal) and words.

The idea that in communication we often rely upon more than the utterance itself, that inflection and movements of the body can play a role in conveying meaning and the idea that the symbolic function involves objects in shared action space are both in conformity with the publicity requirement. Particular bodily movements and inflections of our voices can be governed by conventions in the same way in which linguistic use is governed by rules. Understanding the meaning that another person wants to convey involves making a judgment about what the content is that they wish to convey to us.

These aspects of Vygotsky's analysis of children's language use resonate nicely with some of Wittgenstein's remarks. Wittgenstein's builder who utters "slab" when he wants his companion to bring him a slab makes use of the relationship that holds between language and the world, because when the labourer hears the builder utter "slab" he knows that the appropriate thing to do is to take a slab to his boss as is customary in that context of activity (1989). Wittgenstein would also welcome the idea that different messages could be communicated by changes in inflection or gesture while using the same term. If the builder was to gesture toward a particular slab that was badly made and utter "slab" with an attitude of resignment or disappointment the labourer might well interpret this as referring to the poor quality product that their supplier had sent them. If the builder was to shout "slab" while pointing skyward to the slab that was about to fall on the labourer's head a different meaning would be conveyed, and so on. Therefore context, body language and inflection can have an important role to play in conveying meaning. Wittgenstein does, in fact, spend some time on the way in which the content of a complex structured utterance like "Bring me a slab" would be given by considering the activity in which it had a meaning.

Vygotsky's objection to Stern is interesting because of its implications for the relationship between the propositional content of thought and the development of speech. If it is the case that children with a very rudimentary use of language could associate complicated meanings such as "Mum come over here and pick me up" with a simple word such as "Mum" then their thinking would be far more developed than their use of language would indicate. This would mean that they possessed complicated "inner" thoughts prior to a similar sophistication in publicly accessible language use. Wittgenstein's claim, which seems to be supported by a consideration of the way in which concepts, rules and publicity are all focused on language use, would be that the thought only has the complexity evident in the manifest activity and, usually, as marked by semantic components of the speech of the individual.

Development of thinking and speaking: Two processes or one?

Egocentric speech occupies a central place in Vygotsky's theory because it is the developmental step that explains the vast discontinuity between the capacity for thought and language in humans and higher primates. We know much more about higher primate language use than was known in Vygotsky's time, and it seems that, even if he underestimates the ability of apes to acquire and use language, he does notice the tremendous difference in the fruits of co-operative animal efforts and the fruits of civilization. These are plausibly attributed to the collective development of expertise made available by language.

Vygotsky believes that the beginnings of thinking and speaking in both humans and higher primates are independent, but in our view this is not true. What we can say is that prelinguistic children do exhibit behaviours that show the sensori-motor skills necessary for language acquisition. Infants of about six months often make noises that are similar in sound to speech (for example the chicken noise stage in infants), yet we would not want to say that the infant was speaking in the same sense as an adult. This is because the vocalisations concerned lack semantic content. This is not only in the sense that Piaget identified in his discussion of autistic speech — they do not aim to refer to an objective world of semantic correlates of the words used — but also in the sense that they are not being used as signs at all. The vocalisations of infants at this age do not convey meanings such as "the red truck" or "come to me" in any finely differentiated way. Psychologists interpret these early vocalisations as exercises en route to the possession of sensori-motor skills required for speech acquisition. So there is good reason to believe that there are developmental precursors for speech. We can agree with Piaget that these early vocalisations are not noetic or intentional mental acts because a necessary condition of an intentional experience is that it involves noematic content and is under constraints determined by the content concerned and tied to the (rule-governed) symbolic function or the relation between words and objects or features in the world.

It is clear that the precursors of verbally differentiated thought are not confined to speech behaviour. When a sixth month old drops his cuddly toy over the side of his bed and turns his head so as to catch a glimpse of it we think that the infant knows the toy still exists. The infant is at this stage largely pre-verbal, so it would be hard to argue that his thought is organised by language. What is more there is practical intellect in pre-verbal infants which is often exhibited in the use of tools. For example when you see a two year old pushing a trolley loaded with her toys this is an action that must have an intelligent basis, even though the child is pre-verbal her intellect is manifested in the mastery of practical skills. In other words the infant knows how to put her toys in the trolley and support herself against it, at the same time pushing it forward. So practical intellect has an origin independent from language but, if Wittgenstein is right, practice and meaning are inseparable and language infuses and takes content from the human activity in which it is embedded: "our talk gets its meaning from the rest of our proceedings" (OC #229). In fact, at certain points he goes even further: "we cannot separate his 'thinking' from his activity. … He 'thinks' when, in a definite kind of way, he perfects a method he has" (1967: #101–104).

Vygotsky says that these two functions develop along separate lines for a time in humans and are not connected in higher primates. He summarises this idea:

> In the speech development of the child, we can with certainty establish a pre-intellectual stage, and in his thought development, a prelinguistic stage. (1962: p. 44)

In other words Vygotsky thinks that the crucial difference between higher primate and human development is that for humans, the development of language and practical intellect converge and intertwine. Upon this convergence thought becomes verbal and speech becomes rational. The main function of egocentric speech is the organisation of one's activities, through the organisation of one's thoughts, by attaching one's proceedings to a commentary (which is implicitly social). An adult outgrows this need, so egocentric speech, to a large extent, disappears.

We do not share Vygotsky's nihilism about primate development, however we agree with his assertion that in human beings the juncture of language and thought marks a major developmental point in phylogeny that explains the noetic sophistication of adult humans. We have stated that the aim of this chapter is to offer an explanation of how it is that human thought becomes noetic by showing how noematic content could develop and be practically useful to human beings. We will extend our argument in the next section to suggest that it is the convergence of thought and language in problem solving which provides the noematic content for much of our noetic consciousness.

Concept formation

In *Thought and Language* Vygotsky outlines an experiment on concept formation; the nonsense word "gatsun" was introduced to experimental subjects. The word did not mean anything to the subjects because it was a word which had no prior usage. During the experiment subjects came to apply "gatsun" to a combination of attributes for which there existed no word. They had to perform an intellectual activity with the combination of attributes, so that they needed to be able to combine two properties in order to solve the problem. Conceptualisation did not occur simply by using the word in the presence of an object, it occurred in the process of an intellectual operation whereby the conditions for correct use were defined and the subjects came to conceptualise *gatsun* as meaning something "large and heavy". Vygotsky claims that for a concept like *gatsun* to develop it is necessary that there exists a task to be performed that cannot be solved in another way.

This is an experiment that Wittgenstein would have applauded. Consider again his builders in the *Philosophical Investigations* (PI #2, 8–10). The builders' concepts, such as ⟨slab⟩, arise through their work. The builder needs his assistant to bring him a slab. It is this simple operation that necessitates the formation of the concept ⟨slab⟩ because there also exist blocks, pillars, and beams. The relation between thought and action is a theme that will be revisited and argued at more depth in subsequent chapters, but what is essential is to grasp here is that concepts are not simply formed through repeated presentations, they must emerge through an active engagement by the conceptualiser with the activities and objects that fix their content and that individuate their conditions of application.

In Chapter 1 we argued that noemata are the ideal content specifications that organise noetic or conscious acts. We also argued that all linguistic acts are intentional acts (although we have not claimed that all intentional acts are linguistic). Wittgenstein and Vygotsky refer mainly to linguistic concepts when they use term "concept" but this is usually for ease of exposition. When Vygotsky and Wittgenstein use "concept" it necessarily involves rules and therefore a noema or normative content specification, thus, although not all noemata are linguistic concepts, the role of language in communicating the relative norms is easily demonstrated for a wide range of cases.

Vygotsky claims that in the mastery of speech essential structures of a child's thought are mapped out which enable what Kant calls discursive or conceptual transitions in thought. If this thesis is true then the development of logic can only occur after the child's thought is infused by her language. More importantly, if it is true that much of thought (at least higher psychic processes) comes to depend upon language for its organisation, then the nature of most future developments in human thought will be as a result of both socio-historical and biological factors. The biological factors are necessary so that the organism has the information processing capacity to deal with the distinctions and associations. But language is also dependent upon a socio-historical speech community, and therefore the categories and distinctions required to master concepts in higher human thought are also dependent upon this speech community and the cultural milieu it creates. The nature of this dependency requires careful explanation so as not to slip into common mistakes that tend to lead to a theory of social determinism.

There are at least three conceptions of the dependency between thought, language and culture.

1. First, it might be that making sense of higher human thought necessarily involves understanding the cultural context from which it originates. This idea we call "explanatory dependency".
2. A second interpretation is that higher human thought requires for its development immersion in a linguistic community. This idea we call "developmental dependency".
3. A third interpretation of this dependency is that the structure and content of higher human thought are actually produced by immersion in a linguistic community. This idea we call "ontological dependency".

Which of these theses Vygotsky endorses is not clear. We support the first two and remain agnostic, but suspicious about immoderate interpretations of the third. A defence of our position takes us into details of Vygotsky's account and the distinctions to which he appeals in giving an account of the development of fully contentful or noetically articulated human thought.

Syncretic grouping

At this stage in our argument we have said very little about the processes involved in the convergence of language and thought. We have already mentioned Vygotsky does not believe that children learn language as a result of an intellectual act in which they grasp an inner or mental relationship between symbol and image, language develops much more gradually than this and in relation to objects in a shared domain. In his concept formation experiment adults could form the concept "gatsun" quite quickly when it served as a useful conceptual tool. Vygotsky argues that there are distinct phases to the development of the capacity to form concepts. These stages are of particular relevance to our thesis because they give a plausible story of how the generality of meaning, upon which Husserl and Frege are so insistent, could come to exist.

Vygotsky's first stage involves the development of "syncretic conglomeration". The idea is that at this stage children first organise objects under words. In order to grasp this notion, we must accept that there is no general, abstract, or public basis for the child's grouping of objects under that term, and that the objects placed in such categories are "inherently unrelated"(1962: p. 59). An example of such a grouping is when a child points at a dog and says "woof", and then makes the same vocalisation when pointing at a fridge. There is neither a publicly accessible criterion to validate this reapplication nor anything in common between these objects (except that they are both objects). Thus the grouping under the term is both arbitrary and idiosyncratic. For this reason syncretic conglomerations are not adequate for meaning and understanding, a conclusion which follows from Wittgenstein's claim that a necessary condition for understanding an utterance's meaning is being able to apply the rule which governs its usage in a particular context. When objects are grouped syncretically there is no rule that is followed. The grouping is simply a matter of some contingent and perhaps fleeting connection between two objects. Wittgenstein's observation is similar to Frege's insistence that there is more to the application of a particular word than the subjective inclination of a language user to utter that word. For Frege, the child's utterance of a term used for a syncretic grouping is not meaningful because it does not express a determinable sense or content that can be assessed for truth. Only when we have rules that dictate which words apply to which objects are normative determinations like truth and falsity available.

Vygotsky believes that the way in which young children group objects syncretically progresses through phases. For instance, at first children simply try out a word with an object. When the child utters "woof" in the presence of the fridge, she could be trying out the use of that word with that object without any real sense that there is an appropriate term to apply to a fridge. Such syncretic groupings occur in the "trial and error" phase of concept learning. When the child tries out "woof" on the fridge and an adult says "No, that's the fridge" the child realises that this usage is unsuccessful and aims to alter her behaviour to incorporate the normative response.

If the same child was to point at the first dog or another dog (after the unsuccessful try with the fridge) and again say "woof" she is now performing a slightly different operation. Instead of just knowing how to make this vocalisation and applying it to whatever presentation is before her, the child now is looking for (and has found) some continuity between the two presentations (here they are both dogs) which is the basis of the application of the same term. The way in which the child is grouping objects under the term is determined by their presentation to her visual field but, at a certain point she must also conceptualise identifiable and reidentifiable objects as the basis for the use of terms (arguably this is primitive and first arises in relation to mother and father).

There are two serious problems with Vygotsky's theory of syncretic phases: domain specificity and whether phases exist at all. More recent work on children's speech acquisition indicates that they get good at using concepts from distinct domains at different times (Keil 1989; Carey 1985). We will discuss the problem of domain specificity for Vygotsky (or any other "phase" theorist) once we have finished explaining his theory. Vygotsky does not offer any experimental evidence to suggest that children do pass through various syncretic phases, so we are entitled to treat his assertion with a degree of caution. It may well be the case that when children begin to make vocalisations in relation to objects that they already know that there are correct ways to denote particular objects. There is something very odd about Vygotsky's phase of syncretic conglomeration. It's hard to see why a child would try out a word with an object without realising that there must be some connection between their vocalisation and this object and that there is a standard that applies to this connection. In fact we have taken that to be implicit in the child's moving from the fridge to the dog (again) as a possible point of application of "woof".

Complexes

"Thinking in complexes" is the name Vygotsky gives to the developmental phase that, in his scheme, follows syncretic grouping. In a complex "individual objects are united in the child's mind, not only by his subjective impressions but also by *bonds actually existing between these objects*". (Vygotsky 1962: p. 61) So a key difference between complex grouping and syncretic grouping is that the child realises that it is a bond between two objects that enables them to be classified under the same term, not just connections between her impressions of two objects. The implication is that the child's consciousness is beginning to become less egocentric, he is beginning to understand that words work because they are about things in the world that other minds can agree upon and that there are right and wrong ways of linking things according to the word that is being used. If objects are grouped according to bonds actually existing between objects then it becomes easier to see the basis for the application of a word to an appropriate rather than an inappropriate object. For example when you are reading a four year old a story and point to the picture of the lion you may succeed in making them see the animal as a lion. If you turn the page and there is picture of a tiger it is quite likely that the child will point to the tiger and call it a lion. A three-year-old could make this sort of judgment on the basis of features in common between the objects. Lions and tigers are both big cats, yellow, and wield big claws. The criteria that the child is employing are qualities that actually exist in the pictures, they are not just subjective impressions.

A child that is forming complexes is closer to a fit subject for the attribution of linguistically mediated concepts. Using complexes involves grouping according to bonds actually existing between objects and knowing that there is a public basis to the bonds detected and the application of the term. Therefore it is hard to see how using complexes differs in any categorical way from following a rule, we need to consider carefully the possibility of continuity rather than discrete phases of development.

The child that applies "lion" to the tiger is making some kind of mistake. Features that both objects share, such as having four legs and being yellow, are not the criteria for the application of the term lion. To decide whether such an application is an example of linguistic conceptualisation we must consider whether picking features that two objects share involves following linguistic rules. When the child looks at the tiger and recalls features possessed by the lion perhaps she is thinking ⟨That thing is a lion⟩. The child's judgment is linked to the actual features of the objects but in order to meet the full criteria for a shared (language based) concept she must also appreciate that there are some links that are the correct basis for the judgement in question.

There is a further argument for a continual refinement in noetic content. A child who thinks that a present object is the same as another one seen at another time is manipulating a noetic content. The ability in play is similar to that being used by a three year who thinks about a picture he has seen without having it before him. Representations manipulated independently from a visual presentation imply the existence of an ability to work with imaginative noetic content. Thus the three year old child thinking with complexes is one that would, under our theory of mental content, be exercising reasonably sophisticated noetic abilities. In fact the judgements concerned involve more than just elemental applications of content markers to presentations and representations in that there is also coming into play, an articulated cognitive structure which locates types of items in relation to one another.

Recent research on the way that young children differentiate biological kind terms (like lion and tiger) have shown that kindergarten children and even pre-schoolers have systems of belief which provide the basis for them deciding when an animal belongs to a biological kind. Keil, Jeyifous, Bacillious and Mulvaney conducted a study in which the stimuli were "drawings of a pre-transformation animal, a post-transformational animal and three intermediate stages" (Keil 1989: p. 237). The objective of their study was to see what status children ascribed to animals in the transformational stages. If what Vygotsky says about complexes is true then we might expect younger children to stick closely to characteristic features of the pre-transformational animal. We might expect older children to have formed a better idea of "biological essence". The researchers used a number of transitional animals: chicken/turkey; goat/sheep; horse/zebra; tiger/lion. Participants were told about the following transformational stages between a tiger and a lion (as well as, we presume, being shown a picture of the transformational stage).

> Tiger/lion
> Drawing #1: Scientists took some dye that never comes off and dyed its black stripes orange. Then they put some hair tonic on its head and neck to make some bushy hair grow there. And they dyed the fur on its face orange where it had been white. Is it still a tiger or has it become something else?
> Drawing #2: Next they took the permanent dye and dyed its fur a solid brown colour over most of its stripes. They added more hair tonic on its head and neck to make the hair grow in bushier and thicker clumps. And they dyed its fur brown where it had been white. Is it still a tiger or is it something else?
> Drawing #3: They used some dye to cover all its stripes and white patches and make its fur all one colour. They also added more hair tonic to make the mane really bushy and a slightly bushy end on its tail. Is it still a tiger or is it something else?
> Drawing #4: Last they added more hair tonic so that that bushy hair grew in on its head, neck and chest. And they made sure that the brown permanent dye made every part of its fur brown. Is it still a tiger or is it something else?
> Drawing #5: All the time they were doing this, they changed the way it acted, so now it acts like a lion: it growls like a lion, it eats what lions eat, and it

> hangs around with other lions. When they were all done with it, it looked just like this, which is just what a lion looks like. What do you think it is really, a tiger or a lion? (Keil 1989: p. 237)

If a child with the ability to think about biological kinds were presented with this scenario we would expect him to think that if the tiger started off as a tiger this is what it remained, irrespective of the change that the devious scientist made to it. If only the actual features of the tiger are what counts in deciding whether it is a tiger then if these features cease to be coextensive with the picture in front of them we would expect that this child would cease to see the picture as a tiger and report that it is now a lion or a mixture of a lion and a tiger.

Keil et al. conducted this experiment with kindergarteners, second graders and fourth graders. They measured for the tendency to resist changes in natural kind. They found a trend in the tendency to resist changes in natural kind in children of the older groups ($p < .09$). They found that most children tended to reclassify the tiger as a lion at one of the transformational stages (1989: p. 237). An interesting finding of this study was that children did not tend to think of the transformational phases as blended animals, tiger/lions. With only a few exceptions the children saw the picture as one animal or the other.

This study has implications for our understanding of children's thought.

1. Children tend to resist the idea that a member of a biological kind can change its nature. Thus they seem to have a fairly essential view of what it means to be classified as belonging to a given kind.
2. This experiment does not support Vygotsky's thesis that conceptual development passes through a complex phase. We would expect that if that happened then the ambiguity or mixture of features of resemblance would lead to a similarly mixed conceptualisation whereas children made up their mind and tended to be bivalent in their assignments of objects to categories. This gives us reason to be cautious about believing in the generality and necessity of Vygotsky's phases of conceptual development. It is, however, possible that this is an artefact of the domain of language-involving natural kinds.

Complexes and concepts

Vygotsky believes that complex thought is not the same as thought operating with fully developed adult concepts. The reason for this is not obvious.

Vygotsky says:

> Any factually present connection may lead to the inclusion of a given element into a complex. That is the main difference between a complex and a concept. (1962: p. 62)

So the child that calls the tiger a lion made that judgment because of some features that the objects shared. The adult correcting the child, who knows that the tiger is not a lion because it belongs to a biological kind, must still judge on the basis of features in common or distinct between the animals but takes these as symptomatic of the correct basis of classification which underlies appearance. What makes the difference between the adult's usage and the child's has to do with the generality of the criteria behind the application of the terms and the mastery of the supporting cognitive structure which does not conceptualise things on a basis such as "things that look like that" but rather on the basis "things of that fundamental type".

The (Vygotsky's) child classifies the tiger as a lion *only* because of features that are actually common between the picture animals. The adult is different in that she realises there is some sort of general, and perhaps non-evident, criterion that is necessary for applying a given term correctly. The child's application is simply on the basis of actual features that exist in the two presentations. Thus we could consider complex grouping as "subjective" (or at least idiosyncratic), to indicate that there is nothing objective about the method by which the objects are grouped. Think again of Wittgenstein's builders, if the builder's assistant did not realise that when his boss said "slab" that there was a determinate meaning to this term then he would be very unsuccessful at getting the slab. We could also think of Husserlian noemata or Fregean senses where the contents are not based on the links made by individuals but are normative and essentially binding on all competent users of the concepts concerned.

As we have already hinted it is hard to see how there can exist a significant qualitative difference between complexes and concepts. Complexes do seem to involve attempts at applying criteria for the usage of a particular term. We have also already suggested that concept use involves following the appropriate rules for the usage of the relevant concept. Given this view of concepts, it is plausible that the mastery of the relevant rules grows gradually and increasingly forges links between different complex-based contents. This more holistic view would be in keeping with Wittgenstein's thoughts on the subject.

> The sign (the sentence) gets its significance from the system of signs, from the language to which it belongs. Roughly: understanding a sentence means understanding a language. (1958: p. 50)

> When we first begin to believe anything, what we believe is not a single proposition, it is a whole system of propositions. (Light dawns gradually over the whole.) (1969: p. 141)

We could similarly argue that the child's growing sophistication with a wide range of concepts helps determine just what is included and excluded by the use of any particular concept. For instance, if the child seems to understand the concepts ⟨prime number⟩ or ⟨marsupial⟩ these carry implications for other elements in the child's cognitive repertoire such that it is not possible that they could be grasped in isolation from the ability to think other things.

Wittgenstein also argues for the publicity of all language, as have we. He observed that the conditions that underpin meaning must be accessible in order for us to know what we and others mean. For meaning to be accessible it must be a function of something public, rather than something private and individual. The same should apply to the way in which young children learn what terms mean. The place that they must start is by asking how adults use the term in question on a given occasion and what things adults group under this term. Vygotsky uses the example of the term "triangle"; the child is shown the sample triangle and is instructed to pick out the other triangles. The only place that the child can start is with the activity that the adult performed and the conditions of its occurrence. Because the child may not immediately grasp the actual criterion that the adult uses in applying the concept of a triangle, the child may not be as successful in a wide range of possible circumstances. However, if a young child on some particular occasion does use a word appropriately, we might think that she has grasped the concept involved. It is not until our experience of the child's usage broadens that we are likely to discover an error and see that she has not fully understood the content indicated by concept. This is additional support for the Wittgensteinian thesis that understanding is a relatively holistic ability. We do have concepts of triangles and other things and, once grasped, they can be employed in circumscribed mental acts but we (and the thinker herself) cannot know that the concept is mastered except through an ability to manifest their understanding in a suitably wide range of mental acts (which for some concepts necessarily involve language).

It's not clear whether Vygotsky thinks that using the precursors of concepts is knowledge based but we have suggested that attributions of knowledge are as secure or insecure as attributions of concept mastery. Keil shows that different concepts develop in different ways and at different times, eg biological, nomological, and natural kinds (1989). Children get very good at using concepts like cat (particularly if their family owns one) well before they fully understand what Venus is or the wider implications of calling something a cat. If it is true that precursors of concepts are a developmental stage en route to full concept use then we would expect children to use them for all sorts of concepts at a similar age. Furthermore, once a child had progressed beyond these precursors had begun to use more adult concepts then they ought not revert to the use of pseudo-concepts or any other precursors. But the Wittgensteinian picture is far more plausible.

A concept, like a complex, involves the organisation of aspects of a sensory presentation and the application of a category. Consider your concept of a triangle, if an experimenter told you to sort a set of shapes into squares and triangles you would pick out the triangles on the basis of them possessing three sides. A child thinking in complexes could possibly pick out the same aspects (three sides) after being shown a sample triangle but Vygotsky would say that the difference between your operation and the child's has to do with the stability and degree of abstraction of the cognitive event that guides your grouping. If you were asked to think upon your concept of a triangle you could offer an axiomatic description of a triangle even though you might, for most purposes, just point to the shape and say "I know a triangle when I see one" with the thought that you are well versed in recognising genuine triangles according to the objective criteria used by all and demanded by the rules governing the concept. The child could only point to the shape of the triangle to indicate the criteria for her grouping and it would be *her way* of grouping things. So the possession of a concept may not simply be a function of which features are attended to by the subject. Both the complex user and the concept user has aspects of the object to which they attend and in the present case they might coincide but the concept user differs in knowing what aspects of a particular object count in qualifying an object as categorizable under the term that marks the concept. The distinction has to do with a conceptual difference between complexes and concepts in terms of the normativity and objectivity (or wide intersubjectivity) of the criteria which the subject uses to unify objects into a group.

Meaning and reference

"Hesperus" and "Phosphorus" are words that mean different things. If you say "Hesperus has risen" you mean the evening star is in the sky but if you say the same about Phosphorus you would be talking about the morning star. We now know that Hesperus and Phosphorus in fact refer to the same thing, the planet Venus but you might not know this and therefore you might say, without irrationality, "Of course the fact that Hesperus is in the sky means that Phosphorous cannot be". Thus, although you mean different things by the terms you use and there is no irrationality in what you say from your point of view, the identity of the objective referents of the terms entail that it is false. You are, in fact, referring to the same celestial body, and the relationship between your words or thoughts and the world is guaranteed by the rules governing the terms "Hesperus", "Phosphorus" and "Venus". When a child successfully uses a complex she also refers to an object but the same implicit engagement in a world of rule-governed contents does not hold. So even if the child says "fire engine" when the fire engine screams past, and even if the referent of her vocalisation is the same as it would be if her mother had made it, Vygotsky considers that it is possible that the child's understanding of fire engine is not at a fully conceptual level. If this was the case the child might describe the ambulance as a fire engine, on the basis that they both have loud sirens, or might not realise that there is a determinate range of things to which the determinate concept, expressed by the term "fire engine", in fact applies. This implies that when the child refers to the fire engine, although she successfully picked out the appropriate object for that term, she does not necessarily mean what her mother means in using the same term for the same presented conditions. The child would be grouping objects under that term according to a commonality between fire engines or even fire engines and ambulances (perhaps because of the siren). If the latter were the case the child is using "fire engine" to pick out something like, ⟨things with sirens⟩. The mother, by contrast, means something like ⟨the truck that fire fighters use as an appliance for fighting fires and transporting equipment and fire-fighters⟩ and that is called in English "fire engine". The mother's concept of a fire engine coheres with general usage whether that follows functional or purely descriptive criteria but the child's does not.

It is not clear that Vygotsky successfully defends a sharp division between syncretic groupings, complexes, pseudo concepts, and full concepts in his discussion. The child seems to have an inaccurate concept of a fire engine to the extent that complexes and syncretic groups, even if they are not completely subjective and involve an attempt at publicly accessible commonalities, are not constrained (and thought by the child to be constrained) by the rules that everybody else uses. As a child can use the same word as an adult in a different way it follows that the use of a word, *per se* or considered in isolation, is not in a fixed relationship with its meaning. If we accept, with Wittgenstein, and it seems Vygotsky at certain points, that the meanings that are attached to a word "evolve" throughout the course of a child's development, we can then explore Vygotsky's description of the dynamic interaction between meaning and word in children learning to speak.

> Semantically, the child starts from the whole, from a meaningful complex, and only later begins to master the separate semantic units, the meanings of words, and to divide his formerly undifferentiated thought into those units. The external and the semantic aspects of speech develop in different directions — one from the particular to the whole, from word to sentence, and the other from the whole to the particular, from sentence to word. (1962: p. 126)

The observation here is that when a child just beginning to learn language uses a word like "drink" what they mean by this is some precursor that they will later come to express by using a whole sentence. This is deeply congenial to recent work on representational redescription by Annette Karmiloff Smith (1992). A child may mean something like "go to the fridge and get me a drink", yet we would not expect the child to think a thought with the complex articulated content ⟨go to the fridge and get me a drink⟩. Due to its limited language ability the child's awareness and articulation in thought is also much more limited. So a child's language develops from the capacity to operate with single terms used fairly inarticulately (in the sense that they lack cognitive and linguistic articulation with other words and semantic units) to operating with articulated sentences and phrases. The capacity to use whole sentences is a necessary condition for breaking a semantically complete objective, such as "go to the fridge and get me a drink" into components. So although when interpreting the toddler's "drink" you would think that they had a disposition corresponding to that utterance the toddler would not be aware of their disposition in the way that we would understand it. The toddler's utterance may, in fact, be causally related to thirst in much the same way as that of an adult (although sometimes toddlers seem to make such requests just because it seems like a good thing to do at the time or in service of some other need like parental reassurance). But there is more to the meaning of an articulate utterance than such a causal origin and this complexity becomes available through the growth of language skills so that both the toddler's utterance and related behaviour gradually take on a more clear and distinct or articulate shape. When we think the toddler wants someone to get her a drink, our thought about her comprises separate semantic entities that can then serve as a basis for understanding her. And here the crucial claim is that thought is formed from separable semantic elements through concepts derived from language so that the toddler's thought cannot be regarded as having the same form as ours. Her insufficient mastery of language (necessary for differentiating thoughts in this way), entails that her cognitive activity is a semantically undifferentiated or primitive reflection of the causal forces moving here. Over time her thought may take on the contents that characterize our thought but she cannot be credited with articulated thought from the beginning.

Vygotsky's point here can be profitably related to Wittgenstein's builders. When the builder only ever requires his assistant to bring a certain type of slab to him the term "slab" is sufficient for instructing his assistant. If the builder requires his assistant to perform more complicated operations or to select from a range of possibilities then the communication needs to become more sophisticated. If there are different types of slab then they need terms that can communicate this difference and if there are different operations available besides simply taking the slab to the builder then there is also a need for terms that can differentiate between them. The general maxim would be that for every new operation there needs to be some linguistic means to mark that operation so that it can be used to differentiate and articulate the relevant co-operative activities. This is important because it is an illustration of two of Vygotsky's (and our) most important theses. First, thought is, to a very large extent, dependent upon language, both in terms of its content and also the general cognitive skills involved. Any general theory that fails to take account of the mutual influence of language on thought and vice versa will miss these important insights. We will emphasise this point when we examine the relation between consciousness and society. Second, thought and language are distinct processes, that develop alongside each other. From the way that language and thought develop from part to whole and whole to part it is evident that the relation holding between thought and language is not one that remains constant through time. The relation might be better described as a dynamic interaction between language, thought, and the world in which the social milieu is a pervasive influence on all three relata.

We have argued that Vygotsky's complex/concept distinction (and in fact any attempt to reify developmental way stations) appears dubious. There is nothing that differentiates between complexes and concepts except that complexes are based upon impoverished criteria which may be idiosyncratic and not therefore have the potential of shared and normatively constrained concepts with their rich cognitive connections and broad domain of applicability (as broad as the co-linguistic group that uses the concept). This is related to the fact that neither Vygotsky nor Wittgenstein appear to endorse a classical view of concepts. A classical view of concepts implies that there are necessary and sufficient conditions for the application of a particular concept and that these are specifiable in a determinate way for every concept. This view implies both that any object may be unambiguously assigned to or excluded from the set of instances that make up the extension of the concept and that any individual may unambiguously be said to grasp or not grasp the concept. But if we allow concepts to be in a dynamic and mutually influential relationship with growing competence in language (as per Vygotsky and Wittgenstein) then this is not the case. Concepts have fuzzy rather than sharp boundaries, a view explicitly espoused by Wittgenstein but also emergent from our interpretation of Vygotskian developmental theory. We will develop this view in more detail when we answer some objections to the Vygotsky's theory in the following sections.

Fodor's objections to Vygotsky

In a 1972 paper Fodor raises objections to Vygotsky's theory of conceptual development. We will outline four of them as follows:

Vygotsky operates with a 'classical view' of concepts;
Vygotsky's adults could not communicate with Vygotsky's children;
Vygotsky offers no viable mechanisms of learning and conceptual development;
Domain specificity mitigates against developmental stages.

Vygotsky operates with a 'classical view' of concepts

> ...it is a serious objection to Vygotsky's account of the nature of concepts that he fails to realise the extent to which each obtains its identity from its position

> in a network which connects them all. We shall see that, like most philosophical Empiricists, Vygotsky thinks that concepts are related to experience by necessary and sufficient conditions for their application, so that whether a given concept applies is, at least in principle, independent of any fact about the world except those mentioned in its definition. (Fodor 1972: p. 87)

Fodor notes that a classical view of concepts has been proven to be problematic by philosophers such as Quine and Putnam. If it can be shown that Vygotsky thinks that fully developed concepts are always governed by necessary and sufficient conditions then his theory of concept development is flawed. We have already suggested that a natural consequence of Vygotsky's view of thought and language tells against this view if we release him from the hard-and-fast distinctions between stages of cognitive development. Others are also ready to defend Vygotsky. Keil thinks that there are two answers to this question (1989). The first is that for some concepts Vygotsky may not be so far from the truth. Some kinds are created by human convention and may have nearly, if not completely, definable meanings. It is no coincidence that Vygotsky has studied concepts of this sort because for Vygotsky and other post-Marxist psychologists there is a close relation between human production and the nature of the world in which our thought takes shape. The concepts produced in a highly humanised environment tend to be either terms relating to artefacts defined in relation to human activity (such as *chair*: a piece of furniture used for sitting on which has a back support) or totally artificial constructs for which definitions are completely clear (such as *prime number*: a number with no whole number factors apart from itself and 1) or at least terms with highly conventionalised meanings (such as *baroque*: relating or pertaining to the baroque era in European history as in baroque music and baroque architecture). Thus perhaps a qualitative shift holds for this special subset of concepts that are well defined from the kind of account that might need to be given for natural kind (or approximately natural kind) terms such as gold, gazelle, or schist.

When we explained how Vygotsky's pseudo concepts were supposed to work we explained how a child may have a pseudo-concept for "triangle". An adult's concept of a triangle does seem to be a concept that is governed by necessary and sufficient conditions generally validated and subject to tight normative constraints. Every adult who has realised that all closed plane figures with three straight sides are triangles has grasped the necessary and sufficient conditions for that concept. We would say that any person who has not grasped the fact that triangles are just and only those plane figures that have three straight sides does not understand the concept, thus grasping that these conditions are unequivocally and objectively definitive is necessary for understanding the concept triangle.

Because the concept triangle is a good candidate for a classical concept, what Vygotsky says about the pseudo-concept *triangle* and the concept ⟨triangle⟩ seems plausible. However the number of concepts that can be described as having such necessary and sufficient conditions is limited and Vygotsky surely wants his theory to be more general than simply for this class of concepts. Keil suggests a more fruitful response to Vygotsky than Fodor. One can adhere to a doctrine of qualitative shifts without holding a strictly classical view. Thus one might argue that all concepts have probabilistically distributed features, not necessary and sufficient ones, but that the nature of such a distribution radically changes, such that young children tend to sum over all attributes and relations that are observed to co-occur with concepts, whereas older children tend to weight just a few features and relations much more heavily. The change occurs, we might say, (after Vygotsky and Luria) as the child learns through language which features are the favoured ones among those who are masters of the concept. Thus, for instance, in distinguishing chairs from stools the existence of legs and a padded seat are not relevant but a back of a certain kind is. It is plausible to take this interpretation of Vygotsky as he does not specify that concepts must be governed by a set of necessary and sufficient conditions. Using ⟨triangle⟩ as an example of a fully developed concept is somewhat misleading as it does suggest that the end point of concept development is always a classical concept and tends to overlook the much more fluid and elastic concepts that hold widely in the domain of human activity.

Vygotsky's adults could not communicate with Vygotsky's children

> If the conceptualisations of children are radically different from those of adults, it is extremely difficult to imagine how children and adults could ever manage to understand each other. All the more so if the alleged differences are supposed to be differences in word meanings, for that is to say that adults and children are, in a fairly strict sense, talking different languages; a situation only barely disguised by the similarities of the phonological and syntactic system the languages employ. (Fodor 1972: p. 87)

In other words Vygotsky's description of complex and concept development amounts to asserting that there can exist a qualitative difference between adults' and children's propositions. If it is the case that the adults use fully developed concepts and a child uses complexes then what adults and children mean by the same proposition must be different. If this is the case then children and adults must always misunderstand each other. This is a problem of which Vygotsky was aware. His idea of the pseudo-concept is an attempt to show how complexes could appear in use to mean the same thing as their concept counterparts. If a child was using a pseudo-concept we would not have reason to suppose that there is a disagreement about meaning. Keil agrees that Fodor's objection is too strong (1989: p. 18). He suggests that we often do fall back on global, primitive, similarity spaces to resolve such miscommunications. What he means is that anyone who has spent time trying to talk with young children about topics that they don't really understand will realise that you often need to point to crude similarities between things to get across an approximation of what you are talking about. For example, if you were trying to explain to an inquisitive four year old what the International Monetary Fund is, you might say that they were a bit like the people working in your bank, in that they lend money to those that need it or if you were trying to explain cloning you might say it involved taking a bit of a grown up and making a whole baby out of it.

Keil suggests that the reason children and adults do not have the problems in understanding each other that Fodor takes to be implied by qualitatively different concepts is because there is often heterogeneity within domains. By this he means that concepts and complexes usually work on the basis of similar features. For example the child that has learnt that the white woolly four legged animal is a sheep and then goes on to call the goat a sheep makes this generalisation on the basis of features not dissimilar from some of those that adults use: part of what makes us decide that a sheep is a sheep is that it has four legs and is white. Of course we have more sophisticated criteria for applying the term and we also know that in order for this to be a sheep it must have wool of a certain type and belong to a particular biological kind. In sum we can conclude that, because concept use in part rests on crude similarities between objects it is not hard to understand what novice language users mean and also to understand why they make the mistakes that they do. Keil puts this point succinctly.

> If more associative structures are intimately related to causal explanatory beliefs and both are fundamental to conceptual structure, then access to such

> structures may well allow adults to communicate with children and experts with novices. (1989: p. 18)

Vygotsky does offer a suggestion about what happens when novice language users and adults communicate.

> In the semantic structure of a word, we distinguish between referent and meaning; correspondingly we distinguish a word's nominative from its significative function. When we compare these structural and functional relations at the earliest, middle and advanced stages of development, we find the following genetic regularity: In the beginning, only the nominative function exists; and semantically, only the objective reference; signification independent of naming; and meaning independent of reference, appear later and develop along the paths we have attempted to trace and describe. (1962: p. 130)

In other words, at the early stages of language acquisition novice language users can agree upon the referent of a word, but may not have grasped the meaning (Sinn) of the word (and hence can mistake what an adult means). Fodor says that Vygotsky's solution is simply hopeless.

> To see that this solution cannot be right, consider the case of witches, ghosts, goblins, and elves. Since these concepts have the same extension (namely, the null set), our discussions with children about which of them rides on a broomstick cannot be mediated by a merely extensional consensus. Analogously, one could hardly teach a child that Lenin was the father of the revolution if you agree on who the terms refer to but not what they mean. On the contrary, the condition upon a statement which expresses a synthetic identity being informative is precisely that one knows what the terms mean but not what they refer to. (1972: p. 87)

Fodor may be premature in his dismissal of Vygotsky's explanation. He is correct that any language user who had only the logical referent for terms like "witches, ghosts, goblins, and elves" could not form meaningful statements about them. However reference is not only a logical process but a psychological process as all those who try to develop theories about non-existent objects know. Most of the time, even if there is an objective extensional referent (for instance for something like the Taj Mahal) many of us do not latch on to that by immediate acquaintance but by some indirect means consistent with our psychological and social ecology. A language user who had only grasped the referent for a particular term may therefore not be able to use this term well. It is important to bear in mind that Vygotsky is an ecologically real psychologist not a logician and that problems of epistemic access loom large for him (as for any naturalised epistemologist). When he states that it is only at the very early stages of mastering a concept that novice language users have no meaning but reference for words he is thinking of simple observational concepts like ⟨cat⟩, ⟨dog⟩ and ⟨Papa⟩ not the kinds of things we learn about through books and stories. Whereas we can be acquainted with the reference of the former kinds of terms the latter are only accessible through indirect means. So we have to adapt the term "reference" from its logical to a psychological use to see what Vygotsky is getting at. If you were reading a picture book to a child of about two and a half and came to a page with a picture of a witch on it you might point to it and tell them this is a witch. At this very early stage we wouldn't expect the child to have a more adequate concept of witch than the referent with which they have been supplied. But the child does not take the picture to have no reference beyond itself any more than she takes that implication from any picture in any book (such as a picture of a dog). We know that witches don't exist, yet we are perfectly capable of saying all sorts of meaningful things about them and the child takes it that we are talking about something not nothing (or "the null set"). To try and crush this psychological or naturalistic story into the tight shoes of empiricist philosophical logic is to be both imperceptive and ecologically unsound. Thus, the fact that most of us believe that the extension of the class of witches is the empty set is a subtlety we do not convey until the child has some inkling of the kind of thing that a witch is supposed to be. For the child, Dummett's maxim that "the sense is a route to the reference" is therefore true and we have to meld this insight with Vygotsky's claim. To do this we have to give Vygotsky a pinch of Fregean salt. Vygotsky is saying that the child does not initially come by a concept replete with all its normative constraints and cognitive connections but rather as a way of thinking about that kind of thing (or the thing represented there in the case of a fictional object). The initial assumption is that things pointed out to them are awaiting their acquaintance in the world and not just figments of imagination. Therefore a child, with no more to their understanding of witches than that they are things of the type that father pointed to, may not realise that they do not really exist. The epistemic mastery required to grasp the difference between as-yet-unencountered-but-encounterable object and non-existent objects is, we could say, an advanced attainment.

This means that the referent, to which Vygotsky alludes, is not the logical referent but the denizen of the situation in which the relevant bit of language was taught and learnt. The logical or propositional nature of the referent may not be clear to the child but some conception of it is grasped as a whole or in a lumpy and undifferentiated or unrefined fashion. When this child becomes more acquainted with witch talk, has other thoughts about witches, and possibly even nightmares about them, there is obviously more to their understanding of witches than a connection to the objective feature of the world to which their thoughts originally attached (or to the null set). One would presume that Vygotsky acknowledges that at this later stage there is more to the child's understanding of *witch* than its referent (even in the naturalised and psychologised version of that term that we have suggested), as this is not the earliest phase of their mastery of this concept and the concept has had time and exposure to discourse to gather around itself a cluster of associations. This child who has nightmares about witches may not realise that the term *witch* fails to refer, or witches do not exist. In fact one of the strategies that you would try with a child having bad dreams about witches is to convince the child that witches do not exist by discursively engaging with them and introducing reason and theory relevant to the concept so as to clarify the issue. As in all Fodor's writing about concepts and their development this objection has a wooden and psychologically obtuse quality about it that fails to do justice to the domain of child psychology with which Vygotsky (and Keil) are both philosophically and empirically familiar.

Vygotsky offers no viable mechanisms of learning and conceptual development

Keil summarises Fodor's objection.

> Vygotsky seems to adhere to a hypothesis-testing model of learning in which the child makes conjectures about possible new relations that might be central to a concept and then evaluates those conjectures against available evidence. This general model of a child as a scientist who evaluates and modifies these hypotheses continues to be a prevalent assumption in much of developmental psychology. But if a child's concept undergoes a complete qualitative shift, any hypotheses made in the earlier representational format is forever trapped in that format and useless to a later one because the later one would be unable to "read it". Learning would only occur within each stage, with no carry-over to the next. (1989: p. 17)

The claim is that if a child begins learning about a concept such as broom stick as being "the thing that my Mother keeps in the cupboard" or "the object that witches ride on" and then later forms a concept that does more explanatory work like "the implement that is used for sweeping floors, has a long handle, its brush is made up of long bristles etc.", he will not be able to use the experience leading to the earlier concept. This concern can be answered in a similar manner to Fodor's objection that Vygotsky's children could not communicate with Vygotsky's adults. Children's and adults' concepts of broomstick may be different. An adult may tend have a more functional definition (the implement that is used for sweeping floors, has a long handle, its brush is made up of long bristles etc). Although a child's broomstick concept may be quite different (witches ride on them, Mother keeps one in the cupboard) there is a commonality both between the features that an expert language user would use and those of a novice and between the reference classes of their term. In other words, even though the adult concept is more sophisticated it incorporates aspects of the child's concept and is ultimately applied to the same set of objects. Even though our concept of a broomstick may be "the implement that is used for sweeping floors, has a long handle, its brush is made up of long bristles etc" it is still something that a witch may ride on or is kept in cupboard. The entry into discourse at one point makes accessible to the child a much wider range of thought and talk about any item conceptualised by the child in two ways:

(i) it exposes the child to language use directed at the object the child is referring to; and
(ii) it exposes the child to cognitive connections between the term the child is using and the expressed thought contents of others.

These two means serve as powerful scaffolding, (once we have abandoned the sharp edged boundary view of the grasp of concepts) for the child to grasp more and more content relevant to the understanding of any given concept. Hypotheses, as any good philosopher of science knows, are rarely accepted or rejected outright but are far more often refined and modified so as to more adequately do their work in a domain of application. Concepts, we would argue, are the same. Again it is the woodenness and ecological detachment of Fodor's theory of content that lets him down.

Domain specificity

> Take a time slice of a child and you will find pervasive and homogenous limits upon the type of concepts it can form. Developmental stages are to be characterised by reference to such limits; ideally, by the construction of

> formalisms which express them precisely. The primary goal of theories in cognitive development is thus to exhibit these changing mental capacities of the child in terms of an orderly progression of such formalisms, and to characterise the endogenous and exogenous pressures which occasion transitions between them. (Fodor 1972: p. 92)

This is a serious objection to Vygotsky's theory only if we fail to realise that cognitive complexity and formal articulation of concepts within the cognitive space of the child both develop along a biological as well as social trajectory and we force Vygotsky's developmental theory into a formal mode. Fodor's criticism of general stage developmental theories is in part fuelled by his obsession with formal cognitive modelling according to a classical functionalist or computational account of representation. Vygotsky need not accept this baggage. Work on domain specificity since the publishing of Fodor's paper has provided more evidence for the contention that domain specific knowledge and growth of general cognitive complexity are complementary developmental strands. Annette Karmiloff-Smith is a prominent Neo-Piagetian who has acknowledged that changes need to be made to Piaget's ideas of general stage development (1992). Her suggestions incorporate both features and link them to language mastery in a way deeply congenial to Vygotsky's overall orientation. The child learns tricks in different domains and develops fairly lumpy or undifferentiated representations in that domain. The child then increasingly masters the use of terms with a complex and articulated position in linguistic space and uses those terms to representationally redescribe their cognitive attainments.

We have already mentioned that it is possible to read Vygotsky as pointing to some interesting features of knowledge development that are highly convergent with this idea. Fodor might well point to the fact the Vygotsky was heavily influenced by Piaget and therefore it is likely he intended his theory to be read as about general stages of concept development. However, as one of us has previously argued, a Vygotskian theory is best read as an account divergent from Piagetian orthodoxy (Gillett 1987: p. 101–12). If this is the case we would reiterate that Vygotsky's theory tells us an interesting story of about how qualitative phases within specific conceptual domains can occur. Vygotsky is the champion of language related social cognition (as a neo-Marxist psychologist). This implies, as a general theory, that concepts develop and change. Perhaps he erred in reifying and attempting to precisify cognitive stages but that fault seems vastly outweighed by the important points he makes about thought and language.

In summary, Fodor's arguments and our discussion of them do rule out several modes of qualitative change. They do rule out global qualitative shifts in the manner of representation and processing such that children in an earlier stage are fundamentally unable to have representations available to an older group. When the global change assumption is replaced by a domain-by-domain assumption, the arguments are weakened somewhat, and work against any claim that a child at any given stage is unable, even in a restricted domain, to have conceptual representations of the sort possessed by an older child or adult. The grasp of the content of concepts is, we have argued, a matter of degree and not an all or none capacity such that the more a child becomes competent in a variety of situations and appropriately uses the concepts applicable to that domain the more detailed one can be in content ascriptions to that child. We would therefore contend that rather than exaggerating Vygotsky's fault in his tendency to over specify the distinctness of stages of concept development (as Fodor does) it is better to stress the relation between thought and language and assimilate Vygotsky to Wittgenstein when the latter claims, "Light dawns gradually over the whole." (1969: #141) Thus, even on a domain specific basis, claims of fundamental competency changes in the manner of processing and/or representation are exceedingly difficult to defend. And along with this we have implied a deep suspicion of any attempt to over-formalise (in computational terms) the cognitive mechanisms of a child. The child has a burgeoning interactive competence that is not easy to neatly divide into cognitive or representational chunks each with its own little package of content.

Grammar

Language has both semantic and syntactic properties. It also has grammar. Vygotsky claims that there exists a grammar of thought that exists independently of linguistic syntax, a claim which resonates or appears to resonate with some of Wittgenstein's remarks. Vygotsky calls the grammar of thought "the syntax of word meanings" (1962: p. 128). At first this thesis is alarming; can it be that thoughts, especially if language is important for their development, are regulated by a different set of rules from the grammar of natural languages? The claim becomes more sensible once it is unpacked and expanded a little more (particularly if we enlist some help from Wittgenstein). Language is not a linguistic replica of thought with its own set of rules; when I double negate in language I affirm the thought expressed and one cannot imagine thought having any other rule. What Vygotsky claims here is really just a restatement of a familiar Fregean and Wittgensteinian theme. The theme is that any item in thought or language in part functions as it does because of the place it is stationed. Thus, if a friend said "I am thinking of an exit" and you replied "That sounds a bit alarming and impulsive", they might say "Oh no, not suicide, merely the exit of the local cinema." Here the meaning of the term "exit", the thing being thought of, could only be gleaned from some scene setting or contextualisation. Frege's decomposition principle seems to catch this feature of language and thought in that it begins with the complex sentence or proposition and assigns meanings to component parts according to the functions they perform in the whole. Frege's thesis is explicitly developed for use in philosophical logic but Wittgenstein's use of the term "grammar" is somewhat broader while still covering Frege's context principle "the thesis that a word has meaning only in the context of a sentence" (Dummett, 1981)

Wittgenstein remarks,

> What belongs to grammar are all the conditions necessary for comparing the proposition with reality — all the conditions necessary for the understanding (of the sense). (*Philosophical Grammar* #45)

This remark is of interest because it implies that thought has more than a syntax but in fact a rule governed semantics which is itself articulated in complex ways. Vygotsky's remarks, particularly when we note that he explicitly mentions *word meanings*, are deeply congenial to this suggestion. The child is in the process of mastery of a highly interconnected set of rules which organise cognition and behaviour along lines which represent a dynamic interplay between language and thought. This implies that we need no special grammar for thought over and above the grammar discussed by Wittgenstein; that grammar allows us to appreciate the constituents of propositions and the complex relations between sentences and the world in which they are used.

Our analysis of concepts and complexes has shown that the key difference between them is that complexes may be idiosyncratic but concepts involve an abstract representation in the judgement of whether it is appropriate, in terms of objective linguistically dictated criteria to apply a predicate. Full possession of the concept involves convergence with the prevailing norms maintaining co-linguistic thinkers and that relates both to application and to cognitive role. For triangles the norm was axiomatic and formal and defined the concept of a triangle but for other things such as butterflies there are a range of possible thoughts and practices that would certify the subject as a possessor of the concept.

A parlour game, popular at the moment, involves a person who is drawing trying to make players on her team guess a word by drawing a picture. One of the fascinating things that happens when you play this game is that people who know each other particularly well or think alike seem to be quicker at guessing each other's pictures. Some married couples have an almost uncanny ability to guess a complex word from a single curved line on the page. This phenomenon is, however, not just a curiosity of parlour games (as Tolstoy noted); it holds for all communication. For spoken language the degree of complexity necessary to convey a phrase can vary according to the knowledge of the person being spoken to. There are obvious examples such as the schoolteacher who deliberately chooses short words and sentences when speaking to a room of new entrants or the two deer hunters who need the merest gesture to convey a complex pattern of action and intention. It is surprising how little needs to be said to some people in order for them to grasp your meaning. For example your son comes home from with his report card. Before reading it you say "Happy?" to him. He knows that your question is asking him whether the marks that he has received for different subjects are at a level that you and he will find acceptable. Your son says "All right", meaning that you should be prepared to be a little disappointed, some of his marks are good, but there are some that are not as good as they should be. So the meanings that are conveyed in this example are complex and complete, despite the limited use of language. Vygotsky's claim about there existing a separate grammar of thought can profitably be seen as a claim about the distinction between formal or lexical meaning and the thought conveyed by an utterance. If we understand meanings to have their own complex articulation with the rest of our proceedings (a la Wittgenstein) this allows us to escape formal specifications of the signifying aspects of a word or phrase when we understand the range of thoughts that a given sentence may provoke depending on context or the varying contents that may be communicated by the same term given different contexts of use. On any formal account of language and meaning your conversation with your son is hopelessly under-determined in its content and therefore quite unclear.

Conclusion

We have argued that the relationship between thought and word is one of dynamic interdependence yet not identity. Words have uses that are validated and constrained by shared norms. But for a word to be a word it must embody, or be accompanied by, word meaning. Word meaning is the most common unit of thought and is contributed to by the uses of a multitude of competent speakers. In this chapter we have outlined examples, provided by Vygotsky, of how word meanings could develop and become linked to objective concepts. This thesis is important because, if we are correct in the claim that an adequate general theory of the origin of word meanings must exhibit their engagement with what Wittgenstein calls "the rest of our proceedings", it fingers a serious inadequacy with all theories that claim word meanings (hence words) lie in a simple, causal correspondence relation with objects in the world. It is hard to find a good argument in support of this atomistic claim, however this does not mean that it is a trivial or obsolete claim. If it is true that all word meanings develop then it cannot be the case that word meanings are the result of a correspondence between a pattern of sound or writing and a simple impression, or sensory presentation, or even extensionally specified item in the world. A rejoinder might be that concepts are formed in this way but word meanings do not come about simply by a one-off presentation and correlation but are formed after a series of associations between a presentation and a word. The thesis would be that after sufficient simultaneous occurrences of word and object the individual grasps the meaning of the word by relating a word to an object: "Ah it's that thing in front of me". But we have argued, after Vygotsky and Wittgenstein that words relate to senses or intentional specifications of objects and in fact, participate in the formation of the contents of thought.

If what we have argued in the proceeding sections is true, Vygotsky's theory of the development of the child's comprehension of word meanings (simplistically interpreted with its stages fully reified) is inadequate. In order for a concept to be associated with a word a series of qualitative changes must be undergone which involve not only abstraction and generalisation but a recognition of the community of thinkers in fixing the meaning of a term and the content of the related concept. Because the processes by which this end is achieved involve active engagement with others, we cannot do justice to the complexity of the operation to suggest that word meanings (concepts) lie in a simple causal correspondence relation with features of the world. We are now in a position to say why this is so. Grasping a new concept involves knowing (at least to some extent) both the criteria for applying that concept and knowing how it relates to other concepts. Thus there is a level of cognitive sophistication that must be reached before certain concepts can be formed. For instance one cannot have the concept of murder before one has the concepts of death and of a deliberate action to produce death. This implies that concept formation is not adequately explained by comparison with mirroring, in that concept formation is the result of purposeful activity on the part of the conceptualiser and a congruence between the thinker and others. Thus the idea that concepts are somehow "stamped into us" or impressed on us by our sense impressions of objects and the relations holding between them neglects the development and activity of the child in its own dealings with the world and in its participation in a human community.

Children learning concepts within a domain often pass through phases of understanding — from the picking out of individual features that seem to the child to be common to the objects grouped under a concept to more generally applicable and shared criteria. In doing this task thinkers develop the cognitive skills necessary for concept formation, application, and manipulation. Whether conceptual development does or does not conform to the stages that Vygotsky outlined is not crucial for the thesis that we wish to establish here. In any case it does not necessarily follow that when a child or an adult is learning a new concept they must also pass through all of these stages. Grasping concepts involving colour words affords a skill at a more general level that can be generalised to other situations and related colour concepts. Knowing how to operate with colour words and concepts involves normative constraints upon their use that are indifferent to shape or composition of things. For example, you know that when someone applied a colour predicate to an object that the predication attributes a universal property rather than gathers the object under a type-term (such as "dog" or "frog"). That is, applying a colour term to an object — as in "the damselfly was red" — implies a specific type of relation between the damselfly and the colour universal concerned. As a result, an accomplished concept user's ability to form perspicuous representations using concepts means that they are capable of grasping concepts without working through any of the preceding stages and they know what follows and does not follow from, say, the attribution of colour. Because you know the linguistic norms that will govern the use of say *Turquoise* (after being told that it is a colour) you are a reasonable distance down the track towards forming a concept of *Turquoise*. You may never have seen this colour, so it would be implausible to suggest that you could have a fully developed concept of it because it would seem to be impossible to form a concept of a colour that you have never seen. But this is not true of all concepts: the snark does not exist, yet we may have a good concept of what it would be like if it did. Most of us have not seen (or sensed in any individuating way) electrons but we can still have a workable concept ⟨electron⟩ and a grasp of what it means for something to be an electron.

We began this chapter promising to provide support for the following assertions:

1. Children's consciousness does not involve the same degree of noetic sophistication as adult consciousness.
2. An examination of the transition from children's consciousness to adult consciousness reveals that adult consciousness relies heavily upon language acquisition and mastery for its noetic sophistication.
3. The normativity or generality of noetic consciousness is generated by the appropriateness of one's conceptualisations in relation to others.
4. The fact that noetic consciousness involves content being socialised provides a means for naturalising the noema (or ideal to which the concept conforms).

Vygotsky's ideas about there being qualitative shifts in concept development suggest, we have argued, only that cognitive development involves increased sophistication in concept use. We have not made explicit in this chapter the increased possibilities for consciousness and action that are created by conceptual sophistication. This will be our task in chapter five where we will continue the development of our theory of mental content, with an analysis of consciousness and action.

The phases of conceptual development and the pressure for increased sophistication in concept use are driven by attempts to use words more accurately. Thus one of the driving forces behind the linguistic and noetic sophistication of children is the drive to improve the propriety of one's language use and conceptualisation in relation to others. This theme will reappear in later chapters where we argue in more depth for the normative constraints governing our conscious acts.

Vygotsky's work on the phases of conceptual development shows that the kind of changes that might occur in conceptual development are the result of attempts to be a better language user. Concept development involves a series of shifts involving increased sophistication and abstraction leading towards rule governed mental content. As we develop cognitively we come to use language, consciousness and the proceedings of self and others to understand what is happening in the world around us. The grammar of thought and language are intertwined, as Wittgenstein realises, and refer to the complex set of rules that articulate thought and language mastery. This enables each of us to both deepen and broaden our appreciation of the objects that surround us and to participate in the society where language itself is living and growing in part by the contributions of all of its users.

Chapter 3

The objects of consciousness

We have outlined a view in which intentionality as *directedness toward an object* or *aboutness* is an essential feature of consciousness. We have argued that consciousness is typically a state in which one is currently exercising or could exercise a number of skills structuring human interactions with things around them. We have argued that the fact that these skills involve relations to things in a shared environment yields a robust intentionality condition for consciousness. However we now have to say something more about intentional relations to the objects of which we are conscious and attempt to fashion an account that solves certain problems arising in this area to do with the nature of the intentional object and the features of intentionality already discussed. The first of those problems is *the inference to the external object* (from the private content), but there is also the problem of *the link between an actual object and a singular thought, the paradox of intentionality*, and finally *the co-referentiality problem,* which we have already noted.

The problem of the relation between thought and object

We have already made some use of the parallelism that some authors have noted between intentionality and its objects and the structure of meaning (Sajama and Kampinnen 1987: p. 10). For instance, in the theory of mental content we would note the parallels between, on the one side: the mental act, its content and the object of the thought grasped in the mental act and, on the other, the word (or term as used), its meaning, and the referent of that component of the linguistic act. We have gone beyond this to suggest that language and, through language, culture have a formative influence in the shape of human cognition. This brings us to a problem which both philosophy of language and philosophy of thought have in common and which is central to any account of intentionality: the problem of the actual object and its relation to the content of thought.

We have already noted that intentional objects have a number of features that distinguish them from objects as undistinguished things or referents. There are two of these that are particularly relevant to externalism or idealism about the objects of consciousness:

i. the referential opacity feature;
ii. the possible non-existence feature.

First, an intentional object has to be picked out according to some conception in order to individuate it. Thus, for instance, I might be thinking of the object in my pocket but not thinking of the knife my father found in Italy although these two specifications might, in fact, pick out one and the same thing. On this basis, if I were asked whether the object in my pocket had ever been in Italy I might genuinely not know whereas were I thinking of it as the knife my father found in Italy I would know. *Second*, an intentional object may not exist. Thus I can think of the golden mountain hidden in the Andes without there ever being such a thing. These two features require us to say something more about the object of thought than just referring to the particular in the actual world of which a thinker is thinking.

However we cannot easily collapse the idea of the object of which I am thinking into the idea of the content of my thought conceived as some representational, ideational, or mental item. Some have taken this to be Husserl's agenda when he makes remarks that seem to indicate a kind of idealist commitment.

> Objects exist for me, and are for me what they are, only as objects of actual and possible consciousness. (*Cartesian Meditations*, as in Hammond et al. 1991, p. 65).

This is clearly not Husserl's intent nor, arguably, the intent of the later Brentano. In fact the passages we have selected from *Ideas* indicate that Husserl thought an idealist reduction to be absurd.

> The tree plain and simple, the thing in nature, is as different as it can be from this perceived tree as such, which as perceptual meaning belongs to the perception, and that inseparably. (p. 240)

The attempt to reduce objects of thought to mental contents neglects some important considerations.

First, when I think of the effect of fire on my body I am thinking of what an actual fire would do and not thinking of the effects of an idea of fire. We could call this the gap between living an experience and thinking of the experience. Second, if my relation to things in general is only indirect, in that my mind is acquainted or in contact solely with mental items, how do I know that there are things to which those mental items relate? Thus if my intentional relation to a fire is only via an internal mental representation or content, then how do I know anything about actual fires as distinct from my thoughts about them. To put this worry in another way: how is it that I have an idea of intentionality or directedness towards external objects as distinct from contentfulness or topicality of thought if it is the case that I have only contents or topics of thought on which to base my thinking? We could call this the problem of *the inference to the external object.*

We seem to be caught between the Scylla of collapsing intentionality into contentfulness and the Charybdis of gesturing at a doctrine of intentional relationality that struggles with the distinction between extensional and intentional specifications of the objects of thought. This shows up sharply in the possible non-existence problem and the fact that the relations between thoughts and objects are essentially specified or individuated by their intentional content rather than a bare connection to an object. In an attempt to resolve this dilemma, we will try to flesh out an account of intentional relatedness between subjects and actual objects of thought beyond the mind which does not interpose representational items in the O position of the S – O relation.

Aquinas and Brentano

The problem of specifying the object of an act of consciousness has a long history in that it has exercised thinkers since Aquinas wherever they have wanted to go beyond the rough and ready idea that we receive sense impressions and build complex ideas out of them. This model has dominated empiricist writing about intentionality and leads directly to the reification of representational objects resisted by Husserl, Merleau-Ponty and others. Haldane has labelled the problem of the object 'Brentano's problem' and considered it in its general form: what sort of thing is an intentional object such that a mind can relate to it? (1989) He makes an extended appeal to Aquinas, who clearly delineates the elements of an adequate account of our conceiving of objects:

> The conception is ordered to the thing as an end: for the intellect forms a conception of the thing in itself for this reason, that it might know the thing understood. (Aquinas)

Aquinas asserts that the conception of an object is essentially directed at the object itself, not at a mental or ideal substitute for it. The conception is however a creation of the mind and as such uses the cognitive equipment to compose the conception. If therefore intentionality consists in directedness towards something in the real world we must show how our cognitive equipment, through the use of concepts, can put us in touch with something that is not conceptual. Kenny analyses Aquinas' doctrine of intentionality by building on Aristotle's thesis that the mind is a mode of functioning of human beings as rational, social animals (1984). The apprehension of an object of thought is a modification of mental activity by both a form and a "context of sense and imagination". He concurs with Haldane in arguing that Aquinas has no sympathy for the introduction of a mental *relatum* to do service in the intentional relation. In discussing Aquinas' view of ideas, Kenny remarks:

> The ideas are not intermediate entities that represent the world; they are modifications of our intellect consisting in the acquired ability to think certain thoughts. (1984: p. 90)

Kenny's "modifications of our intellect" gets beyond a reified representational or intra-mental item and suggests a mode of relation as carrying the content. However, we cannot simply accept the characterisation of the mental act as "being appeared to Xly" because this suggests that a combination of universals is the basis of our apprehension and Kenny is careful to try and meet the obligation to say something about particulars and not just universals in his exposition of Aquinas' views.

> Of course material objects are not to be identified with universals. They are objects which are thinkable in their potency: their thinkability, their intelligibility, is their capacity to be brought under the universal concepts of the intellect's creation.

This has advanced the exposition of the intentional relation only to the point of noting that the forms or concepts of the intellect give form to the intentional object and through that form determine the content of the thought. However, it has not yet told us how to forge the intentional link between the mind and the object, particularly in the case of an identifiable individual whose link to the mind is an essential feature of the content of the thought (thoughts of particulars of this type we will call *singular thoughts*). The problem for a theory of intentionality constituted by the need to reveal *the link between the actual object and a singular thought* is also articulated by Wittgenstein:

> That's him (this picture represents him) — that contains the whole problem of representation.
> What is the criterion, how is it to be verified, that this picture is the portrait of that object, i.e. that it is meant to represent it? (*Philosophical Grammar #5*)

Wittgenstein goes on to remark that the criterion of identity for the intentional object cannot be, as it is tempting to think, *similarity to an actual object* because, particularly if one selects a cubist or expressionist influenced portrait, the visual resemblence may not be at all clear and decidedly not individuating and yet we would still count the portrait as having an intentional relation to a unique object — it is of, say, Peter. In fact more generally one can see that whatever it is that appears in thought or language is intrinsically unlike an actual thing one encounters in the world. Kenny expresses the problem thus "what makes a picture of X a picture of X, what makes an image of X an image of X, what makes a thought of X a thought of X". (Kenny 1984: p. 82)

Both Wittgenstein and Kenny ask for an account of the connection between the thought and its object. In fact a link of the type we are seeking will evidently link the subject and the object of thought and not just by some coincidence of features between the content and an object in the world because of the obverse possibility to that in the connection without resemblance objection. Imagine that I came across a painting of a man's head that caused me to say "That is a painting of Peter". However, when I asked the artist he denied that it was and in fact had painted it in the antipodes from where my friend Peter and I lived. Here we have resemblance without connection to go with our connection without resemblance described above. To get over this two-edged objection (connection without resemblance and resemblance without connection) we want some account of how the object itself, presented according to an intentional specification, enters into the individuation of the thought.

Sharpening the problem

We have sketched a theory of consciousness, which is heavily conceptual in nature and therefore rests on the recognition that conceptual content is essential to the nature of what is being thought. This exaggerates the problem created by the insight that actual things in the world rather than general concepts should figure in intentional specifications of conscious or mental phenomena. The problem is made vivid when we consider an object whose existential status is unclear.

1. Travellers in the Himalayas fear yetis.
2. A yeti is a humanoid creature that lives above the snowline in the Himalayas.
3. There is a humanoid creature who lives above the snow in the Himalayas and who is feared by travellers.

The train of thought here seems to be clear and clearly involves just the oblique contexts, which we discussed in Chapter 1. The initial thought or fear implies that there is a relation between yetis and travellers. The problem is that we do not know whether yetis exist and therefore that relation, and consequently the thoughts of the travellers may have a non-existent intentional object. This example presses our problem because, on the one hand, their thoughts about yetis seem to require a similar analysis whether or not they are true (to preserve the normal inferential links between items of mental content) and, on the other, it is impossible that there could be a relation 'thinking of Y' between a thinker and a non-existent Y. To further explore Brentano's problem we could therefore focus on *'the paradox of intentionality'*:

i. X's thinking of Y is a relation between X and Y;
ii. X's thinking of Y is the same kind of thing regardless of the existential status of Y; but
iii. there can be no relation if Y does not exist.

The yeti problem raises *a fortiori* Reid's observation, that we have thoughts about things not the ideas of things: "This one object which I conceive, is not the image of an animal — it is an animal" (p. 230). He goes on to make the intuitive distinctions of "the vulgar":

> all mankind, both those who have contrived language and those who use it with understanding, have distinguished these three things as different — to wit, the operations of the mind, which are expressed by active verbs; the mind itself which is the nominative to those verbs; and the object, which is, in the oblique case, governed by them. (Reid [1785] 1983: p. 140)

It is clear, for instance, that when I think or worry about a yeti I am thinking or worrying about a real yeti that might or might not exist and do me an injury and not merely my idea of a yeti. But arguments against ideational objects of thought leave us without clear direction in trying to understand intentionality. An analysis which preserves our intuitions about there being a relation between thoughts and their objects seems to entail that if there is no physical object then the might must relate to non-existent or purely mental objects.

Our problem is intensified even further if we explore further the implications of the idea of singular thoughts — thoughts that are essentially about a given particular. Consider the following case.

Xavier thinks of an apparently yeti-like creature he saw while he was stranded on a particularly difficult rock-face. This individual seemed to show him the way to get off the rock-face safely. He often thinks ⟨I wonder if I really did see *that creature*⟩. In this example, it is possible that Xavier is thinking of an actual creature, in which case its content is derived in some way from the thing he saw. But it is also possible that there was no creature and the content of his thought cannot be derived in that way. Now, if the first alternative is correct, there is a relation between Xavier and the creature such that we can investigate it to elucidate intentionality but this characterisation (and therefore the analytic project based on it) is problematic if ⟨that creature⟩ does not refer to anything. We therefore need an analysis of intentionality whereby Xavier's thought has content and the essential structure of thought is preserved whether or not the 'yeti' exists.

In the post-Cartesian empiricist tradition there seem to be two major mutually exclusive and bivalently exhaustive positions available.

1. The idealist view just accepts that what is in the mind cannot be an actual concrete thing, such as a brick or an elephant. It then opts for the thesis that the mind does not deal with actual concrete or particular objects but rather with mental correlates of objects (called, usually, ideas, representations, or some other name which allows them to exist in a different mode from the actual things they are ideas or representations of).
2. The realist opts for the view that the mind relates to objects themselves. A realist can *either* be a direct realist and rely on a metaphor such as the mind 'contacts', 'directs itself upon', or 'apprehends' the object *or* she can be an indirect realist who believes that some representational intermediary comes between the object and the mind and that the mind relates to the object via this intermediary. We will examine this latter view in its prevalent or empiricist version in order to discuss problems common to both realism and idealism.

Enunciating these problems will bring us to a more adequate view of our consciousness of objects as things, independent of our minds, about which we can frame thoughts. Both of these are wedded to the reification of the object of thought and a doubly substantive view of the S–O relation. Reid has suggested, somewhat akin to Kenny's "modifications of the intellect", a more dynamic view in which the mind is a nominative for a number of functions exhibited by human beings. This, we shall argue, is a far more fruitful path to take.

Empiricism and the universalist view

The problem that creates pressure towards some variety of idealism can be outlined in a set of premises that we could dub the *Idealist Representational argument.*

IR1. When one thinks of an object that object is in some sense in the mind.
IR2. The contents of the mind are mental or conceptual in nature.
IR3. Objects are actual and concrete not mental.
IR4. Objects themselves cannot be contents for the mind.
IR5. Therefore the mind contains things that correspond to the objects we think about but not those objects themselves.

Each of the first three premises is independently plausible but, as we have seen, Reid and the phenomenologists want to reject IR4. We must now see whether they can do so.

We do use the phrase 'to have something in mind' when we are talking about a person's thought and we do seem to believe that it is the actual thing to which we all refer when we designate a given particular that is the something concerned. Thus, we might say "He has Aethelred in mind" and be meaning to refer to the actual Saxon king but not for a moment think that his head has somehow expanded to contain a sweaty, living, breathing, mail clad Saxon: the intuition that is recorded by IR5 and given a particular nuance by the preceding premises.

When we refer to somebody, say Fred, having Aethelred in mind we would usually, if pressed, explain what we meant in terms of something like a mental image, copy, or conception of Aethelred which belonged to Fred and which Fred called up or activated whenever the situation called for thoughts about Aethelred (Reid p. 221). In this sense we tend to think of consciousness as a kind of inner display on which mental copies or representations of objects appear, act out their brief part and sink back into unconsciousness.[8] But notice the reification of the representation that springs so easily into the argument and is implicit in this picture. The same implicit reification is found contemporary philosophy of mind when it refers to objects in the mind as tokens of a mental content type whose nature is given by some specification in conceptual terms. Once again we strike the problematic view, that conceptions of objects and not objects *per se* are the objects which indwell or in-exist (Husserl) our intentional states. It is natural therefore to try for a conceptual specification of a particular object conceived of in a given way that has two types of features:

i. universal or qualitative (descriptive) features which characterise the object;
ii. indexical features which link it to a given particular.

i. This is sometimes called a dual-component thesis and is embraced, for instance, by McGinn. Haldane expresses a sophisticated version of this view:

> The conceptual component of a reality-intending thought consists in the articulation of wholly general features. When these duplicate an existent state of affairs and are exercised in association with some feature of the thinker the cause of which is traceable to that state of affairs then the thought secures a reference. (1989: p. 29)

On its common interpretation, the universal or descriptive features add up to something we might call a quasi-individuating likeness or qualitative specification of the object. Wittgenstein notes the essential features of this view in his discussion of resemblance (e.g. to the subject of a portrait). In particular, he notes that any resemblance cannot be unspecified because the idea of resemblance *simpliciter* is empty and should be linked to some feature or respect on the basis of which the things resemble each other.[9] He remarks, the idea of the same and the idea of a rule go together as we have discussed above in relation to consciousness; the rule giving a principled way of identifying the dimension of resemblance (1989). We are compelled to specify the principle or dimension of resemblance because any particular, *a*, can be said to resemble any other thing, *b*, in some respect or other, for instance (minimally) in that

8. For the time being we shall neglect Freudian distinctions between the subconscious and unconscious which will become important in Chapter 8.

9. Resemblance — everything resembles everything else in some way or another.

both are particulars (which might mean that they resemble each other no more than the spiral nebula and a Christmas pudding). Any overall resemblance, on this view, is a sum of specifiable and limited resemblances each of which has some conceptual content; this is, in fact, reminiscent by Brentano's discussion of distinction and comparison between objects of consciousness. On this account, if one were to think of 'the big red umbrella with the green and yellow wooden parrot carved on top' one would have in mind a conceptual specification in universal terms which is unlikely to leave anyone in serious doubt about what is being represented even though one can imagine a situation in which it might not be a singular description. This is good enough for most naturalistic theories of the individuation of objects of singular thoughts because we are plausibly designed to achieve good-enough specifications for our domain of cognition and action and not absolutely individuating specifications. However it does rest the focusing of attention on a particular on the conceptual specification of that particular rather than an actual link with it. We shall later pursue the implications of rule-following and the learning of language (as discussed in Chapters 1 and 2) to arrive at a neo-Wittgensteinian account of the intentional link but for the moment we can rest with the claim that we need, in addition to a general specification or a set of universal characteristics, some way of forging a link to the actual object of thought.

ii. The indexical features are meant to fill this gap. They fix which item of a given type one is referring to in thinking of a particular object. However, it is tempting for a thorough-going universalist or descriptivist to cash this out in terms of objective spatio-temporal indices such as 'the one standing in the umbrella stand in Mr Jonabad's front hall yesterday'. It should be evident that this move merely shifts the problem to the indices used to individuate the item concerned and their status in terms of features of the contents of consciousness. Are the indices which link my thought to the actual object themselves actual or intentional? If they are actual then we must explore what the connections actually are and this account must provide a mechanism sufficient to fix the semantic relation in the actual world. If we opt for mental indices in a notional or experiential world then we have something like Ayer's view (1979).

On this version of the descriptive view the objects of thought are denizens of a realm of mental images and it is the pattern of connections between these Cartesian (or inner) experiences that allows us to infer beyond them to the world that is causing them. This thesis confines itself to the epistemic discipline of exploring our experience, idealistically conceived, and the knowledge that can properly be grounded on the content available to an idealist when we bracket any assumptions about the external world. Husserl is often thought to recommend this picture but it is unclear that his bracketing is supposed to operate in this way. Some argue that his bracketing is meant to suspend our natural metaphysical assumptions, for instance that mental contents are built out of simple elements available to a mental analogue of our physiological receptor systems (*Ideas* Ch. 2; Hammond et al. 1991, Ch. 1). If it were not for Ayer's prior commitment to the empiricist picture he inherited from Locke, Hume, and Russell, we might, however, call his study a phenomenological exploration of the world of experience.

The discipline of attending to what is within experience and bracketing (or excluding from our thesis) any assumptions about *what the experience is an experience of* is more rigorously followed outside the empiricist tradition and particularly within phenomenology. This more rigorous analytic discipline was embraced both by Kant and Husserl in their attempts to provide an account of the objects of thought. It will serve us equally well in the present project.

A foray into Kant and post-Kantian phenomenology

Kant aims to define the conditions under which a thought can be considered well formed so as to qualify as a thought of a determinate object. He derives from his table of judgements in the transcendental deduction of the First Critique a series of categories that, he claims, underpin thought about objects in general. The categories are *quantity, quality, relation, and modality;* what Kant means by them is, however not clearly evident until he describes their application to thinkable states of affairs. Here we find them expressed in the "principles of pure understanding" (B187). It will be helpful to list and explicate the principles in relation to the associated judgement and category types.

QUANTITY: *The axioms of intuition* are based on the principle that "All intuitions are extensive magnitudes" (B202). This principle covers the fact that in any thought of an object that object must have certain determinate (however vague) spatio-temporal characteristics. Thus it makes sense to ask of any object of thought what sort of dimensions in space and time might it be expected to have were one to encounter it? Notice that this is not an empirical generalisation based on multiple encounters with objects but an *a priori* condition on an item of consciously apprehended content that one would be prepared to grant the status of being an object.

QUALITY: *The anticipations of perception* are based on the principle that "In all appearances, the real that is an object of sensation has intensive magnitude, that is, a degree" (B207). Here Kant is appealing to the idea that a thinkable object, were it real, ought to impact to some degree on the thinker's sensitivity. Even if invisible it would still need to be detectable in some manner, i.e. to give rise to some quantum of detectable sensation in order to be considered an actual thing worthy of attention by a subject attempting to gain knowledge about the furniture of reality.

RELATION: *The analogies of experience* have given rise to volumes of debate because their basic principle seems overly rationalistic: "Experience is possible only through the representation of a necessary connection of perceptions" (B218). Pared down to its essentials we find that Kant is wanting us to consider the ways in which the putative object of thought fulfils the conceptual requirements of either object or property, enters into causal relations with other objects, and has a place among a community of objects. It certainly seems basic to any topic of thought that we should know something of its metaphysical status: whether we should think of it as a particular or universal, its causal properties, and its community of interactions before we could say that we have any clear idea of the type of thing in question. Consider, for instance, *the colour red*; of this object of thought we would say it is a universal and therefore bears comparison with other universals but does not enter into causal relationships except through its instances. By contrast, *a bee* is an object that instances a general type, which has causal relations to other physical objects, and which could be expected to interact with any other object occupying the same tract of space-time. It is in such terms that judgements of RELATION tell us what constitutes being an object of a certain type. If we, as Kant did, confine ourselves to judgements available within a world of experience, these categorical judgements of relation can only be explicated as necessary or *a priori* connections between appearances otherwise considered as comprising a continuously varying flux of unrelated impressions. But we have not accepted this Humean starting point so need not adopt the rationalist and Cartesian reading that is often given to the analogies. What we can do is accept that these a priori requirements are dictated by the internal connections that are essential to our conceptual system that is the milieu of all of our defensible and rationally orderable judgments about the world around us. On this ground we might claim that even if the objects we are talking about are actual objects with an existence independent of our ways of knowing about them, then the way that we conceive them must respect the categories of Kant's deduction.

MODALITY: This category gives rise to *the postulates of empirical thought* and requires the thinker to have knowledge of the modal status of the object of thought. A moment's reflection suggests that it would be alarming if any thinker claimed to know what she was thinking about and did not know the modal status of the object in question. Think, for instance, of someone who said they had in mind a person called Albert and then could not say whether Albert was an actual being, a possible being, or a necessary being; one would have to conclude that the thinker in fact did not have a clear idea of the object the thought was directed upon.

If these categories seem not to have the status that Kant claimed for them, try to think of any object about which you have a clear idea and in relation to which you are genuinely in doubt about how to make any one of these judgements. It is, it seems to us, a futile effort. Nevertheless, we can only conclude that Kant shows us what it means to think of a thing as an object: we are thinking of an intelligible object whose metaphysical features are determinate when we are able to satisfy these categorical conditions in relation to our conception. Or, to put it in another way, if we cannot specify these features of our apparent object of thought then we do not have any clear idea of what kind of thing we are thinking about. We are still no closer to having a clear account of the link between a thought of the object (with all these essential features suitably filled out) and the actual object that the thought is a thought of. On this subject, Kant admits that these principles are only regulative of our alleged knowledge and he appeals to the manifold of sensory matter which alone can establish the existence of something which is the actual object of thought (B222). On the connection between sensory matter and the thing itself he is apparently silent. We will later argue that he provides a condition that does the business and thereby converges with Wittgenstein and satisfies what we have called the co-referential condition.

Husserl explores the nature of objects of thought by using a set of quite distinct analytic tools: *the transcendental object*, *hyle*, *noesis*, and *noema*. An object is given in thought when the mind contains hyle or sensory matter similar to Kant's matter of sensibility. It is then structured by noemata so as to have noetic content. For Husserl, as we have seen, intentional contents are informed by meanings or *noemata* (ideal forms of thought) and not identical to real world objects transcendent of experience but they are not 'shadow' or 'inner' objects. They are *noetically constituted* in that they are apt to be thought about or figure in acts of consciousness. Therefore we must provide an interpretation of mental relations which does not assume inner mental objects and yet allows that things are thought of as being thus and so where the 'thus and so' is a placeholder for an intentional specification and not merely an extensional designation. For instance, 'the morning star' is a mental categorisation that, absent human beings and their diurnal rhythms of life, would not be applied to Venus (the term 'Venus' itself, has of course a rich cultural history). Husserl distinguishes between the (*noetic*) "proper components of the intentional experiences, and their *intentional correlates*" (1931: p. 237) where the latter are the objects of thought on the one hand and the *noemata* or forms of meaningful experience and cognition on the other.

The *hyle* or matter of the object structured by *noesis* yield the proper components of any phenomenological event, say, of seeing a tree; and these components are intentionally real or in-existent (to use Brentano's term). They are meaningful in virtue of their relations to the actual tree (in the world). But the *noetic content* that is structured by its relation to the tree is 'steered onto' or related to its object (the actual tree) by the *noema*. The noema is an intentional correlate of the experience itself and is therefore ideal not real. To look at it otherwise, *noesis* is a faculty intrinsic to or immanent in acts of the mind and noemata are transcendent of the mind but in a different way from the (actual) object. Both are transcendent of the real content of experience because they are not contained in the experience even though noemata inform the experience (1931, p. 261). The *noematic* refers to contents in a similar way to meaning (*Sinn* 1931, p. 238) refers to the objects we speak about and is unchanged in different *noetic* phases of contact with actual objects. Thus, at one point, Husserl remarks that the actual colour, shape or nature of an object manifests itself through a "hyletic phase" of concrete experience that takes varying perspectives on it. These are united as referring to the one thing by the meaning constituting function of the *noema*. Husserl's view clearly preserves for *noema* (or *Sinn*) something which transcends an individual moment of experience as it appears to the subject but which is intrinsic to the meaning of that experience.

Let us take a further example to try and clarify Husserl's view. I walk around a Henry Moore sculpture. I am struck by various impressions of solidity, contour, surface, space and mass, and so on. Each of these is informed by its own noema but all the noetically constituted moments of my experience are united into one over-arching mental occurrence — my total experience of the Moore sculpture. The sculpture is inert if salient, the impressions are inherently shifting but they are drawn together in relation to their intentional focus — the sculpture itself. This focus as the object of my mental act embraces or includes the moments of my (potentially disjointed) perception. The noematic correlate, my ideal specification of the sculpture as such, is therefore as transcendent of my (actual) perceptual series as the (actual) object that I see as a sculpture. Thus my immanent or real experience has two intentional correlates:

i. the object (in the world);
ii. the *noema* which unifies it and relates it to that object.

Note Husserl's contrast between consciousness and reality or what he calls actuality (1931, p. 121). [In *Ideas*, Husserl uses the term 'actual' for the familiar sense of 'real' and his technical use of 'real' refers to the occurrent contents of the mind]. The ideality of the *noema* and its role in fixing the object of the thought in a way that does not depend on the occurrent mental goings on of a subject combine to suggest that the *noema* determines what counts as an integral part of the experience e.g. of the colour red, a tree, the Moore sculpture, or Dvorak's 8th Symphony. This aspect of Husserl's view allows the essential or canonical content of a given thought not to be a function of occurrent ideas, which Frege calls "men's varying states of consciousness" (1977: p. 25).[10] It also parallels Dummett's insistence, in his philosophy of language, that the sense of a term should guide a thinker on to its reference (1981: p. 47). The problem of the link between the actual object and the singular thought implies that the actual object must somehow figure in the determination of the noematic structures and the related workings of noesis that yield an object of consciousness. How that might be is not solved by a universalist reading of noetic content.

10. We shall indicate references to Frege's *Logical Investigations* (1977) by using the abbreviation LI.

Husserl clearly embraces the thesis that the contents of consciousness are intentional and not to be reduced to or simply equated with actual objects in the world. Husserl's (Aristotelian) terminology for the analysis of content has made visible the distinction between what can properly be said to be immanent (real) in the mental activity of a subject — *hyle* and *noetic contents* — and what is transcendent or cannot be contained there — the actual object and the *noema*. Husserl's exclusion of the *noema* — the objective sense, or meaning — which determines the content given by *noesis* to an intentional object, suggests that if we find a location for noemata we might also solve *the co-referential problem* and *the inference to the external object* problem. For Husserl the *noema* defines, in the case of an intention directed upon an actual object, its actual world reference. If somehow we could forge a robust link between the reference and noesis that transcended the individual mind and its acquaintance with the reference we would also have solved *the paradox of intentionality*. It remains to see if we can turn this trick.

We have accepted Frege's argument (echoing Reid) that this cannot be a function of individual or collective impressions but we have also noted that a noema is not the kind of thing that happily inhabits a world of actual objects. Therefore we have, in driving for our account of the relation between consciousness and its objects, to avoid the trap, into which Frege (and to some extent Husserl) fell, whereby we are forced to posit a 'third realm'. This (noematic, objective and ideal) realm is supposed to be distinct both from the world of objects and from the consciousness of thinkers and it provides the forms of contents which individuate thoughts and also determine their truth or falsity when those thoughts concern actual situations. The problem is particularly acute in the case of objects like Yetis whose metaphysical status is indeterminate. How do we fix truth conditions for these?

We have noticed that when I quake with fear at the idea that I might ever confront a Yeti I am not fearing an image in my own mind for images cannot hurt me in that sense. Neither am I fearing an abstraction from various inscriptions or utterances because, again a la Reid, such notional objects hold few actual terrors. I am fearing a thing which, endowed with the properties described in popular folklore, might destroy me. For Husserl, there must be a *noema* correlated with an act of thinking about a Yeti. The *noema* has a prescribed and meaningful form that constitutes different *noetic* moments as *hyle* through which the actual object — correlated with the *noema* — presents itself (1931: p. 261–2). It is clear that essential to this particular *noema* is some reference to traveller's tales from the Himalayas. We therefore, on Husserl's behalf, must provide a conception of *noemata* which, in the present case, satisfies the dual constraints (i) that the Yeti *noema* may indicate an object or a fictional creation; and (ii) that it must be objective in the sense of normative in relation to individual ideas about Yetis. If we solve this we then have to address Husserl's 'real' contents: What, for instance, is the *hyle* for a Yeti?

The *hyle* comprises the unstructured appearings that are informed by the *noema* (itself normative and related to the actual object if there is one) so as to become noetically contentful. Specifying *hyle* is a fairly daunting problem even where they can be related to an actual object (and thereby the object related to the thoughts of a thinker). At least in the actual object case there are actual or causal connections that could link the thinker to the object and serve as some kind of grounding for the *noetic content*. For a Yeti such causal connections are themselves in question and with anything remotely like the object of mystery and imagination it is said to be requires a different account of the noematic constitution of the object.

However, we cannot, because of Husserl's distinction between *noesis* and *noema*, allow our account to lay too much stress on the creative role of the apprehending mind. If we were to do that we would lose sight of the transcendence of the *noema*. What is more, a further question would then arise: How does an actual or possible object become determinant of the *noematic content* and thus constrain (and not merely get created out of) the *hyletic* and *noetic* content which have mental (real) existence? We must conclude that although Husserl rejected idealism he failed to link his intentional objects to the world in a way that made clear the semantic or intentional relation between consciousness and its objects. Thus both Kant and Husserl, while clarifying certain cognitive and logical conditions for a thought to count as a thought of an object have left one of our central problems (the link between the actual object and the thought) untouched.

The unresolved problem of the link to the object

Recall Reid's common sense realist claim: when I think of an animal I am not thinking of an idea of an animal and when I fear the flame and the sword I fear the impact of the actual flames and swords, not ideas of them. On an indirect realist view, the states of mind are caused because the presence of the actual things I fear usually accompanies my ideas of them even though I have never been acquainted with those things except through their mental counterparts. We therefore seems to have two choices: either

a. one can accept that we have no knowledge of what the world is really like "out there" so to speak, and therefore no knowledge of what it is for an idea to resemble an object (and so have to concede that *the inference to the external object* is a "shot in the dark"); or

b. one can claim that the reason I know about what things out there are like is that the ideas are the way they are because they resemble their real world objects.

The first option, which could be taken to involve a sparse version of Kant's *noumena*, is considered by most to be unpalatable. The second does not solve the two-edged problem that we identified in relation to Wittgenstein's remark: we can have resemblance without connection and connection without resemblance. This problem can be made quite pressing if we imagine a representation R_p that resembles an object O_o that it is not a representation of more than its proper intentional object O_p or does not resemble its intentional object at all. Consider the following story.

> Zena paints Piotr. Her painting looks like a yellow box with black edges and three appendages, one red, one orange, and one purple. In a country to which Zena has never been and of which she has never seen any visual image, a schoolchild has made a cardboard sculpture that looks just like the object in Zena's picture. Zena's portrait of Piotr, along with another painting called 'Sculpture' is shipped to that far country but en route the case is broken open and the contents vandalised so that one painting is destroyed. In that country the cardboard sculpture has become well known through a well-publicised hoax played on a gallery owner. When Zena's painting arrives, as part of a damaged shipment said to include 'Portrait of Piotr' and 'Sculpture' it is immediately given the second title.

Now we know that the title is wrong but it is true that it resembles the child's sculpture more than, to most people, it resembles Piotr. Nevertheless the real intentional connection is not captured and we have to have an account other than resemblance to elucidate what this intentional connection turns on. We have already argued the general case that what goes on in the brain cannot "resemble" in any straightforward sense what it is properly to be regarded as a representation of and, given that the contents of a conscious act, absent a strong identity thesis, are not physical events at all they cannot resemble their objects (which may be physical things or events).

We have already discussed the epistemological conundrums of inference to the external object and co-reference to which any internalist view (such as the indirect realist view) of intentionality gives rise. One obvious candidate to yield the link between the object and the conscious act directed toward that object which we have not yet scrutinised in any detail is a causal version of the indirect realist view.

The causal indirect realist response

One plausible response to the need to specify the intentional relation goes back to Locke's indirect realism. He is happy to assume that there is a causal connection between the object that gives rise to a thought and the ideas making up the thought about that object. This causal connection is all that he believes necessary to tie thoughts to the world at sufficient points to enable us to say that those thoughts are about a world out there. The causal connection is also invoked to ground the actual connection between a mental act and its proper object. On this view the object of any conscious act is the object which causally gives rise to the contents of that act.

There is also a plausible and relatively straightforward way to flesh out this skeletal answer. The account begins with an empiricist view of the so-called "chain of perception" and uses this posit to ground the chain of reference. Perception is said to be a matter of receiving impressions that are based on excitation of the sensory receptors. The resulting nerve impulses are passed through structured causal channels in the nervous system. This path which leads from the object to the processing centres of the brain responsible for conscious content results in an object of thought being registered in consciousness. Thus, in any act of reference to an object of thought, we need only find causal connections or intermediaries between the person and the object to secure the intentional relation. The intermediaries, in a non-perceptual case may be such things as memory traces or even names, which themselves have causal connections to the object and establish the link between the mind/brain state of the conscious subject at the present point in time and the object that subject has in mind (whether present or absent). There are, however, some serious problems for this view. We will mention five (some of which have already been discussed).

- the problem of the intentional terminus;
- the problem of conceptual structure;
- the problem of the non-existent object;
- the co-reference problem;
- the problem of referential opacity.

The problem of the intentional terminus

Once the idea of the causal chain has been sketched for us, the most serious problem for this thesis immediately comes into view. Which point in the causal chain is properly designated the object of my thought? Whatever else we can say about causality, it is fundamental to a causal view that there should be an unbroken causal chain stretching through any designated point in that chain to link antecedents and effects. How then does one privilege the point at which the intentional object is located? What distinguishes, for instance, *the figure seen in the mirror* (or not seen in the case of Count Dracula) from the light source in the room, the light pattern on the surface of the mirror, the stimulation on the surface of the retina, or the pattern of excitation in the first receiving centre in the brain, as the object of thought? Why should a particular sample of "middle sized dry goods" occupy this privileged place in an unbroken causal chain that, in purely physical terms is quite egalitarian as to the significance of events at any point? In a sense we have already supplied the answer by talking of referential opacity, conceptualisation, and the need for co-reference, themselves problems for the causal view. We will argue that these answers lead us into a theory of intentional content closely linked to linguistic meaning and, in particular, is a far more complex matter than can be analysed in terms of causal chains (on the basis of the role of rule following in the theory of meaning and conceptual content).

The problem of conceptual structure

We have already discussed this at length and, at this point, we need only note that it excludes an uneffaced reference to the object of thought (as physical-causal existent) as a suitable place-holder in the explication of the intentional relation. Count Dracula known as Count Dracula and not just the pleasant central European aristocrat who has welcomed me into his castle is the object of my fear and it is not until he is seen under that (intentional) mode of presentation that he stands in the right relation to my conscious act of fearing him. But the object who is Count Dracula is the very same physical object who appears to be the pleasant European aristocrat. This means that the only specification of the object, a physical specification, fit to figure in a causal chain cannot do the work needed to flesh out the intentional relation which occasions the to-be-explained mental act.

We have argued that referential opacity which defeats any purely physical or extensional account of the object of thought is important in understanding the way that objects figure in acts of consciousness. We have also argued that intentional specifications are built out of concepts. Concepts, in turn, embed normative constraints or rule-following in the individuation of their contents and thus the explanation of their role in conscious thought. But rule-following is not just a matter of being caused to act thus and so by an object but of obeying certain norms in how one responds to that object. Thus conceptual specifications of content are not simply given by causal features of objects and do not have any natural place in a specification of the causal chain linking object and subject. Thus causal chains are blind to intentional content and will not fix the object of thought as it figures in mental explanations.

The problem of the non-existent object

The problem for a causal thesis here should be obvious. Here there is no terminus causally standing in relation to stimuli impinging on our receptor systems. We therefore do not have the close analogy with perceptual objects needed to render the causal view plausible and must find some other type of analysis; we suggest that the rule-following analysis does the job well.

The co-reference problem

It is fundamental to my grasping the intended reference of the sense central to my thought that I refer to the same object as others. We have already discussed the normative nature of this requirement and the inefficacy of substituting an internal equivalent or something that functions only because of its causal relation to my inner workings. My object of thought must essentially be the same as your object of thought if the truth of our thoughts is to be tested against the way things are with a common referent. Thus my referent cannot be a distinct although notionally equivalent causal source to whatever it is that stands in the right relation to your thought. If it were I could only guess its identity on the basis of some happy similarity between my words causally based on representations in my mind and yours based on quite other causal connections in yours.

We consider that these objections are conclusive and demolish the thesis that causally based internal events and an account of the causal chains between thinkers and objects in the world can form the basis of an analysis of objects of thought.

Singular thoughts revisited

The class of thoughts called singular thoughts (an example of which was Xavier's thought of the yeti) will, we believe, allow us to escape our impasse in elucidating the intentional relation. A singular thought is a thought of a particular object just as Zena's painting was a painting of the individual she knew as Piotr. Again an adequate understanding turns on elucidating the intentional or 'thinking of' relation. Despite the fact that a causal connection will not do the job of fixing this relation, some actual connection is needed as can be shown by considering a purely conceptual specification offered by Prior.

Prior's suggestion about the 'thinking of' relation where Y is a real object turns on a logical relation between thought and object. He claims that when there is an object, Y, in the next room of which I am thinking ⟨that is a violin⟩, that the relation between me and that object is: *Y is the object which makes my thought true*. He elaborates this "bare" account in an attempt to distinguish thoughts about an unknown object, A, that A is X and thoughts about an object, B, known to the thinker that B is X by using the apparatus of quantification (p. 134ff). This allows him to make a principled distinction between Othello's thought that someone (he knows not who) is unfaithful to her husband and Othello's thought that someone (Desdemona) is being unfaithful to her husband. Prior has it that the first thought can be formulated *Othello believes that there is an X who is unfaithful* and the second *There is an X such that Othello believes her to be unfaithful*. That this is not a perspicuous analysis of all the thoughts in which we are interested in the relation between the thinker and the object of thought can be seen from the following two cases.

> Vera tells Wallace that she will put a boiled sweet in the box on the kitchen table. During school, Wallace thinks ⟨there is a sweet for me to eat in the box on the table⟩.
>
> Leticia calls to Milton as he goes out the door to school. 'Look,' she says 'I am putting this boiled sweet in the box for you to eat when you get home'. Milton, at school, thinks ⟨there is a sweet for me to eat in the box on the table⟩.

Now Milton and Wallace both, on Prior's analysis, have a thought such that 'the sweet in the box makes his thought true' but they have different thoughts (or — thoughts with different content-types). What is more they each have a thought such that both *W/M thinks there is a sweet for me in the box* is true and *W/M thinks of the sweet in the box that it is there for me* is true so the quantification move does not work. We therefore have failed to capture the special relation between the object and the mind that gives us an adequate analysis of the intentional relation as it applies to the content of the singular thought. We can bring this out if we have a third person exchange the sweets during the day. In this case W could arrive home and take the sweet thinking, mistakenly, ⟨That was a nice sweet which V left for me⟩ but M is epistemically placed such that he can think ⟨That's funny, that's not the sweet L put in the box⟩. This difference between their two cases makes it clear that there is a different type of content involved in each thought although both are made true by the sweet being in the box (Salmon, 1992) and they both satisfy the quantificational alternatives. The distinction between contents is such that there is a richer relation between M and L's sweet than between W and V's sweet. The richer relation is not captured by the indiscriminate characterisation implicit in Prior's 'Y makes S's thought true' nor by Prior's attempt to advance beyond this austere characterisation.[11] Prior himself notes the need for something more than an analysis in terms of concealed quantifications:

> under what conditions can we be sure that, in someone's belief, fear, assertion, etc., we *do* have a genuine relation between the man who believes, fears, etc., on the one hand, and the individual that his belief, fear etc., is 'about' on the other? (p. 137)

When we look for a characterisation that does provide this assurance, we are often left with a term like 'acquaintance' which goes along with the device of logically proper names. This may seem intuitively clear but we have found

11. See, for instance, *Objects of thought*, p. 140.

reason to argue that such a relation resists any simple analysis — such as a causal analysis. In the most straightforward of cases it seems to rest on a metaphor such as the idea that such names have as their function "to drag some bit of the world right into what is being said" (p. 147) and things only get worse when we move beyond straightforward cases. It is much less clear when we broaden our gaze to the general class of intentional objects.

In the yeti case, we encounter our problem very acutely. Xavier is not sure whether he saw a yeti. We therefore cannot say *Xavier thinks that there is a creature who is a yeti,* nor can we say *Xavier thinks of that creature that he saw that it is a yeti*. Xavier is thinking of a particular encounter with the world that it might have been an encounter with a yeti or "I, Xavier, saw something but was it a yeti?"

We must now try and capture the link implicit in this thought in such a way as to understand how it can yield a connection between the mind and an intentionally apprehended object.

The information link

Gareth Evans has attempted to capture the richer relation that grounds thoughts about particulars in a way that goes beyond dubbing it 'acquaintance'. He claims that the difference denoted by the term 'acquaintance' is that there is an "information link" between the thinker and the object with which he is acquainted (Evans p. 121ff). This appeals because, in some sense, M does have information *from* the sweet that L put in the box whereas W only has information *about* V's sweet. What is more, M's information seems to be a function of his contact with that particular sweet whereas W's information is inherently general — it could relate to any sweet with the descriptively specified properties (a distinction able to be captured by a suitable quantification — *there is a sweet in the box*). Because M's thought individuates L's sweet but W's thought only provides a conceptual slot potentially able to be filled by any qualitatively similar sweet, we are justified in saying that M has an *essentially* singular thought of just *that sweet* whereas W, by contrast, seems to have an *essentially* descriptive or general thought. We need therefore to flesh out the idea of 'information' so that what the thoughts have in common and how they differ both become clear; this should prepare the way for a richer characterisation of the intentional relation between thought and object. If this is successful then we may be able to give an analysis of thoughts sufficient to deal with thoughts about both existent and non-existent objects.

Evans discusses two types of essentially singular thoughts in which the information-link is particularly clear: *recognition-based thoughts* and *demonstrative thoughts*. A recognition-based thought typically involves the subject having a kind of 'gestalt' based on information gathered from the object. This may not be reducible to a combination of descriptively specifiable features sufficient to individuate that item as is illustrated by the common experience of being stumped for individuating features to describe to one friend who has an appointment to meet another friend in a public place. The existence of such an irreducible, recognitional, 'information package' (which cannot be specified in terms of descriptive elements) from an individual implies that at some time one has been in perceptual contact with that individual and thus been able to demonstratively identify it or pick it out (as ⟨that object⟩) (Snowdon 1981). But notice that here we have started by discussing a recognition-based thought and arrived at a demonstrative construction — ⟨that object⟩. This implies that, of the two types of singular thoughts, demonstrative thoughts are basic to our identification and understanding of objects in general (see Gillett 1988).

The apparent basicness of demonstrative thoughts has broad relevance to human thought and experience and is supported by a consideration of the way in which we learn concepts. A thinker who is developing competence in dealing with the world is dependent upon things being picked out as instances of certain concepts. The thinker learns what features of the world occasion the application of a given concept, such as ⟨dog⟩ or ⟨apple⟩, through concept instancing items — here dogs or apples — being picked out and marked by the use of a certain term in demonstrative judgments or speech acts such as *'that is a dog'* (see Ch. 2). We take this to be the thought behind Quinton's suggestion (1964) that the situations in which language is taught and learnt are the basis of all our empirical knowledge. The many transactions where human beings use expressions such as 'that is red', 'that is a ball', 'that is Aunt Emma', and so on, on this account, play a central role in experience and the mastery of concepts used to organise it. Their cumulative result is the developing thinker learning a set of intelligent skills enabling her to apply concepts to the world around her. These skills are themselves of considerable philosophical interest.

The mind does not passively receive pre-formed conceptualised content apt to ground (neo-Fregean) thoughts (Millikan 1991 p. 100). To think of a thing as instancing a concept, the thinker has to select that colloquy of key features that tend to warrant the application of the concept in question (e.g. ⟨dog⟩ or ⟨electron⟩). These features occur as part of an indefinitely rich array of information potentially available in any given situation. If the information satisfies the conditions under which a certain judgment is warranted, then she can make that judgment (e.g. ⟨that is a dog⟩, ⟨that is an electron⟩). For the thinker to get the right application for the terms involved (and therefore for the shared concepts they express), she must therefore master a range of techniques of collecting and selecting information from the environment according to the 'canonical' basis of the application of a given concept.[12] These 'canonical' features do not relate to an ideal language but merely to the norms governing the relation between the concept or term and its conditions of use. For instance, in learning the conditions that ground the use of the term 'cat'; she must focus on the cat present on each occasion of (demonstrative) use and not on its colour, its size, its location, its movement, or any other incidental feature extraneous to the fact that there is a cat present in the situation.

Wittgenstein comments on *seeing* a thing *as* being thus and so in the following terms: "the substratum of this experience is the mastery of a technique" (PI# 08e). The technique enables one to recognise that in a given range of conditions a certain judgment is warranted. A linguistic term typically serves as a sign or marker for the cognitive skills that underpin this technique.[13] Such a technique is not inferential in that it is not always explicitly based on reasons for judging thus and so but it does obey rules or normative constraints that govern judgments of the requisite type (Gillett 1989). We have already noted that techniques of picking out objects as instances of this or that conceptual type, confer on us the ability to think about a world of objects.

A further ability comes into focus when there is a particular object to be identified and reidentified. Evans refers to this function as 'tracking' that object (1982: pp. 195–96). Perceiving an object as a thing of a certain type (e.g. ⟨that dog⟩) is only the beginning of being able to think of that object. The

---

12. I draw the term 'canonical' from Peacocke (1985).

13. One of us has discussed this in *Representation, Meaning, and Thought* (Gillett 1992). Quinton warns us against over-intellectualizing this process by, for instance, claiming that hypothesis testing is the basis of perceptual knowledge, as if there were necessary and sufficient conditions licensing an inference to the conclusion that a concept — such as <red> — is instanced. The use of a sign or marker does not rest on such a quasi-ratiocinative process or function.

thinker must also be able to conceive of it as distinct from other objects of the same type. This implies that two things are involved in thoughts about particulars. *First*, there is the idea of things of a certain type or kind: "We cannot just re-identify a thing, or recognise it as the same thing, without making use of its being a thing of a certain kind" (Strawson 1966: pp. 83–84). *Second*, there is the identification of this instance of a thing (of a certain type) as being the particular one that ____ (some individuating specification).

According to Evans, we individuate things by locating them on a cognitive, spatio-temporal map. However, this seems too restrictive in that I might, for instance, carry the idea of a particular beggar in mind without knowing just where or when I saw him; I might think, say, 'That beggar that haunts me, where did I see him?' But to frame coherent thoughts about that beggar, I must at least have an idea satisfying the individuation conditions of some type of thing. For a beggar, the type is *human being* and the conditions include a certain persistence in time, physical and causal constraints on spatio-temporal alterations, and so on. I could not, for instance, think of a human being as the same human being if I were to see him as a young adult in a photograph from 1920 and a child in 1989, or if he shifted and changed form and substance like a cloud (barring some strange metaphysical beliefs — see Seddon 1972). There are, we might say, a set of informal and familiar constraints which apply to what Evans calls "the fundamental idea" of a human person (or, in general, any object of a given type).

This view embodies a kind of essentialism about types of things. For instance, it implies that there are certain critical characteristics that determine which individual a given type of thing is. Thus, a radical change in shape may not alter the identity of an amoeba but it would alter the identity of a statue of Apollo. On this view it is plausible that a human being is individuated by time of origin, sex, location within a family group, and so on. Thus one can imagine two possible worlds in which at time t' a baby was born. If, in W1, A and B were the parents and in W2 C and D then the babies would be different individuals. Alternatively, if in W1 A and B had a boy and in W2 A and B had a girl then, again, it would seem that there were different babies involved. It is debatable whether, given all else was identical, the fact that A and B's baby has red hair in W1 and blonde hair in W2 would make them non-corresponding individuals. However, Baby1 could be born in London or Bristol depending on the parents' movements in the respective possible worlds without thereby being a different individual. Different types of fundamental idea would individuate musical motifs or chess positions.

One of us has argued elsewhere, that although spatio-temporal location is basic to our ways of thinking of many types of identifiable and reidentifiable objects, other features may play a similarly fundamental role depending on the type of thing concerned (Gillett 1987; 1992). This should be evident from the examples of the beggar and the musical motif, but other types of individuals that are not primarily individuated on purely spatio-temporal grounds might be ice creams, acrobatic turns, and vintages of wine.

If spatio-temporal information is not the only kind essential for the individuation of items but is still important, and we allow the further claim that an idea of a world is an idea of a set of particulars which instance concepts/universals that are individuated in some discourse or other around here, then it would appear that spatio-temporal location and the individuation of particulars are pivotal features of conceptual thought.[14] Such features allow us to move from the grasp of a general function of judgment exercised in applying a concept to the ability to make particular truth-accessible judgments.

The difference between the general function of judgment (as in judging that a thing is or is not *red* or *a frog* and particular truth-accessible judgments (such as ⟨that frog is red⟩ emerges from a comparison between Frege and Kant. Kant argued that judgment is always required when an appearance is taken to instance a concept.[15] Thus, in using a concept such as ⟨red⟩, I judge that I am warranted in making certain links between my present and other experiences. The links concerned unite this experience to those others in which I have confronted things which count as red so that, whenever I judge that, say, *a is red*, I am, in a sense, activating an appreciation of what is in common between a whole series of experiences which are unified by the fact that ⟨red⟩ is instanced in each of them.[16] Because such experiences are of public situations then the series forms, in principle, a public set of conditions which warrant the judgment in question. It is the ability to make this judgment if and only if it is warranted that constitutes a grasp of the concept ⟨red⟩ (this is

---

14. Which is close to the view taken by Strawson (1959) but not quite the view taken by Campbell (1984–5) although it preserves some of his essential points.

15. The term 'links' is derived from Peacocke's study *Thoughts* (1987), but the idea is discussed best by Strawson in 'Imagination and perception' in *Freedom and Resentment and Other Essays* (1974).

16. Strawson gives a sensitive discussion of this point in 'Imagination and perception', (Strawson 1959).

my version of Kant's claim that a concept rests on a "function of unity in judgment"). But judging that ⟨red⟩ is instanced here and now is not sufficient to develop a truth-linked cognitive map or set of thoughts about the world.

Truth-assessable thoughts such as ⟨the flag is red⟩, ⟨the grass is red⟩, ⟨that is red⟩ and so on are required to ground beliefs which can be built into a comprehensive understanding of how things are. In each of these thoughts a conception of a particular object is combined with a general concept (such as ⟨red⟩) to yield a thought about the world. This is one reading of Frege's doctrine that concepts are incomplete or unsaturated: they must be combined with a conception of an object to yield a truth-assessable thought. This in turn suggests that thoughts about particular things — singular thoughts — based on information links with objects are central in a truth-based understanding of how things are in the world.

This sketchy analysis implies that singular thoughts and information links have certain properties.

i. Singular thoughts can be well- or ill-grounded such that the information link allows for the thinker being mistaken in her judgments. This is because the norms that govern the use of concepts and the formation of true beliefs may or may not be satisfied in a given case. The existence of norms (which are prescriptive in that a thinker ought to follow them) entails that even if the thinker does not always reason about the application of concepts to experience and perception by and large involves a non-intellectual skill, there are judgments involved. These are continuous with the more evident appeal to norms implicit in framing a truth-assessable thought. Imagine, for instance, the subject sees a figure coming towards her on a hazy day and wonders whether it is a mounted samurai. Here her perceptions would be in subtle interplay with a number of intellectual considerations about what is in front of her. In this process, she implicitly recognises that there are reasons that are relevant to whether she ought to see things as being thus and so. She therefore recognises the normative role of reasons in determining the content of her experience and the norms are truly prescriptive (not merely descriptive); they are "norms for persons to follow" (Peacock 1987: pp. 52–53). Prescriptive norms and the possibility of error infect the information link because it is a skill and we cannot drive a sharp analytic divide between cases where the norms are regulative but uncognised and the cases where a thinker makes explicit appeal to reasons and warrants.

ii. The information link does not involve belief-formation but presents material apt to ground belief. Because beliefs have conceptual content, this material must be conceptual in nature; it therefore depends on judgments (which are implicit in the application of concepts). And where shared signs and terms impose definite constraints on the content of a concept, there are norms governing the content-ascriptions involved. These norms necessarily go beyond a specification of the 'inner-states' of the individual (Gillett 1991).

iii. The information link provides different content from that comprising a descriptive thought but content which must take its place in the subject's conceptual system. The difference derives from the fact that information links essentially involve objects whereas descriptive conceptions (even definite descriptions) only contingently do so. But the conceptual nature of the information link implies that cognitive skills exercised in using concepts are also exercised in forming information links with and therefore singular conceptions of objects. Therefore we cannot expunge all traces of Husserlian noesis or Fregean sense from the information-link (pace those who claim that such content is not involved in 'acquaintance'). Whatever is required to determine sense (or conceptual content) is somehow intrinsic to the information-link.

A Wittgensteinian refinement of Aquinas' solution

Recall that Wittgenstein's problem was expressed thus: "What makes my thought of him a thought of him as distinct from a qualitatively distinct replica whom I have never met?" We will now offer a Wittgensteinian refinement of Aquinas' theory of intentional relations between the mind and an object. On this thesis an object of thought known to me as K is *A thing I encountered in the language-related activity where I mastered the use of the term 'K'*. This encounter cannot be understood apart from the human language related activity in which the thing was encountered although the object itself may figure in other encounters embedded in different human (and therefore socio-cultural) activity.

We have argued that in applying a concept in an experience (an encounter with the world), the subject makes a (normatively constrained) judgment. On this view, the content of the concept is given by what is in common between the conditions in which that judgment is made and some (criterial) set of conditions in which the concept has been mastered. The judgments concerned (which enable one to detect what is in common) are, we have argued, governed by rules which prescriptively determine when it is warranted to respond thus and so to certain conditions. These rules have shaped a range of skills or techniques in which the subject focuses attentional and information-gathering faculties on the aspects of a situation which warrant the judgment in question. Furthermore, rule-governed skills shape and therefore determine the ability to keep track of items so as to satisfy the conditions that ground singular thoughts (or the use of individuating expressions). This account of the semantic rules governing general concepts and the formation of conceptions of objects ties the information link and therefore the object of thought to a range of shared practices. The fact that concepts have the same content no matter who applies them is also explained if the grasp of concepts is tied in this way to a range of shared practices. It also implies that something like (Fregean) sense (or a Husserlian *noema*), analysed in terms of warranted use in a specified range of conditions, is primitive in a theory of meaning and thought content.

On this reading, a subject thinks of an item as being of this or that type by locating that item in relation to her grasp of a network of shared practices. In these practices the use of signs (such as the terms of a natural language) have unified her judgments over time and produced an agreement in judgments between herself and others who use the concepts concerned. This claim both embodies Strawson's conclusion that thinking of an item depends on "thinking of its being a thing of a certain kind" and avoids the trap of positing a conceptual or representational realm in which that item appears as a private object. A successful object identification therefore embeds information from the actual item as it was related to in a context which is reflected in the subject's conceptual system and depends on a skill at which she may be more or less adept according to her experience and training.

This view has congenial implications about the types of information that can appear in individuating conceptions. Because the signs (or markers) involved in conceptualising particular things are drawn from the expressions in a natural language, the objects individuated by using them engage with the subject's mental economy in ways that are linked to conceptions formed in ways other than through perception (e.g. by testimony). Therefore to say that X is thinking of an object <u>a</u> is to ascribe to X a conceptual 'slot' into which a conception of <u>a</u> could fit and to ascribe to her the ability to track <u>a</u> through her interactions with the world by using skills honed while learning a language. These skills are obviously broader than perceptual skills and capitalise, among other things, on the subject's knowledge as to how it is with things of that type.

This yields a promising analysis of Xavier's possibly singular thought about the yeti that he might have seen.

Analysing singular thoughts

X has a conceptual 'slot', prepared by his grasp of the concepts ⟨white⟩, ⟨furry⟩, ⟨humanoid⟩, ⟨Himalayas⟩, ⟨fearful⟩, ⟨elusive⟩ and so on, which jointly inform the concept ⟨yeti⟩. He also had an experience in which he found himself so placed that he was inclined to fit whatever it was he confronted into this conceptual slot. The situation in which he judged ⟨that may be a yeti⟩ may not have included any object approximating his concept of a yeti but the conditions disposed him to judge that his information might derive from such a source. He can now think of the conditions that provoked that judgment but be unable to deliver a conclusive verdict on his warrant for it. His inability to deliver this verdict, which would make available to him a range of further singular thoughts (such as ⟨I wonder what that yeti was thinking⟩, ⟨I should have offered that yeti some chocolate⟩ and so on), is based on the fact that he is unsure of the applicability of the skills properly described as *yeti detecting* in those conditions. Absent any assurance about the adequacy of his perceptual skills to warrant the judgment ⟨that is a yeti⟩, he is also unsure about the many judgments (such as ⟨there really was an animal of some kind there⟩, ⟨it was humanoid⟩, ⟨it was white and furry⟩ and so on) that would support or warrant the yeti judgment if they themselves were true. In another possible world called Schmearth it might be that X has considerable yeti-detecting skills such that his conception of a yeti is more recognitional than compositional. In Schmearth he would, perhaps, have asserted ⟨that is a yeti⟩ based on an unassailable *gestalt* the elements of which he might not be able to unpack.

On the present reading, Evans' information-link is a result of informational skills that involve selective rule-governed responsiveness to conditions falling within the range that warrants the use of some sign or marker. The skills are essentially relational and therefore so is the information link. But the use of that sign/marker rests on techniques (of attention focussing etc.), and therefore it can falter or even miscarry. The subject may gather and assemble information in an unwarranted way because of inexpertise, difficult perceptual conditions, inadequate supporting knowledge, or even motivational pressures (the last producing *akratic* misperception). A concept user and her skills are therefore central in the information gathering that grounds mental content/thoughts. These features, and the prescriptive nature of the norms that the concept user obeys, entail that more is involved in the information-link than the causal production of certain 'mental states'. Notice that the skills do not merely tell one how to characterise a given item but also, and *inter alia*, enable one to judge that in certain conditions there is an item to be characterised, that a concept, say ⟨F⟩, is applicable, and therefore that it is right to characterise the situation concerned as being thus and so.

This general view allows us to give two respectable views of the objectivity of real objects of thought and experience.

Two respectable accounts of objectivity

Kant defined for us the conditions that must be met for one to be thinking of a determinate object of thought. In so doing he secured an intersubjective view of objectivity in which the factual or counterfactual convergence in judgements between two competent thinkers is what grounds the truth of a judgement about an object in the world. In fact he links this to communication and therefore, implicitly language (*pace* Strawson [1966, p. 151])

> The touchstone whereby we decide whether our holding a thing to be true is conviction or mere persuasion is therefore external, namely, the possibility of communicating it and finding it to be valid for all human reason (B848)

If we interpret this fairly modestly, then what Kant is saying is that when a subject finds herself confronted by an object she makes and perhaps expresses a judgement. Another competent thinker does likewise and, over time and a number of such encounters she comes to master the skills of rightly making judgements about the objects before her (B172ff). Through this training she comes to judge in conformity with humankind and establish in her own mind implicit norms as to when she is or is not warranted in making a range of judgements about the intentional contents of her experiences. These judgements are, by implication, relativised to the objects in her shared environment and the judgements she applies are relativised to the discourses she inhabits.

So now we come to Husserl and there immediately comes into view a way of securing the objectivity of noemata and their link to the actual object. An object grounding a noema, say *dog*, is an external thing that I and others have used to fix the meaning of a denoting term such as 'dog'. Generalising this, we can say that the *noetic* abilities required to frame a judgement like ⟨k is a B⟩ depend on being able to gather information from the object 'k' or a general term 'B'. The abilities involved in grasping the content *k,* say Karoly, is based on having a fundamental idea of the kind of thing Karoly is, say a human being. The thinker would also need to understand the conditions under which *B* is properly applied to grasp the predicative or general element in the judgement.

This approach allows us to deal with the problem cases as follows.

The sweet: Wallace and Milton differ because Milton has information from his sweet which has a certain noetic content directly related to his encounter with the sweet in a situation alike in relevant respects to those in which he is used to gathering perceptual information from objects and forming a conception of the object in question. Wallace can only gather descriptive and general information to base his thought of his sweet and, although this may never show up there are easily imaginable conditions, in which it would (the substitution of a recognisably different sweet for the one Milton saw).

Piotr's portrait is of Piotr because of the language related activity of naming which allows us to latch on to and track objects rather than rely on qualitative similarity for reidentification. That we do sometimes, even often, rely on that method does not detract from the general analytic feature of singular thoughts that we can identify and track an object which pursues a complex path through human contexts and is known by an individuating name.

Xavier and the yeti is an example where the noetic content is clear but the existence of any instances that fulfil it is not and so "we know the post where the word is stationed" (Wittgenstein). This yields a place where the noema is located in our conceptual map of the noematic world (Husserl) but Xavier is not sure whether the conditions he has found himself in and responded to satisfy the requirements of the relevant noematic specification.

We can now move on to a consideration of the ways in which intentional contents are dependent for their individuation on the social and cultural milieu in which the thinker is placed.

Chapter 4

Consciousness and action

One of the principal functions of consciousness is to form and execute voluntary actions according to some weighting of the thinker's current reasons, attitudes, desires, and so on. Therefore, in discussing the relation between consciousness and action, one is irresistibly drawn into a consideration of rational or reflective self-control and freedom of the will. We will argue that freedom of the will is secured if the subject can be seen to do things at the behest of his or her own reasons rather than merely as a result of the causal influences in play. We will drive at this conclusion by considering the nature of action and its essential dependence on conceptual or intentional content. In outline we will argue that, this dependence and the rule-following considerations we have previously discussed, it follows that, in so far as we are rule-followers we must be viewed as able to obey rules rather than merely being caused to act thus and so by antecedent conditions. Rules are normative regularities that give us reasons to conform our activity in the light of certain thoughts. Therefore our account of consciousness and action implies a defence of a moderate theory of freedom of the will.

Our first major claim about actions is that they are, necessarily intentional in two senses:

i. they have intentional content; and
ii. they are purposive.

Our acts themselves and their aims are therefore potential objects of conscious reflection. Secondly, we will claim that the purposive mental acts guiding actions actually explain the relevant actions. Thirdly we argue that action types are individuated by the semantics of the relevant purposive mental content. These theses taken together tie the conscious and intentional nature of actions together to just the right degree in that the more automatic or unconscious an action is seen to be, the less explicit and unambiguous its intentional structure is conceptualised as being. It remains to make these claims good.

Sartre is notorious for his optimism about the human capacity for free will and his existential humanism stakes out one limit on the dimension along which we might align action theories. Thus we need to pay special attention to the strengths and weaknesses of Sartre's theory of action.

In Chapter 1 we explained that when we used the term "intentionality" it should be understood in wider and more basic sense than mere purposiveness. Intentionality as we have used it so far has denoted the aboutness of consciousness and we have argued for the joint theses that the things that intentional states are about are objects in the world and that each object is cast in a certain light when it appears as the content of an intentional or mental act. We have also defended a strong connection between intentional contents and linguistically mediated concepts. To avoid confusion we shall, throughout this chapter use the word "purposive" to refer to mental content that is goal-directed or has some aim (intentional in the psychology sense) and preserve the term "intentional" for its use as we have defined it.

Actions defined

In *Search for a Method* (1968), Sartre prepares the way for his second major philosophical work *The Critique of Dialectical Reason* (1976). The *Critique* was Sartre's attempt to revamp historical materialism so that it was more congenial to his existential phenomenology. In particular Sartre was concerned about the tendency of some Marxists to attempt explanations of human behaviour that ignored the purposiveness of human action and the meaning-giving activity of human thought.[17] We need not concern ourselves with the Marxist project here, but it is relevant to the present study that Sartre rejected action explanations that ignored intentionality (both in *Being and Nothingness*

17. "We must resolutely reject the so-called "positivism" which imbues today's Marxist and impels him to deny the existence of these last significations [action's goals]...The supreme mystification of positivism is that it pretends to approach social experience without any a priori, when in fact it has decided from the start to deny one of its fundamental structures and to replace it by its opposite. It was legitimate for the natural sciences to free themselves from the anthropomorphism which bestows human properties on inanimate objects. But it is perfectly absurd to introduce by analogy the same scorn for anthropomorphism in anthropology." (Sartre 1968: p. 299)

(1958) and in *Search for a Method*). In his discussion he argues that actions (like consciousness in general) are not only intentional in that they are directed towards those things that give them content but are also purposive and understandable in terms of the kinds of things that we find people doing in the ordinary situations in which we have learnt to use language.

> If my companion suddenly goes toward the window, I understand this gesture in terms of the material situation in which we both are. It is for example, because the room is too warm. He is going "to let in some air." This action is not inscribed in the temperature; it is not "set in motion" by the warmth as by a "stimulus" provoking a series of reactions. There is present here a synthetic mode of behaviour which, in unifying itself, unifies before my eyes the practical field in which we both are. (1968: p. 297)

Sartre's companion has performed an action. Actions are behaviours that are, in some sense, brought about by people as a result of purposive mental acts. The content of the mental act accompanying an action gives meaning to that segment of his activity. Thus we explain the behaviour of Sartre's companion by remarking that he is motivated by the fact he is too hot and as a result he "goes to let in some air". If asked why he went to the window Sartre's companion would say it is because he was too hot and his action bears out this explanation as part of synthetic unity which embraces the relevant features of the context within it. The motive explains his behaviour in terms of his thoughts and their reason-giving contents and the reasons are directed towards his situation in an environment. What is more, the "because" does not necessarily imply that actions have causal relationships with preceding dispositional states, a view that we shall consider later in this chapter. At this point all we wish to glean from Sartre is that for every action there exists a corresponding purpose that must be identified if that behaviour is to be seen as having the content that marks it as an action. The behaviour is necessarily in a contentful relationship with a set of mental acts such as beliefs, intentions, desires, expectations and so on that tell us what action it is and how it fits into the pattern formed by the agent's engagement with the world or "the practical field in which we both are".

It is also worth noticing from Sartre's example, the intuitive level at which one's understanding of another's behaviour takes place. We can, it seems, literally read the behaviour of others as having a certain content in virtue of what we understand about the project or ongoing activity in which they are involved (sometimes, in fact, we need minimal cues, because the action is so self-evident in its intent). In this example, the movement toward the window brings into focus the whole complex situation according to a conception that assigns meaning to all its components.

Identity Structure

Thus far we have claimed that for a behaviour to be an action it must be structured by mental content which individuates it not only as a purposive action, but also as a particular action. So the fact that Sartre's companion is doing something purposive not only implies that there exists a corresponding purposive mental act — an intention, but also that the state has a particular content. In this case, the contentful mental act which organizes the behaviour is ⟨going to open the window⟩ rather than just ⟨moving about the room⟩. Some have interpreted this as the requirement that every action takes place as a result of a *trying*. Tryings are usually invoked because at a certain point in the genesis of an action it is posited that the agent has done all that she can do and then it depends on the interaction between the bodily movements set in train and the environment what happens. However this seems to be an unnecessary ploy. We could alternatively claim that any intention structures a tract of behaviour so that it typically has a desired effect in the domain where the behaviour is occurring and that it is only when something breaks down that it miscarries. That things do break down is a natural fact about the world and therefore the fact that beginning a project that should effect a certain result may not always mean that the result is achieved is also a fact about the world. It seems to go too far to jump from that observation to the idea that some parcel of mental activity that contains the action in all but realisation exists in the mind before the action is executed and brings it about.

We can support this view by returning to the claim that there is an internal relation between consciousness and intentionality. Actions are conscious acts and therefore, even if they are not in any full-blown sense a result of voluntary tryings, they are all intentional and contentful. But we have argued that intentional content is world involving. This is highly congenial to the view that actions are essentially operations on the world rather than Cartesian events (like pre-formed tryings). If, therefore, all purposive mental acts are intentional and the identity of an action is given by the content that explains it then the explanation of an action by appealing to its intentional content tells us something about the engagement of the agent at that time with the (shared public) world.

Action theory has not been neglected by contemporary psychology. Vallacher and Wegener (1987) describe how people come to know the actions they are performing. They define an action's identity structure as follows, "act identities bear systematic relations to one another in an organized cognitive representation of the action — the action's identity structure". Thus, people have in mind a certain idea of what they are doing or want to do and use this prepotent identity as a frame of reference for implementing the action, monitoring its occurrence and reflecting upon its attainment.

We could try and describe an act as a series of limb movements but this is ambiguous in terms of the identity of the act. A complex jerk of the limb or ballism might have the same neuromuscular structure as throwing a stone but in the latter case what we are seeing is not just a complex jerk of the limb of that type (here a mechanical description) but a throwing of a stone at something. We are immediately led to ask further interesting questions: "What was her target?", "How practised is she at throwing?", and so on. The intentional description reveals the action in a way that is interesting for psychology whereas the mechanical description does not. The "identity structure" or intentional content of the action tells us what conditions in and features of the environment are giving the act its distinctive shape. The action identity structure maps the behaviour onto the environment telling us what conditions it will be sensitive to, what changes of condition will change the shape of the action, and so on.

What is more, the current content of the identity structure "tracks" (or varies with) my conscious focus. For example, I am driving casually and chatting away to you and then I begin attending closely to the road ahead, the lanes and the signs and move over to take a turn off. The change in my attentional behaviour indicates a change in the identity structure of my intentional action from an automatic overall content of driving to the theatre to the more detailed task of trying to make sure I turn off at the right place on my way there. This example shows that actions can nest within each other and that, in explaining the detailed shape of my activity, any observer is required to track the contents of my consciousness and their articulation with the structure of my ongoing purposive activity. Already there begins to emerge a clear account of the intimate relation between the intentional directedness of attention (or consciousness) and the structure and control of action.

We can develop this idea further by using other examples where our consciously directed activity and our purpose go completely hand in hand. We have already discussed one of Brentano's best illustrations of the directedness of consciousness in which he discussed a hearer listening to a chord and directing attention either towards the individual notes of that chord or the chord as a whole sound (1966). The directedness of consciousness is, as we have repeatedly stressed, a feature of its intentionality and is specified by specifying the object which forms its content and the way in which that object is noetically engaged with by the subject. This directedness is clearly pivotal in a discussion of the "identity structure" of an action. We have seen that a particular tract of behaviour, while part of an over-arching action, may have a more particular action identity within that whole depending entirely on the way in which consciousness is engaged. Imagine you are presenting a paper to a conference, reading from handwritten notes. While doing this you scan quickly across the sentences. To your horror page 5 was written while the plane (upon which you were travelling to the conference) hit a prolonged period of turbulence. Your handwriting is of a similar quality to your six year old daughter's (it is actually slightly worse than her best). In an attempt to make sense of the handwriting you concentrate upon the individual letters of the words, trying to put together a sentence. When the level of directedness of your consciousness changes in this way the identity structure of your action has changed (in mid-stream as it were). Not only has the direction of your consciousness shifted, but the content of your behaviour at that time has also changed from the point of view of anybody trying to give an accurate account of what occupies your mind in performing that behaviour. Your mind is no longer focused on the larger project of presenting the paper but on the more detailed sub-project of deciphering what you have written (and perhaps even on the possibility that your faltering delivery at this point may impair the larger project).

This fact about our conscious tracking and the intentional and purposive structure of action is important when we consider reductive accounts of human action, for instance, those that attempt to reduce the content of action to some function of the underlying brain states involved. Some, struck by the realisation that the mind is somehow really the brain may wonder if the neurological events in your head determine in some way the corresponding changes in the direction of your attention. Indeed one might see an extension of the "tryings" analysis in this direction. If such a reduction was possible then an account in terms of identity structures and the intentionality of consciousness could be short-circuited by an explanation in terms of the underlying brain states. This would imply that even if the mental or intentional accounts were illuminating to some extent, the real explanatory work would be done by something that was much more clearly part of the fabric of biological science. There are however reasons to do with mental content why that train of argument will not go through. We could call this the *ineliminible reference to mental taxonomy argument.*

It may be possible for a scientist to track the firing of neurons when you focus your attention upon the components of the words. It seems reasonable to suppose that a really good neural scientist might be able to identify the complex neuronal event that corresponded to your change in conscious attention. And if the scientists did tell us that the neural event causing your change in conscious awareness could be traced as a result of other neural events of which you had no knowledge then you may begin to feel uneasy about how much control you really had over the things that you did. Let us, for the sake of argument, say that you do consciously read a sentence "Discourse is the product of culture" and that we call this conscious act C1. When you have trouble reading and begin concentrating upon the components of words we shall call the conscious act C2. The two neural states that the scientist isolates, corresponding to C1 and C2 we shall call N1 and N2.

Now we must ask: Why did the scientist come to pick out N1 and N2 as states of an identifiable type? Not because they were primarily distinguished as identifiable types of neural state but only because they corresponded (in some way yet to be specified) to C1 and C2. If it were not the case that the mental acts were identifiable and distinct then there would be no reason to differentiate the two from the ongoing neural stream or from each other. Thus the individuation conditions of N1 and N2 (the conditions which distinguish them as metaphysical types) are secondary to mental (or intentional) categories.

Can the scientist make sense of the change from N1 to N2 without reference to the move from C1 to C2? It seems hard to see how she could even look for the distinctions without C1 and C2 being distinguished. It is the fact that the change in the attention has shifted, due to an unexpected challenge encountered while performing a certain task, that has brought about the change C1 to C2 and therefore made the corresponding change in neural states worthy of note. But if the scientist cannot make sense of the shift from N1 to N2 without reference to consciousness then she must concede that neurological talk about actions is dependent on mental individuation conditions and therefore that the types in her explanatory ontology are not intrinsic to (or self-contained within) the realm of law-like generalisations she is attempting to work with (neuro-physiological generalisations). Therefore she is under some obligation to say how it is that she can talk sensibly about N1 causing N2 when she lacks self sufficient descriptive categories which tell us which states and events we are talking about and therefore also lacks the ability to generate laws connecting such states and events.

The identity structure of the action to be explained is mental: the change in the focus of your consciousness is explained by the fact that you are reading in front of a group of peers, who are expecting you to say something and you cannot read your writing. These are mental, intentional, conditions and given by descriptions which go beyond the confines of neurological state descriptions. They even go beyond conditions that could be specified in terms of the organism alone (a problem for methodological solipsism). This argument undercuts the possibility that there could be principled neurophysiological types or kinds which would be worth worrying about if we did not have the mental act specifications which tell us how to parse the stream of neural activity. We shall reinforce this conclusion in chapter six by canvassing further arguments for the irreducibility of consciousness to independently identifiable neural states and events with a self-sufficient neurophysiological taxonomy.

The mental content that is determining the action which you can properly be described as performing is, because of considerations of identity structure, given by the intentional content occupying your consciousness and is therefore, to some extent at least, introspectible. In explaining what you are doing to another person, a specification of the contents of your consciousness is definitive (even if your complete set of reasons for acting that way may not always be so transparent). This conclusion is secured by the fact that to act you must mobilize certain skills of operating on the environment in order to bring about an intentionally described (or contentful) change. It goes without saying that you as the subject must know what intentional or noetic skills you are using in order to make judgements about their application, satisfaction, adequacy to your current purposes, and so on. Therefore in explaining your action we need to trace thc origins of your conscious act as a contentful act and not merely as a neural event. This explanation is likely to emerge from an account of your life and the meaning of various events to you rather than descriptions that ignore those features.

Daniel Dennett has a further argument on this point (1987). Dennett imagines a group of Martian scientists who want to study human beings with the benefit of tremendously advanced physical sciences. They observe and record a lot of human behaviour (in purely physical terms) and the physical changes within the human beings that cause all those movements. They come up with a set of correlations that are very good and allow them to predict and explain (in physical terms), for instance, what a man will do after he has made a call to his wife and she has told him to get some drinks on the way home (because they have friends coming to dinner).

Now Dennett imagines a human observer who is given the data from which the Martians have derived their specifications and himself makes a very good set of predictions about the man's behaviour of going to a bottle store, buying some drink, and going home with it. They are amazed that, with his impoverished data base and computational equipment, he can be so good at what they do with so many sophisticated and probabilistic calculations and heuristics that our computational systems have never approximated them. But Dennett goes beyond this comparability point and makes a point that suggests a stronger view than his instrumentalism might otherwise be taken to recommend.

> There are patterns in human affairs that impose themselves, not quite inexorably but with great vigour, absorbing physical perturbations and variations that might as well be considered random; these are the patterns we characterize in terms of the beliefs, desires, and intentions of rational agents (1987: pp.13–35)

If he is right about this then there are things picked up by mental, personal, and social language that are not picked up by the physicalist descriptions of the Martians. There are, if there is something to that suggestion, patterns in human affairs that are both significantly explanatory and unavailable to physicalists. This would be a conclusion that is meat and drink to the present analysis and is in close agreement with our argument about individuation of mental types and the inadequacy of physical or physiological categories.

In this section we have argued that it is the mental content structuring an action that fixes that action as belonging to a certain type. In the next section we shall argue that actions, because they are individuated as belonging to a certain kind in virtue of mental content, are individuated in terms of concepts, many of which as we have already discussed, are linguistic in origin. This has certain implications for the related ideas of rational reflection, the control of actions, and the problem of free will.

Conceptual structure of actions

In the passage about window opening, Sartre claimed that his companion's behaviour was a "synthetic mode of behaviour". He proceeds to explain what he means by "synthetic" when he speaks of psychological sets being "abstract judgements that are insufficiently determined", only becoming determined "within the undertaking" (1968: p. 153). We take this to mean that it is only within the context of a pattern of intentional activity that one can determine or make sense of the content of a given action.

Recall that in Chapter 2 we concluded that the essence of word meaning was a rule governed pattern of use that linked a word to certain conditions in the world in the light of some typical human activity or practice undertaken in those conditions. We also suggested that word meaning is the most common unit of thought. Perhaps we can understand Sartre's "abstract judgements" as equivalent to attributions derived from the activity of the agent but underdetermined without a conception of the engagement of the individual with reality of which that activity forms a part. Once we had achieved some precision in such attributions these judgements would yield the "semantic units" articulating the intentional activity. When one sees the four legged object upon which a friend is sitting and applies the predicate "chair" to that object, there is a movement from a range of universals (four-legged object, piece of furniture, chair) to the particular characterisation that is best fitted with what my friend is doing. The concept ⟨chair⟩ is a generalisable classification that applies to a number of chunks of reality and allows one to think of them as targets of certain kinds of activity. But when you look at this four-legged object at this moment and think of it as "a chair" your intentional activity is potentially targeted in a certain way on just one object because of the role it is playing in a currently significant bit of human activity. So the thing in the world only becomes determined as an object of a given type (or significance) by applying some concept and that noetic act locates it in a pattern of human practice (because of the rules governing that concept).

This may seem like a fairly obvious point, but it implies, in the light of our former arguments, that the following of rules is a basic skill in conceiving of an object and constructing an action directed at that object. This is a departure from what some have said about the nature of concepts and mental content. Some would argue that mental representations such as ⟨chair⟩ are akin to little pictures in the head imprinted through association between the object and word and this would neither account for the rule-governedness of concepts nor their pivotal role in action structures. Our claim is that the purposive mental content accompanying an action is given structure by concepts and forms the identity structure of the action because it is framed in terms that essentially link humans and their behaviour to environmental conditions.

You are at the opera with an American friend who doesn't know a great deal about the orchestra. During the overture you notice that the French horn player is flat. During the first interval your friend says "gee that overture was swell". In pointing out that the French horn player had played poorly it becomes obvious that your friend does not know how to pick out the French horn from the other instruments. So your friend has not heard the French horn in the sense that it has not been an individuated focus of aural perception (as discussed by Brentano in relation to the chord and its notes). This phenomenological observation reminds us that in targeting our behaviour or perception on to a particular bit of the environment we selectively attend under the guidance of concepts that we have learned.

The individuation of actions by concepts occurs in the same way that the perceptual activity was individuated at the opera. The difference between you and your friend at the opera was the mastery of certain concepts. Similarly a skilled batsman has at his disposal a much more complicated range of concepts to guide his action than the social cricketer. When the skilled batsman sees a delivery coming down the wicket that he judges to be ⟨full of length, slowish, and turning towards off stump⟩ this conceptually sophisticated observation will have implications for his action. He has decided that any ball that fits this category he is going to ⟨reverse lap⟩ rather than try to play a drive or a sweep. This approach to his action is one that the batsman has thought through at some prior time. Quite likely he has rehearsed physically the shot that he will play when presented with a certain type of delivery. His basis for selecting this strategy is a calculation that a selection of the right kind of shot for each ball bowled is likely to lead to be an approach to batting which maximizes safety and scoring rate (which is not to say that he laboriously calculates as he faces each ball — the milliseconds available for decision do not allow that). Obviously he cannot do this unless he can judge what each ball is doing according to a range of concepts and then select from a range of shots adapted to each type. And equally obviously these have been smoothly incorporated into an almost instinctive performance by practice. The social cricketer may not have at his disposal the same conceptual framework and skills to differentiate deliveries in this way and be able perform the same actions. His approach to batting involves swinging as hard as possible at anything within reach.

In considering the rule governed nature of concepts, including the concepts that govern action it is clear, as we have argued at length, that there are norms that apply to their use. Thus when the social cricketer says, after going out to a lofted slog straight to square leg, "my defensive shot didn't come off" he is making a mistake about the sort of action he has just performed. Really he "ought" not consider his action to be of that type because it does not fall within the range of cases covered by the concept ⟨defensive shot⟩. This crucial dependence of concepts on rule following undermines the view that an action, when thought of as an intentional action, is caused by the events preceding it. The skilled cricketer when he sees a short pitched delivery coming towards him is not causally compelled to think ⟨that is a bouncer⟩ but it is in his best interest to think of the delivery in that way. Having conceptualised the trajectory of the ball in this way, the batsman must then react quickly in the light of the implications this delivery has for behaviour and its outcome. Doing nothing will mean he gets hit in the head. Ducking will mean he doesn't get hit but also he doesn't score. The batsman may have noticed prior to the delivery that that there was no fine leg or square leg, thus the hook shot to the bouncer (which will send the ball in the direction of the non-existent field placements) is a good option. If the batsman did not have at his disposal the concepts ⟨bouncer⟩ and ⟨hook shot⟩ then he has a good chance of being struck in the head by the ball or not scoring both of which do not fit his overall project of scoring runs.

For the moment we need to turn our attention to the reason why it would be mistaken to claim that he is causally compelled to think of a delivery as a bouncer. The mistake arises because the application of concepts like ⟨bouncer⟩ involves judgment. So in the brief amount of time available as the ball is coming towards him the initial awareness of the delivery is that it is one that is going to bounce halfway down the pitch. Now this observation does not in itself determine that that the delivery will bounce up to a height qualifying it as a bouncer (head height). If in fact it does not rise to a difficult and dangerous height then it will not be appropriate to consider it a bouncer. Thus when seeing a delivery coming towards him the batsman must always make a judgment about whether this is the appropriate way to think of and respond to this delivery according to the norms governing the appropriate concept —

⟨bouncer⟩. He can only judge in conformity with these norms if he has mastered those skills (of attention, perception, and judgement) required to use the concept correctly which is not just a matter of the way in which he is causally affected by what is happening.

It is tempting to watch a batsman playing shots and think that his actions seem instinctive, perhaps almost reflexive. There is something to this idea, in that when a skill is well-practised it does not require deliberation but it still requires the agent to judge that the situation is appropriate to use the action type concerned. In fact, a very large part of success in sport derives from the player's ability to predispose themselves to act in ways most likely to lead to their success. What is automatic in such a situation is the sequence of detailed movements that is exhibited but these would never have been molded into a identifiable sequence or action type if the concept unifying them had not been mastered and then applied in the circumstances where the action occurs.

Understanding actions

Thus far we have considered mainly the cognition of the agent but in Sartre's case, his view of his companion's doings was an important part of the story. The passage about the window actually involves a number of claims about the way that Sartre understands his companion's action. We have already noted that when we explain why a person performed an action, an adequate description of the intentional or purposive state that guided the action is a necessary component. Thus we say "He was opening the window", "She was looking inside the box", or "He was trying to look nonchalent" and in each case we impute mental content to make sense of what is going on rather than just describing the actions in a mechanical way.

We have considered what Sartre meant by a synthetic mode of behaviour. The idea is that semantic units (noemata) give structure to the specific features of behaviour and are synthesized together in the conception which structures the act. "Practical field" has not been explained yet. What Sartre is referring to is the situation (the room) that he and his companion are in and their overall orientation within that domain. Getting to the window to let in some air may require that his companion steps around a desk or performs some other practical operation. Different types of windows require different methods for opening. So if the window demands you move a lever before pushing the window open this has implications for the way in which you achieve your end. Sartre's companion, prior to getting up and walking to the window may have appeared uncomfortable, perhaps perspiring a little and not paying strict attention. Sartre may have thought briefly that something was not quite right with his companion, maybe he had bad news to tell that he was postponing, or he was feeling unwell. When the companion rises from his chair and walks to the window, the realisation that he is going to close the window and has been uncomfortably hot gives meaning to his previously unexplained, unarticulated, and unnamed discomfort. Not only does the grasping of the purpose guiding the companion's action give meaning to what had gone before, but it will give meaning to some of what happens in the future. So when Sartre's companion steps around the desk after he has realised that she finds the room too warm he also knows that this behaviour is "avoiding the desk so as to reach the window, so that she can open it and let in some air." Sartre's conception of what his companion is doing involves a synthesis of his activity under a certain conception in a given field that maps that activity onto its context. To think of this as a chain of causes and effects is to limit the explanation so as to lose sight of the identity structure or conception structuring the action which may embrace a whole series of events connected in a psychologically significant way. In fact we use this "synthetic", "field-relative" mode of explanation in a wide range of situations.

Notice, however, that the only successful way to map a person's intentional activity onto the local environment is to have some command of the concepts that that person is using (where these conform to public and shared criteria of application and connectedness). We cannot hope to map the activity of somebody whose activity is structured according to inaccessible concepts.

Imagine, for instance, that you are watching a cricket game. You are unfamiliar with the game and have to be told that the person you are talking to is about to go in to bat. In he goes and you see him take a stance in front of some bits of wood, try and hit a ball that is bowled to him and run to (or nearly to) another set of similarly disposed pieces of wood. After doing this for a short time he comes back to rejoin you and you say, "what was that all about?" The batsman might then tell you that he was trying to score quickly for his team which means hitting the ball and running from one end of the pitch to another. Each completed run counts as one for his team. Now you begin to see that if the next batsman has the same agenda, you will again see the batsman trying to hit the ball whenever it is bowled to him and even if he does not hit it well running quickly between the wickets to try and complete a run and score. So when you see the player playing aggressive shots with his bat and running quickly even if the ball has not been hit a long way then his previously stated intention to score quickly enables you to see his running as trying to score runs (you may even be told he is "taking sharp singles") and you see this overall pattern of activity as one which experienced cricket players use to score quickly. Your introduction to the concepts in question allows you to put an intelligent construction on what you are seeing whereas without the relevant concepts you would not be able to do that.

Acting in accordance with a concept

We argued in Chapter 2 that language had a significant role in structuring thought. Word meaning, we argued, is the primary (and most common) unit of articulated thought, in that thought takes shape in association with language and both have a holistic and interwoven development. Once a person has mastered a linguistically mediated and therefore shared concept they are able to perform a range of cognitive operations with that concept and others can make sense of their trains of thought and action. So when I master the concept ⟨window⟩ I can perform a range of mental operations, such as that involved in thinking ⟨windows when opened can let in fresh air, its too hot in here, so I should open the window⟩. If such concepts create possibilities for our thought then they must also create possibilities for our actions. If an action is a behaviour that is produced as a result of a conscious purpose and purposes are framed and articulated in terms of the concepts corresponding to semantic units in the language then actions are best understood in semantic terms. So when Sartre's companion ⟨moves towards the window⟩, ⟨loosens the window latch⟩, ⟨pushes the window open⟩ her purposes are constructed in terms of concepts and governed by the semantic connections between thinkers and the world that the constitutive semantic units determine.

Not all concepts are in fact linguistic. Think about how you would push a window open, play a difficult arpeggio on the piano, ride a bicycle, or execute a telling brush stroke in a painting. The actions that are performed when doing any of these things cannot be spelt out using linguistic concepts. The best that you can do is give (via linguistic concepts) some general guidelines about what actions they are and, if the person is at a loss, try and make connection which convey a sense of what they should do to perform the action in question: "Well you exert steady pressure upwards even on both sides and the window should go up". So it is possible that although all actions are capable of being consciously reflected upon and that a description of what you are trying do is what individuates your behaviour as a certain action, that not all purposive acts can be easily articulated by recourse to language. In either case the purpose or intention is constructed from semantic units articulating the person's activity with a shared world and only in that way does it become explicable as having a certain content or thought structure which guides it.

A great deal of a person's success at a practical skill like playing cricket, painting or riding a bike is going to be determined by how readily the person "takes to it", or masters the skills involved and not just how good your instructions have been. Therefore we could say that are two components to such mastery:

1. purely practical sensori-motor skills;
2. judgment in applying the relevant concepts.

Something happens when Sartre's companion attempts to open the window involving both bodily function and conceptual activity. The purpose of the action is to let in some air, because it is too warm. This purpose is semantic in nature and practical in expression. The realisation that it is too warm involves making sense of a bodily experience. Once the person has realised that the bodily state is too hot the person is then can go on to make a series of judgements about how that undesirable state of affairs might be corrected. The making of such further judgements depends in an entirely obvious way on the application of and transitions between the concepts that are going to structure the action. All the relevant concepts such as ⟨too warm⟩, ⟨window⟩, ⟨open⟩, ⟨cooling draft⟩ and so on are essentially semantic in that they concern relations between minds or thinkers and the world. The response therefore has the same characteristics; the semantic connection between the concept of warmth and the real world result of an action to alter the temperature in the room completes the cycle between mind and world that ensures that the action is effective. Notice that the fact that the change must have an inner effect on the body in order for the effect to be produced (by opening the window) does not imply that the ability to form such judgments is an exception to the publicity of linguistic concepts. Bodies exist in shared space, Sartre noticed but did not clearly appreciate the nature of the bodily disaffection of his companion, and a change in a shared domain of activity resulted from the action. This is all able to be characterized by a system of shared signs between suitably similar creatures, nothing need be hidden here even though one of them is internally sensing changes in her own body and acting on that basis.

Take the learning of another skill that involves techniques of coordination of your own body. When you learn how to ride a bike often a big part of your success is couched in copying what an older sibling does when riding. So after falling from the saddle you may watch your older sister with a sense of fierce determination. You might realize that when riding she begins with a certain amount of speed or you might try to get someone to tell you what you are doing wrong or give you some pointers. Such communications give you a clue to the kind of physical actions that might help you to ride successfully and as you bring the activity under increasingly articulate and therefore conscious control it takes the form of an intentional action. The techniques that you adopt are therefore shared and public although your exercise of them in your own case is something tied up within the intimate relation between you as a subject of experience and your own body. Any action therefore is built from the same (shared) resources that ground your concepts, allow you to consciously think about your world in the terms that others use to do that, and use those thoughts to structure your action.

What is important here is that judgments involving concepts that are not obviously linguistic in kind are very similar in structure to the acts of judgment involved in a more obviously linguistic case. The cognitive ability to apply a generalisation, be it derived from an activity or from a linguistic class of objects is very similar. Actions structure behaviour according to conceptual rules however linguistically explicit (or inexplicit) the rules and embedded norms are. Norms of all these types, when used in the task of structuring behaviour, allow what we could call cognitive penetrability and intentional restructuring of thought and it is this condition that bears on the problem of free will or self-control of purposive activity.

Action, character and freewill

Many of Sartre's critics attack him for his over strong theory of free will. Daniel Dennett sums up a problem with Sartre's position that should be familiar to any student of Locke.

> An individual human being starts life with a problem: learning how to control himself or herself. As in all problems, one starts in a certain position with

> limited resources, and must then bootstrap those resources somehow into a solution. This may sound trivial, but it flies in the face of a very influential — if ultimately incoherent- vision of self-choosing: Sartre's idea that one chooses oneself completely by a "radical choice" that brings none of yesterday's baggage along. In Sartre's view it is as if one could create oneself *ex nihilo*; as if, to borrow another familiar bit of philosopher's Latin, the self at birth were a *tabula rasa* or blank slate. We know better. (Dennett 1984: p. 83)

Dennett's point is that human beings always exercise freedom within a certain situation. Situations in turn always carry constraints upon the possibilities that can be performed. So if you are lost in the forest, that situation places limitations upon the actions that one can perform. In an obvious sense being lost in the forest means that one is not free to watch television or eat junk food as these actions can not, ordinarily, be performed in that environment. But this external kind of constraint is not the only one operating and, ultimately, it is not totally separable from another kind of constraint that is, in the event, much more damaging to a metaphysics which argues for total libertarianism in the existentialist mould.

Dennett's argument focuses on the more subtle point that needs to be made. If you were lost in the bush and knew nothing about bushcraft then your options would include such things as seeking shelter or some sort or panicking. You would have no idea how to eat, and very little idea how to stop yourself getting further lost or how to get yourself safely out of the situation. If you were an experienced tramper, you would be able to use features of your environment more wisely, such strategies as building a bivouac, finding food, making a signal that could be seen from the air, heading uphill or downhill consistently and so on would be at your disposal as would a set of recognition skills for features of your environment that may help you in some way. Thus freedom is not constrained only by the situation that one is in, but also by the possibilities for action created by the cognitive skills one possesses.

Sartre's view of free will is captured in Dennett's phrase *ex nihilo*. For Sartre, human selves are always capable of posing the question "How do I want to be". Sartre argues that everything we do requires us to choose one possible way of responding to the world rather than another. Let us say I decide to A, then doing A requires a valuation of the state of affairs that will exist after A above the state of affairs that would result if I did something different say B. Now neither the state of affairs that will exist after A nor that which would result from B yet exists so they must be imaginatively created by the agent and then differentially valued in order to guide the selection of action. Thus the action is dependent not on an antecedent state of affairs but on an intentional or imaginative creation of the agent and on the agent's valuation of those creations. Sartre would argue that both the imagination and the conferring of value are agent-dependent occurrences and therefore that any action is not determined by antecedent events.

An obvious way to counter this argument is to claim that the imagining or valuing is a state of mind prior to the action or intention and that a state of mind is a state of the brain responsive to events occurring before it occurred therefore the future-directed nature of action does not negate the possibility of antecedent determination. Sartre would stick with his ontology of nothingness as essential to future-directed thought and deny the determining causal link. We have already given some reason to worry about physical priority over mental characterizations and will offer further reason to suspect that claim in discussing consciousness and the brain. However for the meantime we will concentrate on the content of action and offer an independent argument for a substantial conception of self-control and freedom of the will.

The anti-metaphysical claims of existentialism provide the philosophical basis in existential ontology for agents to continually recreate themselves because there is nothing they are, by nature as it were. According to Sartre, any person is an uneasy conglomerate of being (which has a certain metaphysical nature) and nothingness (or not-yet-existent possibility) such that one must decide or choose what one will become. But there is a conceptual gap between demonstrating phenomenologically that one can pose the question about our future selves and genuinely being able to use one's preference to shape what one actually becomes and thus, as it were, continually and freely recreate oneself. For a phenomenologist the datum of personal freedom is no more in doubt than the intuitions underlying our perceptual judgements and so it is absurd to state that theories based on our observations about the world could disprove our conviction of personal freedom. This argument is in the same tradition as existentialist claims and, although phenomenology aspires to stand in judgement on metaphysical theories, for many of us a kind of naturalism is the background against which we would assess philosophical claims rather than the bracketing position adopted by, for instance, Husserl (and followed by Sartre). We do therefore need to give some argument as to how it is possible that a penchant for naturalism and scientific theory could have erroneously led us to the thesis of causal or psychological determinism. What is more, if there are significant deficiencies in the existential account of free will and one cannot accept the evident data of phenomenologically real personal freedom as a conclusive argument, we need a conceptual justification for belief in free will. Here we should not overlook the possibility that taking a normative ("Ought I to do this?") attitude towards oneself is important not just phenomenologically but as a clue to human nature. In fact, if that possibility is pursued, it offers us a slightly different argument for freedom and one much more accessible to those who do not locate themselves in the Continental tradition.

We have argued that human beings have and exercise the capacity to make normative judgments about the appropriateness of their predispositions and propositional attitudes. In a moment we shall say what is wrong with Sartre's claim, but first notice a point where Dennett may have been a bit swift. We would argue that Dennett is correct to scorn the existential view that until I make my choice, the slate of intention is a *tabula rasa.* In fact we have claimed that the acquisition of skills as a cumulative lifetime experience of acquiring techniques and we have emphasized the role of predispositions to latch on to what other human beings do as a basic mechanism in human development. We have considered the prelinguistic roots of language (infant's pre linguistic vocalizations that are important for sensori-motor development necessary to vocalize language) but these are, in fact just a subset of the stage setting that needs to go on to develop fully adult behaviour. In relation to language use we have emphasized the normative responses that correct and refine a child's responses until they fit the practices of accomplished language users. But we also argued that concept use had the same normative features. Dennett's comments on the barrenness of the Lockean conception of a new-born infant's mind does not touch the significance of this fact. But the implication of this fact is that in becoming concept users we become creatures who respond to rules and not just law-like processes of configuration by the events which impinge upon us. Indeed one might realize a disposition in oneself (perhaps as a result of some defect in one's training) that needs correction in order to ensure that one does follow the rules governing a certain concept. To the extent that I can reform myself to correct this disposition I am capable of re-creating a feature of myself that is at variance with the way that I have been caused to develop. Now Dennett might say that, if a mature adult was free to recreate him or her-self in this way then that implies that there is nothing that is essential or fixed about that person's self but that is the move that is too swift.

I am a certain embodied being with a certain trajectory that can take control of myself at certain points and influence that trajectory — but it is still my trajectory. If we allow that much of what we are depends on the ways in which others have influenced us then we will have to say that we can change, at first perhaps uncomprehending but increasingly in ways that are purposive, towards the ways of being that others commend. We could say that maturity is the increasing ability to consider all the ways we are being influenced and take an attitude as to whether we will allow them to influence us. This much is implied by certain basic considerations about rule-following as the skill underpinning the use of concepts.

A rule does not cause me to act in a certain way it gives me a reason to do so if I intend to follow the rule (as discussed with the batsman's choice of a hook shot to a high bouncing ball). The rule tells a person what to do if they have mastered the skill of following it. It may do this informally (Call red things red!) or formally (1 + 1 = 2!), explicitly (when a thing is that shape call it a square!) or implicitly ("That's the way to go!"). But a rule of the type involved in concept use presents a set of alternatives of the following form: Either do it like this and learn the skills that allow you to engage in our practice or do not and be deprived of those skills. Of course, given the natural human propensity to try and latch on to what others are doing this is not a choice *ex nihilo* or on a *tabula rasa* but it still does not have the structure of a caused pattern of activity as would be required for any interesting kind of psychological determinism. Thus we argue that built into the fundamentals of concept use is the submission of oneself to certain norms which entail to some extent the fact that you could have done otherwise. This basic conceptual presupposition of mental talk means that if actions are, as we have argued, essentially specified by their identity structures and therefore ineliminibly mental in nature, that the very idea of human action entails some kind of freedom of the will.

However, all this does not secure Sartre's strong libertarianism. At the most we can say that there is an underlying conceptual presupposition in ascriptions of mental content that the agent is a rule-follower and that his rule-following ability is basic to understanding him as having the rich intentionality required for human action. We must now turn to the background against which an agent's conscious action is what we might call an *authentic action* of that agent.

Note that the existential question "Who am I" involves the recognition that one is a certain way, and can be thought of as having a kind of identity. In fact our normal presuppositions about action build on this fact, as was recognized by Hume and is exploited by Dennett in his argument. My actions are the sort of actions I might do, they are in keeping with my character even if on each occasion I make a choice as to how I will act. A series of haphazard acts which evince no consistency or sense of my being a certain sort of person are not what we normally see and call free actions. Sartre, however, seems to leave very little room for an action to show the character of the agent in the way that our normal assessments of moral praise and blame seem to presume. This is made vivid in the case of the habitual gambler. If, for instance, you have a gambling problem and are in the process of stealing funds from your employer, you could take a normative attitude toward your behaviour. Here I am stealing from my employers, I am a thief, yet is this the way that I want to continue to be? (Note that if the gambler was to say that they were causally compelled to steal through their addiction to gambling this would be a prime example of Sartre's "bad faith").

Sherbourne notes both the strength and the fatal flaw in Sartre's theory of free will in considering the gambler and the predispositions towards certain types of action that the gambler or any habitual actor evinces…

> In the reformed gambler case it is indeed true that Sartre is making the point that his assumption of the primacy of disruption has no binding power over the way that choices are made at a subsequent moment — we must choose again, and again, and again. Fine. But what assumption lurks beneath the argument and example. Precisely the assumption that the reformed gambler is tempted. (1994)

The ex-gambler who walks past the casino every day must, on each occasion, choose whether or not to go inside. So the gambler is constantly faced with the challenge of choosing not to be a gambler whereas another person would not be. The problem is that Sartre has no way to explain how it is that the ex-gambler is continually having to choose where another person does not have to live with this fact about himself. Why is it that the gambler finds it so hard to walk past the casino? This very real fact about action, habit, and character is much more understandable on the account we have suggested than on Sartre's account. One could think of ours as lying within the broad swathe of Aristotelian accounts of human action and character. Such accounts concentrate on experience and training in the development of human character as a stable set of features that constitute the psyche of a person.

We have argued that our freedom and responsibility are based on our nature as rule-followers rather than just mechanistic responders. The rule-follower develops and refines a certain kind of skill so as to be able to participate in a particular human practice. But in describing this human characteristic it emerged that it was built on human dispositions to act in certain ways and to develop habits of responding which are more or less congruent with others. These skills are developed by convergence with others in dispositions and habits of categorization so as to satisfy the norms involved in the relevant concepts. Rule-following has elements of intending to act in a certain way but also elements of the customary, of going on in the same way whenever the conditions are appropriate. Thus we could say that we are habitual responders with the ability to use our tendency to form habits into complex purposive abilities fashioned in accordance with the conceptual requirements of contentful rules. These rules mark repeatable types of action (such as particular cricket shots or driving through a corner in a fast car). These structured abilities are potentiated by rule-following and shaped by the normative constraints on conceptual content.

It follows from our account that the gambler, and indeed each of us, is predisposed to act in certain ways by the training which has conferred conceptual abilities on us and by the habits we have got into. We go along with some of the dispositions we develop and others we resist. It is therefore understandable that the gambler, who has developed and endorsed his habit so that it has worked itself into his psyche, for reasons perhaps to do with what he finds enjoyable, exciting or natural, must make more of an effort than someone who has never made that part of his repertoire of activities. The irony is that the very capacity which allows us to develop techniques which transform and transcend our natural predispositions is the capacity which makes us prone to develop damaging traits. We have, it seems, a two edged facet to our nature in that the same aspect which carries the seeds of our promise as thinking active beings also carries the seeds of our weaknesses as creatures of habit. We can, in fact, deepen our analysis by considering actions and habits and their relation to consciousness.

Habits, consciousness, and self control

There are behaviours that in one sense are actions yet are not normally the subject of conscious reflection. For example consider Fred who pokes his tongue out when concentrating. Fred may well have slipped into a habit of exhibiting this behaviour. Perhaps Fred has seen someone else doing it and gave it a try. Because he has done this often he fails to be aware when he is doing it. Fred is now at the point where this behaviour is habitual. A female friend watches Fred concentrating intently and thinks it is a revolting thing to do. She weighs the embarrassment for her male friend that will be caused for him when she informs him of his appearance against the ill effects for him of not knowing that it appears so revolting and therefore being ignorant of the resulting bad impressions he will create with other people. She decides to tell him about his tongue poking. Upon hearing the news, Fred will now have to take responsibility for his behaviour. Now he knows it looks strange, he might try to stop doing it or he might say "Dammit, that is me take it or leave it I'm not changing it!" The main point is that having become conscious of what he is doing he is forced to choose whether to take steps to change himself and his ways of behaving or leave himself as he is. This responsibility implies that even if it was originally an inadvertent habit he had developed it has now moved into the realm of action. So he has accepted that it is something that he was doing, and he has now chosen one way or another. If he chooses to take control over it, that will probably involve more than a momentary decision and will require him to begin what we might properly call a project or campaign of "self-recreation". Therefore his ability to name his habit and be conscious of it when it is happening has made his tongue movement, whose origins are in the unconscious and causally disposed features of his activity, part of his action repertoire such that questions of intention and self-control become relevant.

The problem is that this appears to an example of an action that was not accompanied, for a period of time, by purposeful mental content. Of course it was at all times something he could potentially have been aware of (if someone had mentioned to him that his tongue was out he would have become aware of it). The crucial feature of this example for our thesis is that it is possible for this person's behaviour to be either an action or just a habit. What happens in any instance where a behaviour or disposition is named is that the agent becomes aware of his behaviour and can make it an object of conscious attention. This stance, once taken up, entails that the behaviour truly becomes an action and the question of control is a real question that, according to the answer it potentiates, will change him. An agent with a noticed and named habit is, in Sartre's terms, *condemned* to choice and conscious action. For Sartre, every behaviour has this conceptual character and therefore freedom is an ever-present possibility or an essential ontological feature of the human mind. We have suggested that this overstates the case and that it is more true to human nature (a term that Sartre rejects) to recognize that we are creatures who make ourselves because we have the tendency to form habitual ways of behaving. We would argue that the fact that we build our activity on habits but then can revise and refine those same habitual ways of responding, effectively makes us intentional self-creations.

Imagine a further and more ambiguous example. Greta scratches her backside through her skirt to the discomfiture of her staid male secretary and also her parents but to the amusement of some of her male juniors in her office and in her social set. We are unsure whether she does this intentionally or automatically. If we want to find out whether or not this behaviour is conscious and therefore counts as being an action we would have to address Greta as an intentional agent and hope that she was inclined to be sincere. We might ask "Do you know what you do that causes the boys such amusement?" she might look puzzled and shake her head or she might betray the fact that she knows quite well what we are talking about (even if she will not say). We would then have grounds for concluding either (as in the first case) that she was ignorant about her habit and therefore could not be said to be "acting" or (as in the second) that she was trading on the ambiguity of the action to "play with" her secretary and parents. Conversely, she may be quite forthright: "Yes, you must be talking about my bum scratching, it amuses me greatly to see the puerile responses of my male colleagues." Here we would have good grounds for considering her behaviour an action. Notice that we make the decision about purposiveness on the basis of whether she names and can incorporate her behaviour into her thought and reasoning. If this is so, she is conscious of what she is doing which tells us that it has a conceptual shape and it is an intentional or mental act rather than just a habitual movement she has developed.

So the case of Greta illustrates that there are behaviours for which it is not possible to tell whether or not they are guided by a conscious purpose. In such cases the mental state report of the person being observed has an important role in determining whether or not the behaviour counts as an action. What is crucial is the intentional features of the bodily activity and particularly whether the person's ancillary behaviour and reactions suggest that they know what they are doing. If the behaviour has these characteristics it is conscious. If the behaviour has a conceptual content the person must be regarded as purposing to exhibit through that behaviour a certain intentional activity directed at some feature or perceived aspect of the environment. Again it seems that intentional content and conscious control go hand in hand although the conscious control of behaviour is not automatic but an attainment requiring a certain amount of application and effort.

If we borrow from a famous political statement, we could say that the price of freedom is intentional vigilance because the intentional articulation of behaviour brings it into contact with the system of rule-following and self-correction that underpins our grasp of concepts. Rule-following is coeval with changing the self to meet external normative constraints which we apprehend (however inarticulately) as demands on us. This activity is intentional self-formation and that is what is at stake in most important theories of human action and freedom of the will. On our view we cannot think of ourselves as other than free and responsible as soon as we are made conscious of aspects of self and our activity through the ascriptions of content that others are always making. Thus we would argue that it is an internal or conceptual requirement of our understanding of a person as a conscious agent that the individual concerned is thought to exhibit, to some degree at least, freedom of the will.

We can now turn to the complex issue of the embeddedness of the individual in the society that gives rise to the concepts he or she uses.

Chapter 5

Consciousness and society

> Language is as old as consciousness, language is practical consciousness, as it exists for other men, and for that reason is really beginning to exist for me personally as well; for language like consciousness arises only from the need, the necessity of intercourse with other men... (Marx and Engels 1969)

The relationship between society and consciousness

Marx echoes an idea which might be gleaned from the etymology of the word "conscious" which itself is suggestive of a link with society in that it is made up of the parts *con* — with — and *scio* — I know. It remains to be seen whether this etymological clue leads to any fruitful reflections or not.

We have argued for an important link between language and thought in understanding the contents of conscious mental acts. It is evident that this is deeply congenial to Marx's view of consciousness that is also firmly and squarely located in a tradition that emphasizes society and culture. It is not difficult to see the way that language forms the connection between consciousness and society. However, it remains to spell out how far that connection goes and to what extent it works against a robust conception of individual consciousness and the objectivity of certain features of human consciousness as manifestations of the kind of creatures we are relatively independently of the society in which we live.

Language, we have argued, provides many of the concepts and conceptualisations necessary for a wide range of human thoughts. Consequently language and its social or communal determinants have a profound upon the structure of human action in that language allows the consciousness that there is a certain situation to be engaged with, that there is a specifiable action that could be performed, and that the action concerned has a certain significance in human affairs or dealings with the environment. For instance, if I see that a rock is delicately poised on a ledge over a point at which a herd of buffalo pass on their way to drink and I am equipped with stories about using pieces of wood as levers, I might conceive a plan to roll that rock down on the buffalo as they pass and secure a meal for the tribe. Co-operative effort and communication may then allow us to become aware of some means of repeating the trick. If it does then it will be because language has entered, in the precise way that we have already discussed, into the development and understanding of how to perform the action concerned. Language and social co-operation, we might say with Marx, jointly create possibilities for different ways of knowing and behaving. Our language is, however, an artefact or cultural production of the particular time and place in which we live. Thus there is an important connection between our thoughts and a given socio-historical context. Action can therefore be seen in part as just one symptom of a radical role for culture in the construction of mind in that when one comes to behave in a certain way X one adopts a possible way of being, devised in a cultural setting (such as cricket) which may become habitual for human beings who are formed in that setting. An accumulation of such hexes or habits of thought and action then forms the mind of those human beings and influences their consciousness of the world. Our question is "How can one both recognize the obvious role of society in the consciousness of human beings and resist the kind of cultural relativism that threatens the roots of rational debate in many areas of philosophy such as epistemology, metaphysics and ethics?"

Epistemic issues

Social constructionists have a tendency to make bold nihilist epistemic assertions. Robert Nola goes so far as to claim that the impact of Foucault has been akin to an intellectual Chernobyl (1994). If it is true that human consciousness is a product of socialisation, to the extent that social forces sufficiently explain all aspects of consciousness, this would have epistemic repercussions. However, a defensible form of social constructionism must limit itself to the domains in which it is a plausible explanation and pay some attention to the fact that our epistemic equipment has a venerable history with biological influences having shaped certain features of it, all theses mooted by Marx and Engels.

> The production of ideas, of conceptions, of consciousness is at first directly interwoven with the material activity and the material intercourse of men, the language of real life. (1969: p. 287–8)

This passage links consciousness and the discursive or conceptual tools by which, we have argued, it is given form and content, to practical activity in a way that is immediately congenial to the world-involving view for which we have also argued. Marx and Engels begin from the dual realisation that consciousness concerns actual things in a material world with which human beings are engaged and that it is a social product designed to meet the challenges of that world.

> Men are the producers of their conceptions ideas etc. — real active men as they are conditioned by a definite development of their productive forces and of the intercourse corresponding to these, up to its furthest forms. Consciousness can never be anything else than conscious existence, and the existence of men is their actual life processes. (1969: p. 288)

Consciousness is therefore (according to Marx and Engels) from the very beginning a social product and remains so as long as men exist at all. They emphasise the role of social production even while tying consciousness to actual life processes that are constitutive of the material or bodily engagement between human beings and their environment in a way that is meat and drink to the view of intentionality that we have championed. It is an important entailment of this view that the contents of consciousness are constrained by the bodily engagement of individuals in the world and cannot float free of the actual world in any quasi-idealistic way.

> The identity of nature and man appears in such a way that the restricted relation of men to nature determines their restricted relation to one another, and their restricted relation to one another determines men's restricted relation to nature, just because nature is hardly modified historically: and on the other hand, man's consciousness of the necessity of associating with the individuals around him is the beginning of the consciousness of society at all. This beginning is as animal as social life itself at this stage. It is mere herd consciousness. (1969: p. 293)

Notice that the restrictions or constraints that apply to thought and consciousness arise from the relations between human beings in their shared environment and their relation to nature. But at this point Marx and Engels introduce an absolutely crucial point in the discussion of human thought. The environment in which we live is not natural in any sense that can be given by natural science alone in that it is being transformed by human activity into an context for thought which contains agriculture, buildings, artefacts of all kinds and complex social arrangements. Thus the contents of the mind must engage not only with nature and the presence of others but with its own physical and abstract products. What is more we should not move from the acknowledgement that consciousness and its products are shaped by a process of social production to the conclusion that the consciousness of any individual is no more than an artefact which deterministically reflects social norms.

> ...these three moments, the forces of production, the state of society, and consciousness, can and must come into contradiction with one another. (1969: p. 294)

Here consciousness is set against the forces of production on the one hand and the state of society on the other so as it takes on a life of its own in any individual. The possibility of a distinct moment among the forces of social change arising from individual consciousness may not be a universal feature of all varieties of Marxism but it is one that we would endorse. Consider the fact that any individual is exposed to a variety of discursive influences which affect that person's subjectivity or, if you prefer, multiple subjectivities. A moment's reflection reveals that any individual's particular trajectory through the experiences that configure their experience is likely to be unique (if examined in sufficient detail) even though certain general features might emerge as a result of their socio-historical situation. Therefore, if we do take seriously the effect on consciousness of the cumulative experiences undergone by an individual, we are committed to the conclusion that each individual person's conscious life is potentially different in content from that of any other person. It follows that there is a potential tension between a set of social norms for self-configuration and the lived experience of the individual. This is constrained by the socio-historical context of the person but also by their biology in ways that allow for broad psychological generalisations but it is not determined by anything approaching the status of laws of nature. This is because the rule-following basis we have sketched for concepts provides only the tools of thought and the patterns of thought that result can be as original as moves in a game of chess (and even, by use of metaphor and innovative departure from conventional usage, creatively violate the rules).

What is more, it follows from the Kantian and Wittgensteinian considerations that we have already canvassed that, even if the meaning of a term or element in thought can be considered a social construct, this does not mean there is not a real thing to which that term refers in the world and a unique relation between the person engaging with the thing and the thing itself. The fact that each of us has a unique trajectory in the world and that the many discourses which each of us inhabit are forced together by their co-occurrence in one lived bodily subjectivity gives us an *a priori* argument for the singularity of conscious experience as lived by each individual human being. Thus we would argue that two of the most damaging theses developed from the social constructivist position viz. that there is no thing as the individual conscious subject and that thought and meaning are related only to language and not to the world in which that language is developed, are both untenable.

With these provisos in place we will now explore the real ways in which society and consciousness are related to each other and the impact of that view on our understanding of the internal relation between consciousness and intentionality.

The structuration of thoughts

The view defended in the previous section is very close to what Pettit has called "holistic individualism" whereby we understand the individual as she is embedded in a holistic context of social being and thereby relativise the content of his thoughts and actions to that context but we do not lose sight of the fact that she is an individual whose nature must be considered apart from her place as an instance of a socio-historical type. (1993)

Peter Winch was one of the first philosophers within the Anglo-American tradition to bring to our attention the importance of social and cultural factors in the understanding of what he called "meaningful behaviour". (1958) He based his analysis, as we have based ours, on the nature of rules and their role in determining the content of thought and action. But there is also the evident fact, already noted by Marx and Engels, that a social context creates situations and possibilities which themselves constitute an artefactual environment for action. We therefore need both to look at the structuration of thought by the significations made available to us and the structuration of discourse and contexts by social forces to reveal how an individual human subjectivity and the contents of consciousness can be illuminated by the society in which an individual is located.

Since Hegel and Marx charted the historical dialectic and ushered society and the structure of relations in society onto the stage as an important influence on human beings this has been a central theme in continental philosophy. Winch discusses the example of a man N who casts his vote in an election and remarks as follows.

> What he does is not *simply* to make a mark on a piece of paper; he is *casting a vote*. And what I want to ask is what gives his action *this* sense, rather than, say, that of being a move in a game or part of a religious ritual. (1958: p. 49)

The question is rhetorical in that it is abundantly clear that what gives his action the sense it has is not the bodily movements but the social institution in which it is situated. One might expect the same considerations to apply to perception, and therefore the inputs to consciousness, as to action which is the paradigmatic output of a conscious experience. In *Women, Fire and Dangerous Things* Lakoff makes some sweeping claims "What is perceived by human beings as gestalts (that is, overall shapes that characterize basic level categories) do not necessarily correspond to categories of the external world". He applies the same thought to mental images and actions describing the latter as a joint product of what is there and how we respond to it according to the categories we apply to the thing in question. (p 200) Notice, however that the contents of consciousness are not exclusive productions of categorization but joint products of what is there in the world and our ways of categorising things. This reiterates the point we have repeatedly made.

His point is dramatically illustrated by Matsumoto (1996). He describes a situation in which a White European teacher was teaching a game called "Who touched me?" to Australian Aborigine children. After a very short time the children could not be bothered to play the game. The game consisted in the children standing in a circle and one of them being blindfolded. Another child walked around the outside of the circle, touched the blindfolded child on the back, and returned to his or her place in the circle. The blindfolded child was then asked to identify the person who had touched them. She thought that their uncooperative attitude to this game and the activities that followed indicated stupidity or naughtiness. She later found that they thought she was stupid because normal people could identify each other by the prints left behind them in the sand so the "Who touched me?" game was no fun at all (p. 183). This is just one example of divergent abilities to interact with certain domains by using culturally specific techniques. Other examples can be found in the kinds of problems that individuals can solve and the method of using and representing knowledge; Scribner (1979) describes the use of personal experience and anecdote for reasoning by illiterate societies' members, who which are reluctant to use premise based syllogisms to draw conclusions about hypothetical subjects. This finding echoes Luria's work among different strata of Russian society (1976). One can imagine that conjecture and hypothesis rather than real experience would be a very deficient basis on which to form opinions in certain contexts and therefore the utility of such dispositions is clear. However the point being made is that even something taken to be as universal as the kind of thinking involved in propositional or syllogistic reasoning is an inculcated cultural skill for which an individual needs an appropriate background of training or apprenticeship. These examples and the general theoretical considerations about culturally specific content and its role in mental operations jointly suggest that Lakoff is right in his assertions about the importance of culture in the shape of the mind. But here again we need to guard against extremes in discussing the role of culture. Lakoff argues for an "experientialist" position that blunts the most "Chernobyl-like" forms of social constructionism.

> But despite the fact that we rely centrally on our bodily natures and our imaginative capacities, experientialism has maintained a form of basic realism, since our conceptual structures are strongly (though by no means totally) constrained by reality and the way we function as an inherent part of reality. (p. 372)

We ought perhaps to register at least the problematic nature of the word "reality" here while recognising that the theme of bodily nature and engagement of the world is being repeatedly reinforced in these quotations. We can add to the set of constraints created by bodily interaction with nature (or the modified version of it we inhabit) the requirement that subjects interact with other people. This cements the role of others or at least other bits of their own life trajectory in an environment in order to create a normative context for the application of a given rule in a given thought (Pettit 1993: p. 106). We have already outlined the way in which publicity and pragmatics serve to constrain the contents of thoughts to condition which can usefully be referred to as objective conditions in which the use of certain terms, and therefore the related concepts, is warranted or licit. We now need to turn explicitly to the artefact that is our contemporary environment.

The creation of a context of being

Vygotsky, whom we have discussed in relation to language and consciousness, called his studies of psychology a "sociocultural" or "sociohistorical" theory of psychological processes (Cole p. 148). Bruner, a follower of Vygotsky, makes some telling remarks about the importance of culture and societal influences in the world of thought (Wertsch 1985: p. 32).

> The world is a symbolic world in the sense that it consists of conceptually organized, rule-bound belief systems about what exists, about how to get to goals, about what is to be valued. ... The culture stores an extraordinarily rich file of concepts, techniques, and other prosthetic devices (Bruner 1985)

Bruner's "symbolic world" permeated by rules and concepts forms an environment for thought and action that is, as it were, imprinted like a set of roads and paths on the geography of the natural world and creates ways to move between and access different points of perception, thought, and action in that world. Cole uses the concepts of scripts, schemata, and frames to indicate some of the structuration that occurs when individuals put together their conscious lives and experiences using the resources and "prosthetic devices" provided by their culture. He goes on to propose that there is a basic unit common to the analysis of cultures and psychological processes which is "the individual engaged in goal-directed activity under conventionalised constraints" (p. 158).

This is immediately reminiscent of the activities and responses that we have described as forming the basis of rule-following practices which provide the points of application for the concepts used in structuring human thought and thereby the contents of consciousness. The structuration concerned can be seen even in something as basic as the times that rule our lives and thoughts. Lakoff notes that our model of a week is idealised.

> Seven day weeks do not exist objectively in nature. They are created by human beings. In fact, not all cultures have the same kinds of weeks. (p. 69)

He goes on to discuss work in Balinese culture where a lunar-solar calendar and a complex cycle of days are both used and a complex system results to mark significant time units and time junctures (p. 69). Weeks are just one example of structures that can seem written into the metaphysics of the world because of enduring human customs that orient our life and experience in very basic ways.

> Cultural categories are real and they are made real by human action. Governments are real. They exist. But they exist only because human beings conceived of them and have acted according to that conceptualisation. In short, the imaginative products of the human mind play an enormous role in the creation of reality. (Lakoff p. 208)

This truth is uncontroversial but one short phrase from Marx suggests even more intriguing features of the relation between society and consciousness. Marx and Engels wrote: "language is practical consciousness, as it exists for other men, and for that reason is really beginning to exist for me personally as well". This dimension of the formation of self and personality by social reality that is increasingly taking on a reality of its own and transforming the environment with which I am engaged deserves further investigation.

When we turn our attention to identity and personality we must recognize that important features of self are given by locating oneself in a discourse where dimensions of self are perceived, responded to, and used as the basis for defining one's position among others and shaping one's conduct in the world at large. Self as thinker and actor is located according to complex systems of self reference and described using self attributions which reflect the ways in which others have, historically and socially, categorised oneself (Harre and Gillett 1994: pp. 104–5). Harre elsewhere remarks that "capacity for self-knowledge like all other psychological abilities, must be understood in terms of social relations" (Harre 1983) Various categorisations bear on the self according to cultural context and it is from the materials provided by these categorisations and ways of thinking of oneself as a person that an identity or "identity project" (Harre) can be constructed.

One area in which the socio-cultural definition of self is a particularly important topic is in post-colonial societies where individuals have been socialised to a system of self-understanding that does not reflect their cultural origins but rather the categories of a colonial power. Using Bourdieu's theory of cultural capital and the cycle of reproduction that perpetuates social and cultural privileges and ultimately identities, Ranginui Walker argues that a Maori child in post-colonial New Zealand society, important aspects of Maori identity are rejected. Of the Maori child, he says "he is made to feel a failure and accordingly he rejects school and is condemned as a failure" (1989) He describes historical and ontogenetic phases of the development of identity which involve an early rejection of one's own ethnic identity and identification with the dominant group, a secondary move towards acceptance and a more positive sense of ethnic identity and finally a kind of resurgent assertiveness.

> It is this positive embracing of identity which is the driving force of the current regeneration of Maori culture on a wide front in the Maori population (p. 50)

Similar thoughts about knowing who one is and having a place of belonging to a people and a tradition is also identified by another Maori writer who speaks of "Being Maori". (John Rangihau 1992). For both of these writers there is something basic to self and of the utmost importance in standing in an assured and inherited position vis-à-vis one's own origins and investments. This sense of having a place to stand and a cultural identity to occupy in one's own unique way is, in their view, crucial to human experience. It is closely related to Foucaultian themes concerning subjectivity and consciousness found in the work of other contemporary philosophers.

The social construction of perversion and homosexuality

Making up people

From what we have said in this chapter thus far it is obvious that we think there are important connections between consciousness and society. In *A History of Sexuality* Foucault investigates the origins of our sexuality (1978). He claims that prior to the 18th century there did not exist any "homosexuals" (1978: p. 43). Prior to that time there were only people who performed sodomy. Sodomy was an act that was frowned upon, however it was not until the category "homosexual" was invented that being *a homosexual* was a possibility. Ian Hacking begins his paper *Making Up People* with a question that is very similar to Foucault's about "the homosexual". He asks "Were there any perverts before the latter part of the nineteenth century?" He answers in the negative "The answer is no… Perversion was not a disease that lurked about in nature, waiting for a psychiatrist with especially acute powers of observation to discover it hiding everywhere. It was a disease that was created by a new functional understanding of disease." (Hacking 1986: p. 222)

Hacking claims that such identities are instances of what he calls "making up people". The claim is that the category of perversion created a new disease and a new type of person, the "pervert". It appears to be a clear example of what post modernists would refer to as social construction and is what Foucault means by his claim that there did not exist any homosexuals before the eighteenth century. It is a claim diametrically opposed to a certain kind of natural kinds theory about types of human phenomena.

Causal reference theorists

A certain kind of theorist argues that there are natural kinds which exist in the world independent of human beings and whose essence (or natural/metaphysical defining characteristic) is discovered as part of our general epistemic activity. The Putnam, Kripke, Donnellan causal theory of reference explains how the discovery by a specialist of the "essence" of such a natural kind can spread rapidly through a speech community (Donnellan, Kripke, Putnam 1977). Putnam's famous example concerns the discovery that the essence of water is H20. Once it has been established that water really is H20 then any apparent instance of water can not be water unless it is in fact H20, (this is argued in Putnam's twin earth example). Any person insisting that a substance empirically equivalent to water was water, even though it was not H20, would be said to not really understand what water is. (1977: p. 121)

We do not wish to take issue with the claim that water really is H20 nor that there are other good candidates for natural kind terms. However, perversion is a category that did exactly what the causal theory of reference supposed discovery of all natural kinds should, it spread rapidly through a speech community. After specialists had discovered that people who indulged in unorthodox sexual practices were in fact perverts the idea caught on very quickly. Thus the fact that a category spreads rapidly through a speech community following its discovery by specialists should not lead us to believe that the truth about this category really has been established.

Obviously this is a line of thought that must be pursued with great care. There is a crucial difference between the natural kinds suggested by the causal theorists and the supposed natural kind investigated by those such as Foucault, for the obvious reason that perversion looks a bad candidate for a natural kind while H20 looks a good one. The reason for this is that most of us would agree that the scientists who discovered that the essence of water is H2O have really discovered that this is what water is and it would have had this nature regardless of human activity. The subsequent spread of this belief through a speech community and correction of all those who identify that which is not H2O with water seems to be based upon that pervasive independent existence in the environment of all people. Perversion, on the other hand looks like a category that is intimately tied to human activities and beliefs and might be expected to vary with variations in those things.

The view of natural kinds that this analysis suggests is one in which a natural kind term must have a referent that is able to be picked out in all human contexts where the natural kind exists. Supposed examples of natural kind terms such as homosexuality do not seem to be able to be picked out in every human context in that they depend on the human practices in that context and the meanings with which those practices are invested. As Foucault tried to show for homosexuality and Hacking tries to demonstrate for multiple personality, these purported natural kind terms do not have an essence which can plausibly be separated from those two human variables (practices and meanings). Foucault claims that before the introduction of the term homosexuality there existed only persons who performed sodomy and Hacking suggests that before the invention of the diagnosis multiple personality this was a very uncommon psychiatric disorder. In fact we might say that these categories introduced new possible ways for person to be and new meanings with which to invest their behaviour.

These metaphysical reflections suggest that the distinction between good candidates for natural kind terms and the examples discussed by Foucault and Hacking is a distinction between terms that can have a referent prior to their invention and those for which their referent comes into existence alongside the invention of classification. Hacking calls this phenomenon "the looping effect of human kinds".

> People classified in a certain way tend to conform or grow into the ways that they are described; but they also evolve in their own ways, so that the classifications and descriptions have to be constantly revised. (Hacking 1995: p. 21)

Hacking describes this phenomena as a looping effect because not only does the existence of a category create possible ways for persons to be, but also the category evolves in response to changes in the persons that come to fall within it. Hacking believes that multiple personality disorder is a category that has resulted from this looping effect.

The social construction of multiple personality

Hacking offers several examples of "made up" psychiatric disorders. The example to which he gives most attention is "multiple personality".

> I claim that multiple personality as an idea and as a clinical phenomenon was invented around 1875: only one or two possible cases per generation had been recorded before that time, but a whole flock of them came after. (1986: p. 223)

The implication here is that once the diagnosis "multiple personality" had been invented a new way to be also came into existence. This is not to imply (and Hacking is careful to stress he does not want to imply this) that all psychiatric diagnoses make people up. We ought to distinguish this idea from a more extreme version of social constructionism called "labelling theory".

"Labelling theory" was a sociological theory popular in the 1960s. The idea behind it was that the process of labelling creates the possibility for social distinctions to be drawn. Hacking says labelling theory

> asserts that social reality is conditioned, stabilised, or even created by the labels we apply to people, actions and communities. (1986: p. 226)

Labelling theory is not as fashionable as it once was, it has been criticised for its over simplification of social phenomena. Giddens (1993: p. 129) identifies three problems with labelling theory which highlight its oversimplification of social phenomena. First, by focusing upon the process of labelling the processes preceding the labelling may be missed from an explanation. These processes may be an important part of understanding the behaviour labelled. Second, it is difficult to confirm empirically whether the process of labelling does in fact, increase deviant behaviour. Third, labels develop as the result of historical events, for example, the development of modern systems of law. The problems identified by Giddens should be accommodated by any good theory of social construction as it applies to categories of human being. The theory of making up people that Hacking and we endorse is better called "dynamic nominalism".

Nominalism, realism and dynamic nominalism

Causal theorists of reference claim that natural kind terms demarcate essences that really exist in nature independent of human mental activity. Thus when a causal theorist believes that something is a natural kind, they are realists in this sense about the reference of the kind term. Hacking contrasts realism with nominalism.

> ...a traditional nominalist says that stars (or algae, or justice) have nothing in common except our names ("stars", "algae", "justice"). The traditional realist in contrast finds it amazing that the world could so kindly sort itself into our categories. (1986: p. 227)

Thus strict nominalism is the view that there is nothing more to our grouping of objects under a term than a name or concept we have devised and the grouping that results from that. By contrast we have argued that concepts and the terms that mark them pick out features of the world and our activity in it which usefully help us to structure that activity. Therefore our analysis of mental content cannot be reconciled with any strong form of nominalism because to be pragmatically useful there has to be more to a category than the fact that we name it. Hacking suggests an alternative to realism and strict nominalism that can make sense of the making up of people, "dynamic nominalism".

> The claim of dynamic nominalism is not that there was a kind of person who came increasingly to be recognised by bureaucrats or by students of human nature, but rather that a kind of person came into being at the same time as the kind itself was being invented. In some cases, that is, our classifications and our classes conspire to emerge hand in hand, each egging the other on. (1986: p. 228)

Hacking is here suggesting that terms that refer to human artefacts (like pencil, computer and catapult) emerge coevally with the type of artefact, so there really is something in common between catapults, but what is in common between them is, in part, a function of us calling them catapults. So there is a genuine grouping together of objects similar in some way, but this similarity emerges in the context of certain type of (world-involving) human activity.

His claim about making up people should be understood in a similar sort of way. The term multiple personality successfully refers to a psychological phenomenon, but the existence of the phenomenon that this term refers to is contingent upon the existence of the term and of individuals who come to structure their experience in the way that is given by the meaning of the term or its use among those who understand it.

What is in a name?

Hacking offers four categories to illustrate the variety of situations covered by the possibility of dynamic nominalism.

> Take four categories: horse, planet, glove, and multiple personality. It would be preposterous to suggest that the only thing horses have in common is that we call them horses. We may draw the boundaries to admit or to exclude Shetland ponies, but the similarities and differences are real enough. (1986: p. 229)

Although the category "horses" did not exist until we invented it the differences that actually exist between four legged mammals did. It is on the basis of these differences that we can categorise horses as "horses" and chickens as "not horses". Of course what makes a four-legged mammal count as a horse is a much more complicated story than simply being four legged mammals. However, the features of horses that allow us to pick them out as such may not furnish us with an essence of horses that will be explicable independent of the human activities in which we use them and the important practical distinctions required for successful breeding and so on.

About planets Hacking says

> Arguably the heavens looked different after we grouped Earth with the other planets and excluded the Moon and Sun, but I am sure that acute thinkers had discovered a real difference. (1986: p. 229)

What Hacking means by "looked different" is unclear. Some may argue that the actual experience of looking at the sun, dangerous as this is, is no different today than it was two thousand years ago (*ceteris paribus*). What is certain is that in pre-Copernican times the way that people conceptualised the sun was different from the way most of us do today and therefore what they took themselves to be seeing (in terms of both the objects themselves and their relative movements) was different. However the point is not crucial to the argument at hand, those who wish to establish that the Copernican revolution has not provided us with a description of the solar system that is a better fit with the way things really are would seem to have an uphill struggle on their hands.

Hacking thinks that "glove" and "multiple personality" are different yet again.

> I know not what came first, the thought or the mitten, but they have evolved hand in hand. That the concept "glove" fits gloves so well is no surprise, we

> made them that way. My claim about making up people is that in a few interesting respects multiple personalities [and much else] are more like gloves than like horses. The category and the people in it emerged hand in hand. (1986: p. 229)

We have argued that an understanding of intentionality is necessary for understanding human consciousness, that concepts are the raw ingredients from which we compose the identity structures that individuate actions and that actions both make our environments and ourselves. This is evident in the case of gloves but leaves us with a physical product that would be identifiable as an object even by a species who had no hands. Things are somewhat more subtle when we come to Hacking's claim about multiple personality and dynamic nominalism. His suggestion is that the invention of multiple personality created a new possible way for individuals to be.

If Hacking is correct about "multiple personality", then before the invention of this category it was not possible for people to have multiple personalities. To support this thesis Hacking needs to show empirically that prior to the invention of the category there were no people suffering from this condition. In *Rewriting the Soul: Multiple Personality and the Sciences of Memory* (1995: p. 8) he says that there very few instances recorded prior to the invention of psychiatric diagnosis. Without surveying the sources from which he has arrived at this conclusion it is not possible to say with any great conviction that this is true, although Hacking does argue this thesis at some length. Of course once a category has occurred it becomes easier to record and document phenomena. So it may be the case that there were cases of multiple personality before its invention but that lack of documentation has caused them to be lost to us.

We can elucidate the pivotal relationship between silence or lack of social legitimation and thought or consciousness if we consider an example from Alice Walker's book *Possessing the Secret of Joy* (1993). Extreme forms of Female circumcision have been practised in many areas of Africa for hundreds of years. Walker describes a tribe in which older women of the group performed these operations upon the younger women. There were no words within the tribe with which to describe the procedure. Thus it was something that really happened but was effectively silenced from reflection by the group. Another effect of this lack of conceptualisation of the event was that it has taken some time for these practices to become widely known. Here is an instance where something existed, yet due to the silence surrounding it had not been recorded and was unable to be discussed or responded to as a kind of thing that happened. A similar thing may have occurred for multiple personality. It is possible that the invention of the term facilitated people noticing something that had always existed, yet due to the lack of an appropriate concept had remained largely unrecorded.

It is much less problematic to think of terms such as "skilled batsman" as "made up" ways for people to be. It seems unlikely that there were individuals existing who performed all the actions appropriate for a skilled batsman until the invention of the game of cricket of which "skilled batsman" is a result. It is possible for there to have existed a Papua New Guinean tribesman who just happened to perfect, in the processing of hitting thrown objects around in his village, all the techniques that a skilled batsman would have. This is a fairly far-fetched possibility. What we can say with certainty is that this tribesman's colleagues would not have thought ⟨what a great sweep shot, he truly is a great batsman⟩.

Could George Washington have been a pervert?

The original example that Hacking considered was "perversion". The question posed was "were there any perverts before the beginning of the nineteenth century?" If one agrees with this statement then one is drawn into a position on the possibilities of persons existing before the invention of the term.

> ...it was not possible for God to make George Washington a pervert. God could have delayed Washington's birth by over a century, but would that have been the same man? God could have moved the medical discourse back 100-odd years. But God could not have simply made him a pervert, the way He could have made freckled or had him captured and hung for treachery. (1986: p. 230)

The difference between George Washington being a pervert and being freckled (or hung for treason) is, on the face of it, that his being freckled or being hung were things that could happen at that time. During his life Abraham Lincoln did not keep good health. The physicians of his day provided no good explanation for his lack of well-being. It is now thought that Abraham Lincoln suffered from Marfan's syndrome. Its still unclear whether perversion is more like "being a great batsman", "glove", or like "Marfan's syndrome".

What if Washington had a habit of slipping out in the evening and peering through half opened curtains at other people in various stages of undress. This seems to be a perverted kind of activity, and if he had been caught in this manner would likely have seen his high profile tarnished. Perhaps Washington *would* have been a pervert, irrespective of his contemporaries' inability to label him so. Of course it is not possible for Washington to actually think of himself as a "pervert", but if this is all that Hacking seeks to establish this is a trivial point indeed. His claim is that the category "pervert" creates a new way for a person to be. But if it's likely that Washington could *be* a pervert without thinking of himself as a "pervert" then perversion is not an instance of "making up people". This is not to imply that there are no good instances of making up people, merely to suggest perversion is not an unproblematic example. Certainly the full moral condemnation and pathologising of perversion can be linked to its categorisation by "experts", but there is some room for doubt about the behaviours to which it refers. Without question Washington's evening stroll would not be named as a variety of perversion but something like the corresponding feeling of guilt and some awareness of the ways in which this behaviour might look in the light of general moral principles and the opinions of others could still be possible. However the full panoply of articulated thoughts and attitudes that allows discussion and reflection would arguably be impossible without some kind of naming or categorization as in the example of female circumcision.

Foucault's comments about the making of the modern homosexual are useful for unpacking the issue. Before the invention of the category "homosexual", sodomy was an activity that was strongly prohibited. A person caught performing sodomy in pre-homosexual times would have been in trouble as, almost certainly, would George Washington if he had been caught peering through people's windows. The important difference between pre-homosexual and pre-pervert times is that indulging in these activities would not lead one to belong to a particular category of persons and develop a corresponding identity and set of self-attributions. Becoming a particular type of person in this way involves perceiving one's self or identity as belonging to a particular framework which then colours and locates all one's descriptions of self in accordance with social conceptions of that named category.

Limits to a dynamic nominalist meta theory

We have already noted the availability to George Washington and others of a set of judgements about his behaviour irrespective of the labels or names applied to it. As soon as a phenomenon becomes a little more public and widespread than an isolated case here and there and so becomes an issue for a speech community, one would envisage that there would occur a process of forming a category in order to engage in discourse about what was going on. Thus "getting the issue on the table" of public awareness and concern or "raising public consciousness" about the issue, whether by a moral minority or any other group must very soon mean that the simple analysis in terms of labelling theory, with its nominalist implications, becomes inadequate.

> Suppose there is some truth in the labelling theory of the modern homosexual. It cannot be the whole truth, and this for several reasons, including one that is future directed and one that is past directed. The future directed fact is that after the institutionalisation of the homosexual person in law and official morality the people involved had a life of their own individually and collectively ... The past directed fact is that the labelling did not occur in a social vacuum, in which those identified as homosexual people passively accepted the format. There was a complex social life that is only now revealing itself in the annals of academic social history. (1986: p. 233)

The future directed fact relates to Marx and Engels' remark about the relation between consciousness in society and consciousness "for me personally". The creation of this kind of human activity as a phenomenon that characterises a certain type of person begins a new discursive possibility or niche to be filled by those who identify with the category concerned. This then serves as a focus or node around which the many pre-categorisation moral and interpersonal thoughts can be rendered articulate and forged into a self-conscious identity. Even if the only effect of being labelled "homosexual" was that persons sharing this form of sexuality were united as a group or class of person much remains to be said about the forces that will go on and help shape the development of homosexual culture and identity. Sydney's gay Mardi Gras is an attempt to celebrate gay identity that reaffirms the public consciousness that this is an option for narrative choice. Activities of this sort are not simply the result of labelling, they are attempts by gay people to celebrate and publicise the legitimacy of their way of life and to create a human reality in which to locate oneself. To suggest that the identity of the modern homosexual is created by labelling misses an important influence upon the consciousness of the society and the individual. When this is borne in mind, it is clear that labelling does create a separate category of person, and that that can be the catalyst for the construction, primarily by homosexuals, of a project of creation of a cultural reality which then gives a framework for identity where there previously only existed a framework for mis-identity or inarticulate deviance.

The past directed fact is that the labelling of homosexuals did not occur without some way of life, however poorly articulated and validated, for the category to apply to. Same sex sexual activity has probably always existed but not as a conscious discursive framework for self-development as a person of a certain type. Hacking's suggestion is that those who enjoyed same sex activity found ways of seeking each other out and shared ways of life. The invention of the category, and the resulting uses to which it would have been put, certainly did have great impact upon homosexual identity, but homosexuals would have existed as a fragmented and perhaps marginalised, proto-conscious group prior to their classification. Therefore although it would be implausible to argue that the activity or behaviour which yield the criteria for the classification of a person as homosexual did not come into existence prior to the invention of the category the term "homosexual" and the reality of dynamic nominalism entail that what evolves once a category has been articulated for public and individual consciousness, is far more "real" than a thin reading of social construction might imply but different on the one hand from the existence of physical artefacts such as gloves and natural kinds such as poliomyelitis.

Many writers who speak of "social construction" oversimplify and therefore caricature the relationship between the creation of a discursive device, for example theories about sexuality, and the realities that persons categorised by these theories experience. To some, particularly a certain kind of causal realist, the category is nominal and empty and to others, mad dog social constructionists, it is as real as anything else. Both fall prey to the unreflective use of the term real and its subtle role in human consciousness which is always looking to find intentional objects that will be useful in the task of exploring the world we find ourselves in. To his credit Hacking is careful about stressing the complexity of such processes. He realises that in the complex relation between thought and human reality that is the subject of any theory about "making up people", such processes will typically involve different vectors of influence.

> If we wish to present a partial framework in which to describe such events, we might think of two vectors. One is the vector of labelling from above, from a community of experts who create a reality that some people make their own. Different from this is the vector of the autonomous behaviour of the person so labelled, which presses from below, creating a reality every expert must face. (1986: p. 234)

Hacking is correct to be cautious about the metaphysical implications of dynamic nominalism and making up people because the degree to which categorisation impacts upon different ways of being must vary depending upon the particular features of the case. Is popular culture widely affected, are negative stereotypes involved, is there a body of art and literature which engages with the lifestyle choice in question, are there historical roots, is the law involved, do powerful legitimating institutions such as religion and ethnic identity have a bearing, are all questions which pick out important vectors of influence. Dynamic nominalism allows us to bring these factors to bear on a question of the relation between consciousness and the reality of a way of being. For gay identity we might notice the increasing recognition on popular culture, the defusing of negative stereotypes among large sectors of the population, the growth of openly gay art and literature, the discovery of historical figures whose sexual orientation seems to have gay features to it, the lessening of proscriptions in law, the ambiguity creeping into religious pronouncements, the identification of permission for gay identity in certain ethnic groups and the choice of the term "gay", with its positive connotations as a mark of identity. The name therefore does provide a strong influence upon the construction of that particular way of being. The complex object which engages consciousness under the name of gay identity is therefore surrounded by vectors of significance which tend towards a certain set of attitudes on behalf of non-gay society and those who make it up. What is more the creation of a name is only the beginning of the creation of an object which has its own dynamic essence both shaping and responding to the thoughts of those who apprehend it and live it as their conscious experience.

A different example is provided by Multiple Personality Disorder (MPD) or Dissociative Identity Disorder (DID) in which a different set of vectors are at work which give a different shape to the object of consciousness and the consciousness that apprehends it. We have followed Hacking in arguing that there are a number of influences jointly involved in making up people. Hacking has provided us with the idea of a looping effect between the creation of a category such as MPD and the existence of the disorder as a way of being and an entity for serious psychiatric concern. A discussion of MPD will help to illustrate further the phenomenology of societally produced ways of being and its effect on individual narratives. Essential to our discussion of MPD is the breakdown in the unity of self-attribution that is predicated on the fact that each of us appears among others as a single embodied subjectivity. This is a theme that we will revisit in chapters six and seven. For the moment some similar considerations, more germane to the present discussion can be canvassed by discussing a case drawn from the DSM-IV casebook (American Psychiatric Association, 1994).

Society, consciousness and the bizarre

The DSM-IV casebook includes a section of "international" case studies. The reason why the casebook includes such cases is to demonstrate that the DSM-IV can be effectively applied to mental illness in different cultures. But, as the following case illustrates the story that must be told about the case has to take account of the categories and meaningful connections extant in the society in which it occurs.

> A 24-year-old, single, Xhosa man from a small farming community in South Africa was referred for evaluation of his mental condition after murdering a male witch doctor. According to the patient, he initially consulted the witch doctor for a cough, and was treated with "herbs". However, the witch doctor then had anal intercourse with the patient as the passive partner on 3 successive days. Over the next few days, the patient came to realize that he was pregnant by the witch doctor. He consulted with the witch doctor again, and herbs were prescribed, apparently "to take away the baby." The patient fully complied with the prescription, but discovered that his "pregnancy" continued. He returned to the witch doctor a few weeks later — on the day of the murder. By this time, he believed he had developed a *linea nigra* (a line extending from the naval to the pubis that often becomes pigmented during pregnancy), and that his lower abdomen was slightly distended. This time, however, the witch doctor said that he could not help him, and that he should see "the white man's doctor." The patient apparently then became incensed, and fatally stabbed the witch doctor.
>
> On psychiatric examination, the patient was found to have a fixed, unshakeable belief that he was pregnant. He "proved" this to the examiner by pointing to his stomach, to indicate that something was moving inside. Other than the delusion that he was pregnant and its ramifications, he exhibited no other features of major psychopathology. He was well nourished and appro-

> priately dressed. His speech was coherent and logical, and his affect and behaviour were normal. He appeared to be intelligent, and related well. He expressed remorse for his actions and guilt about the homosexual affair. The psychiatrist was surprised to find that on physical examination, the patient did have a *linea nigra*, and his lower abdomen was slightly distended. Findings of the remainder of the physical examination were normal.
>
> The patient had no previous history of mental illness, and had been functioning well as a machine operator. He had always held witch doctors in high regard, as he believed they could effect cures others could not, but had never before had a male partner. There was no history of substance abuse, and no family history of mental illness… The man was judged to be not responsible for the murder because he was mentally ill. He remained in the hospital, and was treated with antipsychotic medication. At first, he steadfastly insisted that he was pregnant, although he did not know how far along in his pregnancy he was or whether the baby would ever come out. "Men generally don't get pregnant, but I am. This is so because God has willed it." When 9 months went by and he had not delivered a child he began to wonder if in fact he was still pregnant. Shortly thereafter he concluded that a large bowel movement he passed was in fact the baby. He then no longer believed that he was pregnant, but it was unclear he still believed that he once was. The stigmata of pregnancy (*linea nigra*, abdominal distension) disappeared. The last follow-up was about one and half years after the murder, at which time the patient exhibited no disturbance in ideation, mood, or behaviour. (Spitzer 1994: p. 433)

This case presents some difficulties for the psychiatrist wishing to make a diagnosis. Having a bizarre delusion such as this would typically lead a psychiatrist in the west to consider a diagnosis of schizophrenia. In western societies a man believing that he was pregnant would seem to be a good example of a person experiencing a bizarre delusion (though the same does not apply to a man who believes he is really a woman). The reason we would think the former belief is bizarre is because we know that it is not possible for a man to become pregnant and certainly not through having anal intercourse.

What complicates matters here is that this man lives in a society where witch doctors are attributed with broad powers so that for him to believe that a witch doctor is capable of making him pregnant is not a clear-cut symptom of individual psychopathology in that the definition of delusion allows for odd beliefs that have some currency in a certain cultural setting.

Psychiatrists who believe that the falsity and rigidity of belief is sufficient for it being a delusion might still diagnose this man as suffering from delusions. His belief that he has in fact been impregnated by the witch doctor is a false belief, even though the man does have some physiological signs that may reinforce that belief (distended belly and *linea nigra*).

Clearly this case illustrates an important connection between the validity of an individual's beliefs and their society. The fact that witch doctors might be able to make men pregnant (and indeed that the Gods might solve the problem and change the baby into a bowel motion) creates a connex of legitimacy for this man's delusion. This case provides an interesting illustration of the possibility of making people up, or social constructionism. The believed ability of witch doctors provides a possible way for this man to be affected by one. The phantom pregnancy is problematic in a way that gay identity and gloves are not even though all could be accommodated as examples of dynamic nominalism.

We have argued that individuals make sense of themselves through a process of narrative reconstruction of their experience using the possibilities that their cultural frameworks provide. Our ability to create meaningful narratives and the forces to which those are subject are evidenced when we try to understand the way in which this man conceptualised what had happened to him. He was not homosexual and experienced guilt at the homosexual affair that he had been involved in. We do not know the full story behind the circumstances that led to him having anal sex with the witch doctor, however it seems likely that fear or respect of the witch doctor's powers influenced his actions here (perhaps an African example of professional malpractice). As becoming pregnant to the witch doctor is for him a possibility, his concern at the events that took place seems to have led to fear that he was pregnant. The relationship between this man's belief that he was pregnant and the physiological symptoms of a phantom pregnancy is a complex one. However it is possible at least that a dynamic link between the psychosomatic changes and the belief helped to fix and maintain his belief that he was pregnant.

His explanation that his pregnancy terminated after a heavy bowel motion can also be seen as an attempt to form a narrative that makes sense of his experience in terms of all the other beliefs or commitments he has. After nine months of pregnancy it is expected that either a child will be produced or the pregnancy will end via other means. Thus at nine months something has to happen. If after nine months of pregnancy there was no explanation for its end he would be faced with the fact that he had not at any stage been pregnant and that the murder of the witch doctor had been on the basis of a false belief. Thus there is likely to have been some pressure on this man to maintain his belief that he was in fact pregnant by the witch doctor. The obvious resolution links the heavy bowel motion to a supernatural termination of his pregnancy and enables him to cling to his narrative that he was a man who had murdered the witch doctor who had impregnated him and thus violated the laws of the Gods.

This story shows us the way in which societal beliefs and deep-seated cultural attitudes that contextualise the life of an individual can play a vital part in one's consciousness of self and what has happened to oneself. To investigate further the complexity of identity formation and its relation to conceptions of value we draw upon the work of Charles Taylor, particularly in *Sources of the Self* where he proposes a bold philosophical approach to the creation of identity and meaning (1989).

Sources of the Self, Inescapable Frameworks

Taylor's (1989) analysis begins with the idea of *Inescapable Frameworks*. Taylor attempts to establish that "selves" are necessarily tied to "frameworks" and that any investigation of human selfhood cannot escape discussion of its associated frameworks. He argues for a deep connection between selfhood and conceptions of the good.

> ...a framework is that in virtue of which we make sense of our lives spiritually. Not to have a framework is to fall into a life which is spiritually senseless. (p. 18)

Spiritually senseless is a vague term but if we were to take it that the human spirit refers to that which invigorates and morally refreshes us then there is an obvious connection with what we have already said about gay identity in that prior to the articulation of gay identity and its affirmation as a positive way of being there is a kind of shady and marginal lack of self worth, casting a pall over those who find themselves engaging in homosexual activities, a fact of homosexual life to which gay spokespeople have attributed many of the problems of self worth and self understanding experienced by homosexual people. There is no doubt that if we read spiritual to refer to the kind of thing that is real for a person who actively endorses a particular religious framework then this can allow an affirmation of identity and a set of images and value which allow one to articulate the outlines of a way of living without nagging self doubt and ambiguity. Taylor elsewhere makes it clear that he means something broader by "spiritually senseless" than religious coherence although the broad-brush outlines of the account are indicated by gesturing at the role of religion in the consciousness of a believer.

> Finding a sense to life depends on framing meaningful expressions which are adequate. (Taylor 1989: p. 18)

The finding of meaningful expressions that are adequate is clearly meant to relate to the composition of a satisfying narrative of one's life. It seems that by using the term "spiritually senseless" Taylor wants to refer to the lack of a set of meanings to act as the scaffolding of a conscious life narrative. Thus Taylor's claim might be read as the claim that having a meaningful life is formed on the basis of frameworks for thought, action and identity.

> What I have been calling a framework incorporates a crucial set of qualitative distinctions. To think, feel, judge within such a framework is to function with the sense that some action, or mode of life, or mode of feeling is incomparably higher than the others which are more readily available to us. (Taylor 1989: p. 19)

So a framework makes some actions, modes of life and modes of feeling higher or better than others. The suggestion is that frameworks provide a set of values against which the contents of conscious choice can be assessed and which therefore become normative for a person's activities in a way that acts at a higher level than the rule-following we have discussed in relation to the articulation of those meanings themselves. To pursue the analogy with chess we could argue that the meanings which allow us to grasp the concepts marked by our words are like legitimate moves in the game but that these norms are like the idea that you play the game to win (or at least put up a good show).

In *Liberalism, Community and Culture* Will Kymlicka talks about membership of a community with sufficient appropriate conceptions of the good and argues that that membership is a necessary condition of having a good life or to revert to our analogy playing the game in a way that you can think it should be played.

> Different ways of life are not simply different patterns of physical movements. The physical movements only have meaning to us because they are identified as having significance by our culture, because they fit into some pattern of activities which is culturally recognized as a way of leading one's life. (Kymlicka 1989: p. 165)

Kymlicka could be read here as outlining a condition for meaningful activity in general but he also believes that the value of life plans (formed from that meaningful activity) derives from the culture(s) of which one is a member. He claims that without a conception of the good (or a range of conceptions from which to choose) it is impossible to live a life that one considers valuable. Taylor's thought leads in a similar direction. A life that is "spiritually senseless" is the result of not living in accordance with a "framework" and therefore not having a conception of a worthwhile goal to invigorate or motivate one's activity. Taylor believes, with Kymlicka, that such frameworks that allow a consciousness of value, are the result of culturally produced ways of life. Taylor's notion of a "framework" is very similar to Kymlicka's ideas about the importance of cultural membership for a good life, in that they both suggest cultural membership is a necessary condition of leading a good life.

The honour ethic and articulability

Taylor offers examples of frameworks. One of the earliest is the honour ethic.

> The life of the warrior or citizen, or citizen soldier is deemed higher than the merely private existence, devoted to the arts of peace and economic well-being. (Taylor 1989: p. 20)

In ancient and not so ancient times the warrior role was conceived to be a good way of life to achieve or aim at. Of course the warrior ethic has not always been valued to this degree, and Taylor contrasts it with Plato's placing of reason at the top of the list of virtues. For Plato and others of his ilk a life lived in accordance with the dictates of reason was a life in accordance with that which was most worthwhile in human nature. Living the rational life implies that individuals reflect upon the framework guiding their life.

An important feature of those living in accordance with the warrior ethic is that their framework, unlike Plato's, is not necessarily articulated by those conforming to that framework. This is important because members of a framework may not be able to articulate in any comprehensive way the framework which ties their identity together but they would typically be able to name some of the goods concerned, perhaps by use of an idiolect — cool, staunch, mana, and so on. The virtues of a "good vintage car restorer" are an illustration of this point. If you asked someone working on an old car about the framework within which their activity was meaningful you might get a response such as "what are you bleating on about?" yet these virtues exist nonetheless. The unwritten code of the vintage car restorer includes mores such as being at all times meticulous about the job at hand, knowing what modern gaskets and seals will fit which vintage cars and having some practical expertise in the distinctive methods of vintage car construction. The possible inarticulability of frameworks may cause some to question their importance for a good life. People cannot always answer immediately why they consider one thing or action valuable and another not. But if frameworks are not necessarily articulable then questions about the conscious reality of the framework seem to loom. However, if we revert to Marx and Engels with whom we began, we might argue that a conscious value framework is an emergent property of a tract of human intercourse or discourse and its explicit formulation for conscious identification may bear a variable relationship to its naming in a way obscured by the claims of labelling theory and nominalist forms of social constructivism. It is consistent with our thesis that discussion of the framework qua framework or its appearance as a possible object of consciousness is going to be closely tied to its naming as a reality which can appear in an intentional relation.

Inescapable frameworks and identity

We have already discussed Taylor's belief that selfhood is necessarily connected to frameworks. Taylor not only believes that living in accordance with a framework is necessary for living a life worth living, he also believes that the self is constituted by living within such frameworks.

> The horizons within which we live our lives and which make sense of them have to include these strong qualitative discriminations. Moreover this is not meant just as a contingently true psychological fact about human beings, which could perhaps turn out one day to not hold for some exceptional individual or new type, some superman of disengaged objectification. Rather the claim is that living within such strongly qualified horizons is constitutive of human agency, that stepping outside these limits would be tantamount to stepping outside what we would recognise as integral, that is, undamaged human personhood. (Taylor 1989: p. 27)

Taylor's claim that human agency is constituted by living within cultural frameworks is a bold one. The case of gay identity has provided some support for the idea that there is an interesting connection between having a good life and frameworks (or cultural membership). It is quite possible that human agency does need such frameworks for lives to be worth living. However, as one of us has argued, thought and action according to rules are possible for a human being considered in isolation (Gillett 1995) and one hears of autistic children who do not participate in the give and take of a human context but develop skills of thought and action which, as it were, emerge absent any of the normal precursors that one would see in other children. Despite these possibilities it is over-whelmingly plausible that we do develop our patterns of thought and action in a way that closely reflects the cultures and frameworks of value in which we are embedded.

Taylor's claim that the connection between the self and its frameworks is *a priori* or internal should not therefore be read as an assertion that absent human contexts with fairly settled cultural values one cannot act or evaluate the actions of self and others but rather it should be read as a remark on the essential connection between society and language, language and concepts, concepts and categories, categories and the contents of consciousness, consciousness and our dealings with the objects and events around us and the emergence of value out of that activity.

We can get a better grip on this if we pursue the topic of moral nihilism. Moral nihilism is the meta-ethical theory that statements about moral values are not statements about anything true of the world. It is usually defended by appealing to the idea that what is true of the world is to some extent statable without making essential mention of our ways of thinking. Thus it is straightforwardly true in this sense that the Nile river runs into the Mediterranean Sea. Some conclude from this that there are no objective ethical values and that morals are a matter of inventing right and wrong. Naïve as this might be, it is a position that many find philosophically appealing and that others have lived their lives by, as if it were true. Dostoyevsky's character Stavrogin was in all aspects of his life a true moral nihilist. This character thought that all conceptions of the good were false. As Taylor has told us, this character's life was one that could be described as spiritually meaningless. This may be the case. However even if Taylor is right that Stavrogin's life was spiritually meaningless he still has a sense of who he is, in other words a sense of self or identity and a project which he carries through. This tends to moderate the strength with which one endorses the claim that frameworks are the essential origin of value, spiritual meaning, and the self.

Thus Taylor's thought that there could exist no frameworkless self whether that be a pathetic worm of a person or a "superman of disengaged objectification" is one that is far from being obviously true. Nietszche's ubermensch are portrayed as pursuing a passionate but completely individual path and the herd with its solid framework of values gets rather bad press from that quarter. But we should note that Zarathustra pursues his lonely quest armed with a full panoply of values and thoughts and conceptions of the significance and insignificance of certain features of life which are intrinsically impassioned and clothed with value. It is more implausible than anything Taylor says to believe that these could arise ex nihilo and much more in agreement with reflective thought about human life and meaning to believe that we draw on and perhaps surpass the many concepts and conceptions which our society gives to us to disclose the significance of the things it encounters and the things it has made.

Although Taylor's views on the social constitution of human agency are problematic and require careful treatment, these last remarks suggest that consciousness is deeply connected to the productive forces that arise in human association and indeed Taylor's overall treatment of identity formation and value are deeply relevant to the issue of society and narrative identity.

Taylor's notion of identity

To illuminate his thesis about the relationship between selves and frameworks Taylor explores the question of identity. Identity, Taylor tells us, is partly due to moral or spiritual commitment. We have hinted at a loosening of this idea from highly articulate frameworks of value but for the minute can explore one such framework to paint the issues in a clear light. When someone explains what they think about a certain issue by referring to their Catholicism they are divulging the framework which justifies their stance of that issue. Taylor claims such frameworks are necessary conditions for making spiritual or moral commitments.

> It is that this provides the range within which they can determine where they stand on questions of what is good, or worthwhile, or admirable, or of value. Put counterfactually, they are saying that were they to lose this commitment or identification, they would be at sea, as it were; they wouldn't know any more, for an important range of questions, what the significance of things was for them. (1989: p. 27)

It is interesting that Taylor tempers his strong counterfactual assertion with the provision "for an important range of questions". If he had not done so his counterfactual would have been easy to refute. The structure of Catholicism is such that it is not uncommon to hear Catholics framing accounts of their moral or spiritual commitments by a reference to their religion. Yet even Catholicism, which does demand that its followers make many commitments on the basis of their faith, does not live up to Taylor's expectations. Natural law theologians attempt to support their moral commitments (which are concurrent with many Catholic commitments) by arguing on the basis of an essential human nature. Such theologians think that the moral dictates they arrive at are not correct simply because they are the current orthodoxy among believers. When they think that something is good they *really think it is good and would be good whether or not one were a believer.*

A person referring to their Catholicism who said "I think abortion is a bad idea" could very easily lose their faith and still maintain that abortion was wrong. Such a person may proceed from justifying their belief in terms of their religion to stating that it really is bad, because it is a violation of what human beings are and should do. Like natural law theorists this person would think that abortion really was bad.

It is significant that Pope John Paul II has made attempts to justify his view of contraception in just this way (see Humanae Vitae 1975). He did not simply claim that this was what Catholics should think about contraception because it was orthodox within their framework. Rather, he offered arguments based upon the negative impact of contraception upon the lives of those who used it. This may seem mere quibbling as Taylor is correct to be insistent about the importance of a framework for living a meaningful life, but the temptation to reduce the identity and values of a person to manifestations that are totally given by their frameworks of belief, and the embedded conceptions of the good, is one that should be avoided. Catholicism is an interesting example in that it has always been a feature of the Roman Catholic tradition that it has sought grounds for its beliefs that are not limited to those available within a prior commitment to the Creed they espouse. Thus, as in any human enterprise, a blind adherence to a way of thinking and acting because it is what is dominant around here is not the norm however deeply ingrained those folkways might be. There are always voices of question and reflection that ask the framework to interrogate itself.

This attempt to move beyond culturally located grounds for meaning is reflected in the general fact that when people say that they think something is bad, they do not just mean "Well, this is bad according to what I believe". When you really think that something is bad, you think that this is true, the fact that it is suggested by one's framework is insufficient for really saying something is bad and were you to seriously think that there was no other reason apart from that people like you think so you would be a strange kind of believer.

At this point we ought to note, in a reflective vein, that it is the wont of philosophers to question themselves and that the role of frameworks might be deeper or shallower depending upon the individual. The possibility we are mooting can be best put by imagining different kinds of adherents to a framework of value or meaning.

1. There is the kind of adherent whose consciousness is totally determined by their cultural framework and the way that concepts are typically used within that framework. Perhaps it is a philosophers' conceit that such unreflective individuals exist.
2. There is the kind of individual who is deeply committed to a framework but whose mind struggles with many issues under the influence of many and diverse conceptual possibilities some of which are quite marginal or controversial in the light of the commitments constitutive of her framework.
3. There is the kind of individual whose thought draws on one or more than one framework but with no deep commitment or engagement.
4. There is the person whose life has moved from framework to framework and who therefore finds within himself a set of conflicts and irresolutions.

For each of these, at least according to our view, it is a *sine qua non* that the tools of consciousness are given by the rule following practices that constitute some framework or other when the topic of consciousness is a question of identity or value. However the degree of strength with which the norms of thought within that framework will have an influence above and beyond the rules for the use of terms is a matter of degree. This claim defeats most types of strong social determinism.

Taylor talks about an identity crisis as an event that occurs when one loses touch with one's framework so that one's identity is cut loose from the structures which enabled it to cohere and be meaningful.

> They lack a frame or horizon within which things can take on a stable significance, within which some life possibilities can be seen as good or meaningful, others as bad or trivial. (Taylor 1989: p. 28)

This conceptualisation of an identity crisis has intuitive appeal but cases 2 and 4 above suggest another way such a thing might occur. One could have an identity crisis not because one lacked a framework but because one had developed commitments to two frameworks that, in some particular situation, potentiated a deep self-threatening conflict. Persons suffering from identity crises do typically refer to the futility of their present activities and life plans. We would argue that this futility can result from an inability to find unambiguous meaning for a situation given the frameworks at that person's disposal.

Taylor's notion of self

Taylor's separate discussions of self and identity suggest that they might be different things. To explain what he's talking about he offers several thoughts about the self and its relation to frameworks of identity.

> ...the notion of self which connects it to our need for identity is meant to pick out this crucial feature of human agency, that we cannot do without some orientation to the good (Taylor 1989: p. 33).

Taylor here links the notion of self to an orientation to the good. Given that there is room for doubt whether the good is anything objective at all and a moral nihilist (one who believes that all moral predications are false) must be presumed to have some conception of self then the "need for identity" has to play a key role. Obviously Stavrogin did have some sense of self. If you had asked him who he was he could have told you his name, age, where he was born and so on. In fact he could have told you enough so that he could be said to have a full sense of personal identity, in the Lockean sense. Taylor's thesis is better illustrated by another Doestoyevsky character, Roskolnikov from *Crime and Punishment*. Like Stavrogin, Roskolnikov freed himself from the constraints on conventional conduct. After committing murder he eventually reorientated himself in accordance with conventional conceptions of the good. What he had, and revised in the light of love, was a need for a sense of an identity that was worth driving at. This started off for him as the identity of a successful law student who by his brilliance would be marked out from others but changed into the identity of one who loved and was loved, faithfully, constantly, and without regard for his station in life. However, Roskolnikov is only implausibly credited with a formed articulation of that view.

A second feature of Taylor's "self":

> ...it is not like an object in the usually understood sense. We are not selves in the way we are organisms, or we don't have selves in the way we have hearts and livers. (Taylor 1989: p. 34)

The point here is that the "self" is not amenable to investigation in the same way as the objects of the natural sciences. Because he believes that selves depend upon their relations to conceptions of good they cannot be studied as objects in the same sense that electrons can and the subtleties introduced by dynamic nominalism and the looping effect of human kinds come clearly into view. Selves are ongoing projects, one might say (echoing Sartre), constantly being compared to and revised in the light of one's conception of a good (or good enough) identity.

A third feature is the linguistic structure of selves

> A language only exists and is maintained within a language community. And this indicates another crucial feature of a self. One is a self only among other selves. A self can never be described without reference to those who surround it. (Taylor 1989: p. 35)

This characteristic we have broadly agreed with while noting a problem with the extreme claim. The concepts applicable to the self are available within a "language community" but one's language community may change (for instance, if one learns a new language) and that may make available new ways of seeing oneself. If Taylor is correct and selves are inextricably linked with frameworks then it is hard to see how a self could be described without reference to other selves and their reactions, attitudes and ideals. In fact the essential relation between self-reflection and the responses of others to oneself is an interesting topic (Gillett 1993).

We have argued that a child's mastery of language is an integral part of cognitive development. Our personhood is something that emerges alongside our thought. The fact that language is something that can only exist in a speech community means that our thought is influenced by the speech community in which we develop. So as our personhood is a reflection of the way that we think it is bound to be influenced by the speech community in which we develop and the way we are regarded within that community. One can imagine a trajectory of lived experience in which the person was always treated as bad or undesirable and it is a small step to realise the hostility towards the framework of value in which one lived that that might engender.

The self as narrative

On page 35 Taylor offers a definition of his sense of self

> My self-definition is understood as an answer to the question Who I am. And this question finds its original sense in the interchange of speakers. I define who I am by defining where I speak from, in the family tree, in social space, in the geography of social statuses and functions, in my intimate relations to the ones I love, and also crucially in the space of moral and spiritual orientation within which my most important defining relations are lived out. (1989)

This remark is very close to our comments above about cultural identity and it reinforces the thesis that our identity, or sense of self is defined with reference to the "webs of interlocution" within which we are involved. Roskolnikov could hold that such webs of interlocution, in his relative isolation as a penniless law student in a big city, enabled him to form a conception of who he was and wanted to be. But the fact that he knew who he was in that sense, did not mean that he had come to a robust and sustainable belief in the good. In order to achieve the latter he had to be drawn into webs of interlocution, in part by the horror of his act and in part by his real engagement with others, which provided "defining relationships" within which his life could move. So the picture that Taylor is sketching is one which highlights the necessity of knowing, by acquaintance and intentional participation our social relation in order to have a sense of identity. Even then our consciousness of having an identity and a self worth caring about is not totally given by any framework but also by what goes on between people who in part constitute that framework.

Taylor thinks he has shown that all issues about the good must be relative to a moral framework. The moral framework he finally offers us is naturalistic but not in any person-independent or even commitment independent way. There is no objective framework of values apart from the way we become involved with each other and make sense of ourselves, just as Marx and Engels (and Sartre) suggest. We are as inextricably tied to these frameworks, as we are to living with each other and making those relationships work by undergirding them with commitments and values. In part those values rest for their justification on the evident goodness of the resulting relationships and the goods they bring into human lives. If to posit this kind of framework is a kind of naturalism then to that extent the present account is naturalistic.

Taylor believes that we make sense of our lives as narratives that trace trajectories through human affairs.

> In order to have a sense of who we are we have to have a notion of how we have become and of where we are going. (1989: p. 47)

The idea of person's identity being like a story is an appealing one. It fits with the phenomenology of who we are. Often we don't take time to reflect upon who we are and why we are pursuing things and it is often not until we meet a person who asks searching questions about us that we have reason to reflect. To convey a sense of who you are to another person will often involve telling them a story about your "webs of interlocution" in pretty much the way Taylor has suggested. Psychotherapy, for instance, demands that such reflection upon our self takes place. Psychotherapy attempts to facilitate the construction of personal narratives that provide sustainable identity explanations to which one can commit oneself and which will support one at points of threat or disorientation. Taylor explains the nature of identity by way of analogy.

> Orientation in moral space turns out again to be similar to orientation in physical space. We know where we are through a mixture of recognition of landmarks before us and a sense of how we have travelled to get here… If I leave the local drug store and turn the corner to find the Taj Mahal staring me in the face, I am more likely to conclude that the movie industry is once again earning its tax write-offs in Montreal than to believe myself suddenly by the Jumna. Part of my sense of genuineness will turn on how I got there. And our entire understanding beforehand of states of greater perfection, however defined is strongly shaped by our striving to attain them. (1989: p. 48)

This "narrative approach" to personal identity is quite comfortable alongside Kant's ideas on the matter. Kant thought that to explain identity we needed to distinguish between the empirical self and an *a priori* principle of apperceptive unity that is necessary to all our perceptions and reasoning. Roughly speaking the empirical self is just like the self that Taylor describes, it is a potential object of thought, and therefore you can think of it as existing in the past or present. The principle of apperceptive unity (the Transcendental Unity of Apperception) records the possibility that as well as this product of conceptualisation and experience there is a subjective aspect of self which can take its own mental life as an intentional object and so become self-conscious. The author engaged in writing the events of his life can, as it were, step outside the stream of narrative and see how he is getting on.

Taylor's idea is really just an extension of this interpretation and amplification of the Kantian theory (one might call it a Transcendental Unity of Narration). Kant, at some points did not stress the importance of a speech community's influence upon general (or discursive) concepts. This underemphasis can be read into his comments about the empirical self. "Discursive theories of identity" fill in the gaps that might be read into the Kantian theory. Such theories imply that to discover, or make sense of who the empirical self is, we must think how this self fits into spheres of interaction, how its actions are consistent, and why it performed certain actions (Harre and Gillett 1994).

Although Taylor is quite right about the narrative nature of creating a sense of identity we must not forget that that agency is not simply constituted by the frameworks that we live in. Paying attention to the other half of Kant's theory of the self will help to avoid the pitfalls of this mistake. There must exist some faculty with which to reflect upon the meaningfulness of the empirical self who can, as it were, distance itself as subjectivity, from the narrative of lived conscious experience and hold it up to the light of reflection. This does not mean that you have to accept what Kant says about the matter. Yet some story must be told about how it is possible to consider one's life meaningful and able to be reformed according to one's current assessments of value without some such faculty of self-distancing. When we speak of agency we mean not just our empirical selves, but also the faculty by which we make meaningful choices and through them influence the unfolding nature of the empirical self. We must, however guard against the mistake of reifying an extensionless point of willing which drives the self this way and that without significant constraint from within the lived narrative. This is, in a sense, a denial of the progressive formation of self and consciousness by lived experience with others.

Taylor thinks there is an opposite kind of fatal flaw in the conceptions of personal identity espoused by Locke and Hume and carried through into the writings of Derek Parfit (1984) where we lose sight of the unifying morally committed narrator altogether.

> ...what has been left out is precisely the mattering. The self is defined in neutral terms, outside of any essential framework of questions. In fact, of course, Locke recognises that we are not indifferent to ourselves; but he has no inkling of the self as a being which essentially is constituted by a certain mode of self-concern- in contrast to the concern we cannot but have about the quality of our experiences as pleasurable or painful.
>
> This is what I want to call the "punctual" or "neutral" self — "punctual" because the self is defined in abstraction from any constitutive concerns and hence from any identity in the sense in which I have been using the term in the previous section. Its only constitutive property is self awareness (1989: p. 49)

If Taylor's conception of the self is right then Locke, Hume, and Parfit all work with an inadequate conception of self. What we want from questions about identity are answers that do justice to the sense of coherence and meaningfulness that make up who we are. Without considering the narrative nature of our construction of the empirical self the point of asking about identity seems to be missed. Our investigation of consciousness is targeted upon the intentionality of mental content. Intentionality highlights the fact that the objects of consciousness are objects that stand in a relation to a subject and the contribution of the subject to the relation that is consciousness is important. Without focusing upon the aspects that are noticed within a consideration of your identity you are left with a rather hollow investigation of this contribution. The process of creating a narrative of the empirical self involves intentional activity that is guided by frameworks only articulable within the language game of a speech community.

Conclusion

Marx and Engels locate consciousness in the intercourse of human beings and their practical embodied dealings with the world. They point to language as the medium pervading this activity and the medium that potentiates many of the contents of our consciousness.

Hacking has shown how some ways of being can be brought into existence through human thought and theorising about the human condition. It is important to distinguish between things that come into existence hand in hand with theories about their existence and those things that exist but are not known about until theories about them are formed. It seems likely that Hacking's thesis that many ways of being human are social productions is correct. Hacking's dynamic nominalism is useful not only for understanding the diversities of identity that are available to human beings but also provides a useful starting point for understanding the relationship between society and possible ways of being.

Taylor's arguments steer our gaze towards moral commitments and frameworks and it is important to be clear about the strength of claims that can be plausibly defended in that area. We have suggested that the essential connection between a person's sense of self and the frameworks to which they belong is not as simple as Taylor might be taken to suggest. We have also argued that an identification of the frameworks concerned with explicit formulated systems of propositional belief is problematic. However Taylor's ideas about individuals creating narratives or stories to help in understanding their lives provides a fruitful analysis of some aspects of human identity and its relation to society. The effect of these arguments is to strengthen the conclusion that society plays an important part in defining and producing the elements that yield the contents of conscious states.

Chapter 6

Consciousness and the brain

We have argued for several theses in our account of consciousness.
i. Consciousness is intentional such that the idea of being conscious of X is primary and the global or holistic state called consciousness being a conglomerate of more specific conscious and intentional acts about X, Y, or Z.
ii. Mental acts are contentful and their content is given by intentional or conceptual characterisations of objects.
iii. Conceptual characterisations are internally related to the understanding of language.
iv. The objects of mental acts are not internal objects in the Cartesian mind but objects in shared space to which we intentionally relate.
v. Intentional relations to objects are evident in both perceptions, and actions.

We now need to spell out how the mental properties we have discerned in our conception of consciousness might be related to the events in the brain that are revealed by using neurological and neurophysiological techniques. In this project we will develop and provide further support for the following theses.
i. Being conscious admits of degrees; one person (or organism) at a given time may be qualitatively and quantitatively more conscious than another.
ii. Consciousness is to be understood as the exercise of a capacity for selective, articulated, flexible, interest-guided activity.
iii. Exactly the kinds of cognitive abilities that are required to perform the mental activity we call conscious are those that are required for contentful thought.
iv. The neocortex is the brain structure that is the neurophysiological substrate of consciousness (though subcortical centres are also required).
v. Even if the brain is the substrate of all conscious activity, conscious attributes do not reduce to physical attributes.

In this chapter we will develop a view of conscious activity which makes clear the reasons why consciousness and intentionality are not smoothly reducible to the aspects of human function which physically realize them and therefore that when we are dealing with concepts such as action, the unconscious, abnormalities of consciousness and animal consciousness the role of the physical should not be given undue prominence. We should explicitly reject the claim by some philosophers that "Psychology, no matter how it is done, necessarily is a branch of physiology, hence biology" (Millikan 1995). We will argue that this somewhat overblown claim is no more true than the claim that psychology is merely a branch of cultural studies (which, in the light of our discussion of consciousness and society, also has some merit).

Neurology and consciousness

A great temptation in studies of the brain and consciousness is to retreat further and further behind the levels of input processing that are revealed by neurophysiologists and then choose some level at which the organism becomes conscious of what is going on. We have suggested that consciousness involves the active engagement with the object using a wide range of conceptually or noetically structured abilities to work with the informational transaction between the subject and the object. We now need to explore how this complex and holistic function drawing on a number of subsidiary functions might be mediated in the brain.

We will begin this exploration by describing some conditions in which consciousness seems clearly to be impaired or altered by what happens to the brain.

There is more to it than meets the eye

Weiscrantz has described a phenomenon that results from neocortical damage and is known as 'blindsight' (Weiscrantz 1987; Parkin 1996). Certain patients with lesions in the parieto-occipital part of the cerebral cortex (the primary and secondary visual areas) or the major pathways serving these parts of the brain cannot report objects in the affected area of the visual field. However they can, when forced to respond, discriminate those objects at better than chance levels from a range of alternatives. They can also detect location, movement, stimulus intensity, and some crude aspects of form and colour (Parkin 1996: p. 37)

So what do such patients lack? The most obvious answer is that they lack the ability to report visual inputs. The empirical data reveal that they also lack the ability to get it right every, or practically every, time and their awareness lacks distinctness and differentiation, so that they lack cognitive accuracy. But this is only a part answer because we cannot equate consciousness with mere efficiency in cognitive tasks nor merely with the ability to make a verbal response to a stimulus. Dennett, at one point, did hold a theory that gave great weight to verbal report or 'public relations' and we will take up and extend what we take to be right about this view. Weiscrantz, himself, offers the following suggestion.

> What I think has become disconnected is a monitoring system, one that is not part of the serial information processing chain itself, but which can monitor what is going on. I think that is the kind of neural organization one is looking for in order to explain awareness. (1987: p. 316)

'Monitoring' the processing of stimuli does offer us a metaphor for what is going on here but it suggests that there is a centre somewhere else in the brain which, as it were, runs its own surveillance on the visual areas and has a close connection with our behavioural output systems. We must cash this out in some way which does not merely put another homuncular box into the analysis called 'the monitor' and leaves us with a mystery as to what that is doing and how it fits into the whole business.

In fact, some revealing phrases do help convey what more is involved in human consciousness. We say that the subject knows or can tell that things are thus and so; or, perhaps, that he can take notice of or reflect upon things that happen; or that he is appreciative of what is around him rather than merely reacting to it. These bear an obvious relation to 'monitoring' but hint at wider connections to do with complex levels of responding. The hint is reinforced when we recall that what we monitor the thing as being and the way we respond to it or act towards it show the intentional content and finely tuned noetic abilities that we have discussed in previous chapters. This, we have argued demonstrates a complexity in the apprehension of an object which a simple specification of how we detect it does not show.

We should also note that a subject can be conscious of an object, X, and, depending on the way he thinks of it or other aspects of the situation in which he finds himself, show no reaction to it or even ignore it quite deliberately. A classic example of this is the case where the hero is being threatened by a thug and perceives, but does not show, any sign of his perception — that his female accomplice is about to shoot the thug from behind. This also reinforces the point that any relatively simple or even surveyable set of connections from visual areas to behavioural (including verbal) areas will not do in finding a "cerebral specification" of consciousness. Somewhere in between the incoming perceptual information and the outgoing response there is a set of processes complex enough for us to allow interests, attention to various aspects, previous conceptual learning, associated experiences, and so on, to happen. We should therefore be able to find brain processes which explain or at least correlate with these phenomena of consciousness. This is a lot of work for a monitor to do; it is beginning to look more and more like a Cartesian omnicompetent "captain of the cerebral ship" (Dennett 1991).

Weiscrantz has in fact extensively updated his opinion, while retaining the core idea, in his shift to the view that "commentary is a *sine qua non* for awareness" (1997: p. 75). He identifies a weak and a strong view of this thesis. The weak view is that "awareness is *enabling* of the commentary, that is allows it to occur" (p. 75) and the strong view is that "phenomenal awareness itself ... results from the delivery or potential delivery of the report"(p. 76).

He garners an extensive range of evidence to support this view. We have already noted the evidence from blindsight but he also considers the so called "split-brain" patients who have had a commissurotomy. This operation divides the major connections between the two hemispheres of the brain to limit the spread of epilepsy in patients with the more severe and intractable forms of that disorder. The operation results in patients with a "split-brain". in the sense that they have severely disrupted information exchanges between the two cerebral hemispheres.

Such patients were studied by Roger Sperry (1966) and his co-workers and came to philosophical attention through the writing of Thomas Nagel (1971) and Derek Parfit (1984). The philosophers accepted the conclusions of some of the psychologists working with such patients and suggested that in these patients there were two streams of consciousness going on simultaneously, one in each hemisphere. The actual data were somewhat less conclusive than this response might suggest.

> What Sperry and his coworkers found was that when they projected visual stimuli to the left, 'speaking' hemisphere, of split-brain subjects the subjects could report seeing the stimuli quite normally and could identify them. But when they were projected to the 'silent, non speaking' right hemisphere, the subjects said they saw nothing at all. Nevertheless, they could be shown, by indirect means, to have identified the 'unseen' visual events. (Weiscrantz 1997: pp. 32–3)

This finding of the splitting of consciousness was big philosophical news at the time and definitely did tell against certain theories which held there was a localized "centre of consciousness" somewhere in the brain. Some, however, rejected that interpretation and argued that we were seeing an internal informational disruption that a conscious person was trying to cope with as best they could (Gillett 1986). In fact Weiscrantz adds a significant piece of information to this debate.

> Indeed those split-brain patients that I later studied no longer denied seeing stimuli projecting to the right hemisphere — they could give accurate descriptions and approximate dimensions of them (1997: p. 34)

Weiscrantz mentions factors such as neural plasticity and "indirect bodily signalling strategems" to account for this recovery but the details are less important than the philosophical significance of his finding. It is clear that the patients did something to reintegrate their fractured cognitive world and repair the internal discontinuities to what they thought of as the one conscious life.

That philosophical conclusion is consistent with Weiscrantz's summary remarks about a range of neuropsychological syndromes and their bearing on the nature of consciousness.

> This is the position: … in every area of cognitive neuropsychology there are preserved capacities of which the patients remain unaware. These range from perception to attention, meaning, long term memory, and language and within each of these there are several different varieties. The blindsight patient can discriminate visual stimuli without seeing the stimuli; the blind touch ('numbsense') patient can locate the position of a tactile stimulus on the arm that has lost the sense of touch. The amnesic patient can store information that can be retrieved by the experimenter but is not acknowledged as memory by the patient. In prosopagnosia there is a loss of specific memories of familiar faces, but the patient demonstrates through indirect means that this information is retained. (1997: p. 228)

He goes on to mention unilateral neglect, language comprehension and anosagnosia (in which the patient denies a manifest defect). Weiscrantz concludes that consciousness is "the ability to render a parallel acknowledged commentary" (p. 228) of what is happening to them. He says "the medium is the message — the achieving of the commentary is the awareness" (p. 76). We have stressed the flexible and open-ended activity that allows such a commentary. We might also acknowledge the component of that activity which draws on the symbolism and meanings available to an individual to make meaningful the contents of their experience. But this is a theme to which we shall return below.

Coma and states of reduced consciousness

The important point here is the fact that consciousness is fragmented by syndromes of disconnection disrupting the holistic function of the higher parts of the brain — the cerebral cortices — and therefore conscious abilities are not smoothly integrated. Note that if there were, as Descartes supposed, a single unpaired integrating organ responsible for the unity of consciousness this would not happen. The organ cannot be the corpus callosum because that is merely a large bundle of brain wiring and not a centre in itself. Furthermore no centre is involved in the lesion so it is plausible to suggest that it is the continuity and interconnectedness of all the cortical functions that is the neural substrate of consciousness. We can now move from a consideration of disruptions in the integrity of consciousness to more extreme losses.

One cannot be conscious of x and asleep or in a coma; to be either of these things is to be unconscious *tout court*. In fact, we can press the inquiry a little further by following this seam in the conceptual labyrinth we have entered. The significance of loss of conscious life for an adequate theory of consciousness can be discerned if we consider what brain structures are involved in such a loss. The crucial and tragic condition where this happens is called the persistent vegetative state. This state arises when the cerebral cortex has (the highest information processing areas of the brain) been destroyed. That usually results from a severe anoxic or ischaemic injury sparing the lower centres but devastating the cortical networks. Such an individual recovers from the injury to a state where the only activity he shows is of a reflex or vegetative type (Campbell et al. 1997; Cranford and Smith 1979). An individual in this state does not track with the eyes, does not show consistent responses to the presence of others, does not show coordinated motor responses or any responses to presented objects, and does not show any emotions. This is because all the (higher brain or cortical) circuitry which normally realises the complex information processing involved in those more complex and structured responses to the environment has been destroyed.

This is in marked contrast to the 'locked in syndrome' or 'coma vigilante' where the individual is cut off from motor expression by a small but critical subcortical lesion and yet, if he recovers, shows an intact (articulated and conceptual) awareness of what went on while he could not communicate (Patterson and Grabois 1986). In these cases intelligent communication through eye blink or upward deviation of the eyes to yes/no questions can be established and the person shows more or less intact conscious awareness of their surroundings. Locked in syndrome is therefore an output pathway problem and the brain mechanisms subserving conscious appreciation of the environment are intact even though consciousness may not be manifest in the way that it normally is (Gillett 1999).

The two lesions are therefore almost anatomically complementary to one another forming what neuropsychologists sometimes refer to as a double disconnection situation. In persistent vegetative state the lesion hits the higher centres leaving the lower centres intact (and destroys consciousness) and the other severs the connection between cortical centres and the pathways they use to manifest their activity but leaves the cortical centres themselves intact (and preserves consciousness). We will later discuss the role of the incoming pathways and their collaterals to the arousal mechanisms in "waking up the brain".

So now, with the help of a bit of clinical neurology, we begin to see an interesting convergence. Weiscrantz's comprehensive review of the neuropsychological data suggested that being conscious is clearly related to reporting or 'telling' (and it surely is not an accident that there is an ambiguity here between eg. 'John can tell an apple from a pear' and 'John tells everybody about his apples') but is not just a matter of reportability. His notion of a commentary was, however, somewhat wider than the idea of a verbal report and included the fact that the ongoing situation was connected to and potentially "commented upon" (perhaps non-verbally) by engagement with a broad set of conceptual mechanisms. One might then begin to conclude that being conscious of X implies that X has a wider and richer role and connectedness with one's life of thought than does merely reacting to X. On this account being conscious of something, in common with being conscious *simpliciter*, involves the capacity to draw on a flexible range of cognitive abilities and use them in attention and action. A conscious person, one might say, has an open-ended grasp of what he encounters so that his thoughts and feelings can explore it or do a number of tasks in relation to its intentional content for him. At this stage a congenial strand of work in cognitive science can be woven into the present account. This view is, in fact, close to the view developed by Edelman which we shall outline below and which deepens the connection between neuroscience and Weiscrantz's notion of a commentary.

Consciousness, concepts, and cognitive development

We have already discussed the Vygotskian thesis that language and thought are intimately bound together and we have examined this in terms of the rule-following that is part of the individuation of meanings and the role of meanings in the structure of human thinking. We have discussed the nature of language as a rich and socially shared repertoire of signs. These tools allow us to signify that things fit this or that categorization and they unite social groups in the ways that members of the group classify things by using language and language-related activities (as we have discussed in the chapter on consciousness and society). We come to this congruence in our categorizing activity because we are all born equipped to detect those things to which other people attend or react. An infant rapidly begins to use this capacity: "studies show that a very rich form of inter-subjectivity is typically in place by the time the infant is two months old" (Trevarthen 1979). We have argued that the development of concepts is a gradual process in which the child comes to articulate exploratory activity directed at features of the environment in ways that are increasingly congruent with adults and thus build on primitive dispositions and instincts to develop a fine-tuned range of intentional activity intimately tied to the linguistic cues (from others) on which the child relies to organize its behaviour in the world. The cues and the responses they unify and potentiate result in conceptual activity, which we have described as a complex interplay of attention fixation, figure ground differentiation, visual tracking, convergence in classificatory judgements, and representational redescription making use of verbal scaffolding.

For our purposes, the interplay of directed gaze, investigative activity, and guided flexible responses to features of the environment mark a being as conscious and underlie the conceptual complexity of human thought. The brain circuitry or cognitive operations that underpin this kind of activity make place significant constraints on any attempts to correlate conscious activity with brain function. In fact, any articulated system of concepts involves just those abilities to correlate a wide range of experiences and analyze them according to different plans and projects according to the shifting patterns of interest that the organism shows. We might note that these patterns of interest themselves demonstrate a fairly high degree of integration and socially or discursively governed construction of tracts of experience and action. In this respect it is interesting that the priority fixing and executive activity characteristic of highly coordinated social creatures such as ourselves has caused some researchers to posit a Supervisory Activating System that allows human beings to exercise flexibility and inhibition of primitive or immediate and instinctive kinds of reactions to situations (Parkin 1996: p. 224). Most workers in the field would identify the brain mechanisms underlying these functions as being parts of the frontal lobe of the neocortex rather than any more primitive centres such as those involved with reflex activity or general activation functions.

Cortical function and consciousness

The cerebral cortex is the convoluted layer of complex neural circuitry that carries out the most articulated and detailed processing of inputs to the brain. It is an elaboration of processing machinery seen in higher animals and particularly those that use learning to develop flexible and complex behavioural repertoires. The cortex includes neocortex, archi-cortex and paleo-cortex. The paleocortex is concerned with olfaction and need not concern us to any great extent. The archi-cortex includes the hemispheric parts of the limbic lobe and is important in understanding the interface between higher level processing and more primitive emotional and memory mechanisms. The central structure in this mixed primitive and more developed system is the hippocampus and it has a prominent role in the formation of long term memories, learning, and encoding salient patterns triggering orientation responses. The neocortex is the highest level of the system and the higher level activity it performs involves wider and wider information connections potentially able to be elaborated in a variety of ways by short and longer term learning mechanisms.

In clinical and experimental neuropsychology conscious activity is usually thought to involve three levels of cerebral function; there are primitive arousal mechanisms with widespread effects, attentional and orienting mechanisms with somewhat more focused excitatory function, and detailed higher-level analysis of information from a targeted stimulus set. Cortical and subcortical function are, of course, intimately linked to the extent that many of the interwoven and dynamic patterns of cortical activity involve subcortical relays. For the sake of simplicity, we could say that the most primitive and general reactions (sleep/wake cycles and also stereotyped patterns of activity) are mediated in the brain stem and the higher — orienting and analysis — processes dealing with occurrent patterns of stimuli are mediated by cortical systems. The more primitive levels of the system are crucial for the relay of information to the neocortex and the access to episodic memories but when the cortex itself is destroyed the content of complex behaviour is lost and the individual enters what we have already described as the 'persistent vegetative state'.

The brain stem carrying all the incoming information pathways from the body and the outgoing motor pathways itself has fairly undifferentiated centres which interface with the cortex through the limbic system and in particular the hippocampus. The limbic system functions with extensive inputs from all areas of the neocortex and also has close connections with motivational and arousal centres (eg. in the hypothalamus and midbrain). It is plausible that this area enables drive-related or undifferentiated cues with novelty or potential behavioural relevance (because say, of their role in learning history) to be stored and then capture access mechanisms which engage processes realised in the neocortical arrays. One could gloss the primitive levels of awareness phenomenologically by suggesting that they are correlated with a vague premonition or 'feeling' that something deserves attention without being able to give content to what it is. The ability to react as if *there is an intentional object worth bothering about here* would be a useful function to build into any organism with limited processing space and a rich and varied potential domain, any segment of which would be a useful target for processing time if it were likely to be worthwhile. To function effectively the mechanism responsible for this kind of presentation would need to be connected to the organism's spatio-temporal tracking abilities, to those centres providing input about drive states and their satisfaction, and to the information in memory. Once these initial access hurdles are overcome the real business of characterizing the stimulus and getting it connected to the higher cortical processing areas can begin.

The object of the exercise would be to deliver detailed intentional specifications of objects of thought as and when these seemed to mesh with the ongoing projects of the organism. Luria, remarking on patients with lesions in the more primitive areas but intact higher (neocortical) processing, notes that the "potential integrity of the higher, voluntary forms of attention in the presence of a primary disturbance of its elementary forms is an important sign distinguishing these patients from those with lesions in other sites" (Luria 1973: p. 273). He therefore distinguishes the orienting type of response as one that does the sorting and selecting task which allows the more detailed analysis of the higher centres to be used maximally in the directed investigation of points of interest in the environment.

It should now be clear why the cortical function is an essential part of conscious appreciation and activity even if that function is potentiated by the activity in the lower centres (reticular formation, non-specific thalamic projection system based in the intralaminar and medial nuclei, and is to some extent directed by subcortical or limbic centres). Whereas the more primitive centres may potentiate conscious activity, it is the structure of cortex that allows the correlative and selective information processing enabling human beings and higher animals to structure their reactions to and activity in the world in the way characteristic of conscious thought. Central in this activity are intentional objects that, according to the present analysis, incorporate ways of thinking and the nature of human interests in their specifications. It is clear that these noetic features of objects are given as a result of complex cognitive processing rather than just being passively "read off" the causal flux between the individual and the world.

At this point a discussion of Edelman's views (1992) renders the current account even more persuasive. Edelman builds his account of consciousness on several foundations. The first is a *theory of concepts*, the second a claim that *human consciousness is our paradigm* for understanding consciousness and we get less tentative as we consider creatures less and less like ourselves, and the third is a *distinction between first and second order consciousness.*

Edleman's conception of *concepts* is as follows.

> Concepts involve mixtures of relations concerning the real world, memories, and past behaviour. .... In forming concepts the brain constructs maps of its *own* activities, not just of external stimuli, as in perception. (p. 108–9)

Taken together these passages indicate that Edelman believes concepts to be a matter of higher order processing of what the brain itself receives from the environment whereas we have stressed the role of language and rules in dictating the proper contents of human concepts. Our view indicates the fact that the construction of categories of those things to be regarded as falling under a human concept is in part driven from and explained by appeal to the socio-cultural milieu outside the person and not just the brain mappings going on within the person (although these must reflect that milieu). Edelman need not dissent from this view because the difference between his account and ours is to some extent the difference between the ways of grouping stimuli and situations that characterize animal consciousness (which he calls concepts) and the ways of doing that which are found in human consciousness (which we call concepts and which are rule-governed in a different way from animal cognitive strategies). He agrees in substance with the resulting view by remarking that:

> Inasmuch as human beings are the only species with language, it also means that higher order consciousness has flowered in our species. (p. 125)

To Edelman this implies that fully developed or human consciousness is a paradigm or "the best canonical referent" (p. 115) against which we assess other types of cognition to try and understand the extent to which the mental predicates proper to conscious beings of our type apply to them. He goes on to make remarks about what he calls *higher order consciousness* deeply congenial to the view developed in our discussion of consciousness and society. For Edelman primary consciousness involves an awareness of things in the world (and therefore is intentional), an engagement as it were with the specious present, the scene in which one finds oneself, or a present that can be related by the individual to past experiences and encounters. The relations involved are not necessarily reflective in that they may result from cumulative tendencies to categorize or group presentations or features of the world. The move to higher levels of consciousness enables the individual to have a conception of self and the experiences of self as distinct from "succession of things that happen". The gap between experiences had by the self and the world as it is around me opens up space for other possibilities in relation to symbolism and action.

> The freeing of parts of conscious thought from the constraints of an immediate present and the increased richness of social communication allow for the anticipation of future states and for planned behaviour. With that ability come the abilities to model the world, to make explicit comparisons and to weigh outcomes; through such comparisons comes the possibility of reorganizing plans. (p. 133–5)

The creation of a conception of self through communication and the taking on of ways of characterizing self and thereby ordering and structuring one's trajectory through the world were all topics discussed in our study of consciousness and society. It is interesting that this sketch of the thought of a neurobiologist has meshed so closely with the themes we have identified. Thus empirical, scientific, and philosophical discussions of consciousness converge.

We are left with the view that conscious activity requires both brainstem integrity and cortical processing and is on the relatively primitive or brute features of embodiment which engage us with a domain of objects. On this basis we learn and develop through attentional selectivity and concept-guided information, links between one array and a wide range of others and these yield the material which forms the basis of conscious appreciation. Finally we organize and characterize the events around us according to socially mediated categories which inform our noesis so that it makes sense out of what is happening to us in a way that is apt for commentary (Weiscrantz). The lower levels of this system are crude, rude, and unrefined and the higher are configured by the influence of society and culture. It is important to note that even the more primitive priming responses are strongly influenced by top-down input from the workings of the neocortex in relation to present and past stimuli.

This cortical activity is itself layered going from increasingly elaborate organization of incoming information within a perceptual modality to complex, multi-tracked, and cross-linked processing. Thus the information arriving in the brain is sorted and responded to according to a wide-ranging set of interactions between any given unit of information and the distillate of cumulative experience in the light of changing interests and assignments of value. New information is, as it were, linked to all the information collected and organized by noetic work during the behavioural history of the organism. In this way a conscious life narrative is built up from the intentional activity of the organism and permeated by techniques of categorization. In human beings, we have argued, there is a pervasive effect of "the codes of language" in the organization of conscious narrative structures that comprise conceptualised activity. When this is correlated with a plausible account of the brain structures realizing consciousness, we are directed toward the cerebral cortex as the organ which elaborates conscious content even though the conscious tone of the organism, and the distribution of *forte* and *piano* throughout the cerebral orchestra may be determined by activity in more primitive structures.

Links to cognitive structure

We have suggested that objects and foci of conscious attention are features of the environment that engage with a diverse and richly articulated set of brain pathways and micro-processing assemblies. These architectural aspects of the brain link the patterns of activity to which objects give rise to other stored and occurrent sources of input and operate in coordination with current goal-directed activity.

The resulting picture, firmly grounded in cognitive neuroscience, has put some flesh on the bones of Weiscrantz's "monitoring" or "commentary" which "enables the animal to think about his own behaviour and others' behaviour, to communicate if it has words, as we do, so as to link objects and events in time and space that would otherwise be separated; in other words, to think and to reflect" (1987: p. 319). Weiscrantz suggests the link to language or something analogous. We have pursued this in the work of Edelman and sketched his theory but could equally have turned down the path that Dennett takes and discussed the potential engagement of a moment in mind/brain life with a range of different connections to other stored patterns of excitation from perception, emotive responses, memory stores, "word demons" (Dennett 1991), action patterns, and an evolving cognitive map that characterizes the cumulative contents of conscious and unconscious adaptive strategies. More primitive and poorly differentiated stimuli do not have this widespread cerebral "fame" (Dennett, 1991) or informational profile of the features that we notice in our more conscious experiences.

The picture of "monitoring" or "commenting" that results from this account is not that of a localized 'second order' processing unit which keeps tabs on the rest of the brain (and continually threatens to become a homunculus which does everything) but of a wide-ranging connectedness in which the information from any given item is articulated by its accessibility to many different information processing assemblies. This confers on the system the physical analogue of the cognitive connections that underlie any account of conceptual thought which pays serious attention to the holism of mental content (Davidson 1980: p. 221). To be able to consider information in the light of this or that other information from the relevant context and as affected by this or that operation is to monitor it or be conscious of it rather than merely receiving and reacting to it in some fairly simple way. Monitoring in these terms is important because it enables flexible goal-directed processing which may alter in its points of emphasis in the light of information contained in wide reaches of the cognitive system. Commentary arises from dwelling or reflection upon that information and its connections.

The development of PDP networks has shown us how the human brain might realize such a multi-tracked set of connections whose weights change in the light of holistic features of current activity. The co-occurrence of inputs (and therefore the possible use of 'teaching cues' in semantic learning) and the formation of stable patterns of connectedness according to cognitive structures constrained by multiple relationships between semantic units, would both be expected to be important in generating preferential patterns even in an undifferentiated network. We have suggested that collateral inputs which select information for processing in detail arise from goal specifications, motor interaction with the environment, markers used in language-related activities, and the manifest reactions of conspecifics to different features of the environment. The words and semantic groupings of a human community, we could say, are markers of past significance designed to make certain environmental patterns salient. But no animal brain starts with a *tabla rasa*; it has species-specific predispositions to react in certain ways so that some patterns of response are natural (and therefore favoured) and others unlikely in the ethological profile of the type of organism involved. The human brain, even from the moment of birth, seems predisposed to making complex use of the responses of other humans toward things in its environment and as cues and signals in reciprocal relationships with other human beings. An example of this is seen in the natural tendency toward congruence and complementarity of responses that are evident in infants and discussed by both Trevarthen (1983) and Bruner (1983). We have outlined ways in which the mind of the child uses the scaffolding of language to organize conscious experience in our discussion of language and consciousness.

Convergences and cautions

Our philosophical study of consciousness suggested that the type of informational capabilities we see in the neo-cortex provide the rich neurophysiological substrate required for conscious thought. The articulation and structure of conscious thought involve selective concept-guided attention and flexible action that are the kinds of functions that the fine topographic organization of the cortex is admirably suited to serve. Such organization enables the common and similar elements and patterns within presentations to be detected or related in complex ways. Only this kind of processing capacity would enable conscious conceptual thought and only conceptual appreciation of what confronts one enables the richness of human response and reaction that is paradigmatic for our most unreserved ascriptions of consciousness. (Here we can recall the verbal and intentional tests that we might apply to assess a patient's level of consciousness at the bedside and the kind of animated attention that is lacking in the PVS patient).

It is clear that an animal may be conscious in so far as it also demonstrates an articulated and flexible responsiveness to its environment. However, the intentionality that is characteristic of acts of consciousness of human beings is going to be problematic for animals, as Edelman notes, because they lack language. The relevant noetically structured intentional detail in their apprehension of the world and their place in the scheme of things is not possible in the absence of language. Some evidence of intentional content can be distilled from the articulation evident in their behaviour and to the extent this can be correlated with the propositional content of human thought it can be interpreted as involving conscious experiential content which shares features with human mental life. Therefore the central or paradigmatic use of the term 'conscious' will be its use in relation to human experience. In this central sense, to which we appeal with varying success when we attempt to understand the thoughts and feelings of animals (what-it-is-like-to-be-a-bat for instance), being conscious and actively detecting and responding to the features of the world that surround one is a capacity in which a crucial role is played by the conceptual abilities realised in the neocortex under the influence of the social institution of language. We shall return to the topic of animal consciousness in Chapter 7.

Consciousness is also a capacity which, in virtue of the way it links our experiences in terms of the concepts that we grasp, enables reason-guided (or inferential) action, another feature noted by Edelman and explored in our discussion of consciousness and action. Conceptual articulation and the intentional content that it yields is connected with other contents in multiple ways determined by the (more-or-less holistic) cognitive role of that content in a total system of propositional attitude ascriptions. Therefore unqualified ascriptions of reasoning, belief, doubt, desire, expectation, anticipation, and so on are appropriate where the subject concerned has the noetic capabilities to achieve a fairly clear grasp of the relevant intentional contents. Where this condition is attenuated as in the case of animals and psychotic or unconscious mental content so also the ascriptions need to be modified in such a way that the content involved is given in a much less determinate form. One further conclusion now emerges. Wittgenstein's remark "Consciousness is as clear in his face and behaviour as it is in myself" records the way that another attends and reacts to things which are manifest to us when we impart concepts to him. Through applying and teaching him to apply rules to his own activity and experience, we make use of his engagement with the world to impart our ways of thinking. Thus, at the heart of the ability to make judgments, "allocate cognitive resources" to an item or use concepts in actual lived experience are just those abilities to respond to things that are manifest or "clear in his face and behaviour" and that constitute intentionality. What-it-is-like-to-be a human being thus turns out to be a dual matter. It involves:

(i) having certain experiences; and
(ii) being able to think about them in certain ways.

The latter involves those rich and varied capacities that a normal human conceptual system makes available. Thus it is quite understandable that a philosopher asked for some specification of what-it-is-like-to-be a bat, a lion, or a human being should despair. Nothing he could say would amount to having the experiences involved and he cannot in any succinct form capture all the ways in which our conceptual system enables us to respond to things (let alone conjecture about quite other conceptual or proto-conceptual systems). One could say that poets, painters, novelists and playwrights are constantly unfolding new aspects of what-it-is-like-to-be human by linking concepts in novel ways and deploying them in novel contexts. The intractability of what-it-is-like-to-be has been used to argue against a smooth identification of conscious events with brain events and thereby the possibility of a mental physical reduction. But it is not just the problem of specifying what-it-is-like-to-be that gets in the way of spelling out the brain events that equate to the conscious events allegedly going on in our mind. We have given positive reasons, in our discussion of consciousness and action, to believe that such identifications and any reduction of the one to the other are just not to be had. In view of the fact that we have spent much of this chapter making out a case for the correlation of neuroscientific understandings of human consciousness with intentional and mental understandings of the phenomena involved, we ought now to summarize the antireductive arguments under two heads: the irreducibility of essence arguments; and the non-mappability argument.

The irreducibility of the essence of mental acts

Functionalism and cognitive theories of consciousness in general come close to the complex conceptual view of consciousness that we have outlined in that they seek to analyze human consciousness in terms of a range of functional or informational processes going on within human beings. Our account implies that functionalism and other reductive models of the basis of physicalist conceptions of mind and cognition are inadequate as an account of consciousness for several reasons.

The basic functionalist thesis is that psychological state types are to be characterized in terms of the functional roles that these states play in a structure of internal states, mediating stimulus inputs and behavioural outputs. (Van Gulick 1990: p. 108)

1. Such theories fudge the levels of explanation.
2. They neglect some questions about individuation and essence.
3. They focus on the wrong kinds of objects to specify the contents of thought.

1. *Levels of explanation*

Imagine, for instance, that we were attempting to give a characterization of the conscious act of seeing red. To do this we compiled a series of disjunctive sets of internal events that went on when a person recognized red. We could specify these in two ways. First, we might try a specification in epistemic or noetic terms making free use of concepts like hypothesis generation, testing, analysis, attention, inference, and so on. But here the elements of the reductive explanation have an undischarged debt to the language of conscious thought. We know what we are talking about when we talk about people doing these things, we know the rules they obey, and we are prepared for the kind of baggage this brings to the theoretical enterprise in which we are engaged. But this entails that the explanations are only pseudo-subpersonal in that we are homuncularizing and we do not quite know what sort of conceptual slips are introduced when we jettison the embedded assumptions about self-reflection, ability to follow prescriptive norms, and conceptualisation.

For instance, were we to claim that we could explain the transformations undergone by visual information as an attempt by the brain to obtain a true picture of the world. This would conflate horribly the picture of the world as we relate it to each other and orient our bodies in shared space (topics located within the study of epistemology) with the systematic transitions that are required to cluster stimuli in terms of patterns betraying enduring objects, patterns which can be grouped because of a shared set of common features, configurations which are evocative of past adaptive responses and so on (topics relevant to evolutionary neurobiology). There is a relation between the two but to say that this set of brain cells or neural assembly infers from x, y, and z that things are thus and so is to bastardize a scientific enquiry in a way that is not conducive to clarity of thought.

2. *Individuation and essence*

To get past these worries about pseudo-explanation or non-explanation, we could take a second option and specify our subpersonal processes by appeal only to descriptions of physical or physiologically plausible computational or brain events. But we have identified a problem about the intentional objects forming the contents of conscious acts if we take this option and there are further problems about the individuation of the events concerned. One has been discussed in our account of consciousness and action as *the ineliminibility of mental taxonomy argument*, (cf. Chapter 4) the second could be called the *mental criterion for essence* argument. It goes as follows.

Imagine that we had taken an averaged measure of brain activity whenever a red stimulus was followed by the remark 'That is red' (or some equivalent signal that the subject was conscious of red). Imagine that we had done this a sufficient number of times to define the 'canonical set' of neural processes which "were" according to the theory, the functional-physiological profile of the consciousness of red. It is tempting to claim that this is the event which is the physical realisation of the occurrent consciousness of red and that having discovered the real essence of ⟨being conscious of red⟩ we can explore the metaphysics of that conscious act by studying the physical event. But now imagine that an aberrant (in terms of the canonical set) physiological complex should turn up after the experiment is over, and the individual still reports seeing red, what will we do? Clearly we must revise our canonical set so as to eliminate the false negative (in terms of our physically-based theory). Therefore the essence, which we regard as invariant in deciding which individual events do qualify as instances of the kind concerned and which do not, is the mental report (of a competent subject in appropriate circumstances) and not the physiological correlate. What happens if the opposite occurs: our physiologically defined set includes event combinations that clearly do not constitute recognizing red on normal grounds (i.e. those governing the ascription of a conscious act of seeing ⟨red⟩)? In the latter case we would also have to abandon the equivalence or modify it to include the new instance. Whether or not this enterprise is ultimately successful, it is clear that we must and do tailor the canonical set of instances (that define the essence of the relevant type) to fit the public intersubjective criteria for being conscious of red. Thus the definition of red in terms of a physiological description ultimately defers to a conceptual specification that is based in interpersonal practices and their norms, it is not and could never be self-standing.

This is related to, but different from, Davidson's argument for the irreducibility of the mental character of Propositional Attitudes. Davidson relies on the norm of rationality which would cause us to adjust our mental ascriptions to a person in the light of the overall coherence of their behaviour rather than according to our best theory of the correlation between the physical states of their brain and the mental states in question. The conclusion is that physiology cannot yield criteria for individuating the kinds of conscious acts we attribute to subjects and therefore that those acts are essentially not individuated within the world of physical descriptions but in relation to a different framework of understanding, a framework that involves intentional, personal, or noetic understanding.

On this basis alone, it seems that ascriptions of consciousness may be essentially intersubjective and ineliminible from our understanding of human behaviour. But there is further reason to suspect any significant mind-brain identity thesis that claims a one-to-one correspondence between conscious acts and physical states and events.

3. *The problem of intentional specifications of objects*

The contents of consciousness are, we have argued, things with which we are engaged in the world. We have also argued that in any conscious act of apprehending an object there are certain concepts or ways of thinking of that object which specify how it appears in the mind. But this has important philosophical implications. Imagine that a stimulus array comes into my field of vision and as a result there floats before my mind the image of an angry football fan. Now consider the physical story. Certain rays of light bounce off bits and pieces of the world around me, some of which are in motion and are registered on my retinae. From here various patterns of excitation pass up my visual pathways. At the terminus of that activity certain cerebral circuits are activated and, in turn activate others. The same or similar things happen to, and in, the rhesus monkey I am taking home to my son. Despite the physical similarities between my visual system and that of the rhesus monkey I think ⟨that is an angry football fan⟩ and the monkey does not. But what entitles me to conclude that what I am seeing is an angry football fan and not one of a possibly indefinite set of other characterizations of the data I am receiving. The data itself does not yield "angry football fan" and looking only at the physical facts about the situation one would be indifferent about that specification as distinct from "red-shirted red-faced Dutchman", or "animated biped", or even "pattern of reflected light". The causal input to the system is indifferent between these alternatives and we have to get to a fairly high level of conceptual (or socio-culturally mediated) sophistication before we get the requisite content specification.

If we are not entitled to treat a causal input as transparently conveying the information "angry football fan" and must be indifferent about that specification as distinct from "red-shirted red-faced Dutchman", or whatever, then descriptions of content are going to be hard to explain if we confine ourselves to those physical terms. Strictly speaking the causal antecedents of the experience concerned do not allow us to make principled discernments between the various content ascriptions and therefore these can only be made if we have some entree to the conceptual world of the subjects of the conscious acts concerned. But we have already argued that that world is replete with the noemata that govern the concepts we use. Therefore, as we have also argued, it is the world of people who are related in various ways to societies and discursive systems and it is not a world amenable to analysis in terms of what is inside the head or indeed in purely physical terms at all.

Non-mappability arguments

The essential irreducibility arguments are sometimes met by the counter-claims that that the mental specifications must correspond to physical specifications in the way envisaged and thus there is a constant correlation between the two. This can be trivialized by making an *a priori* (question-begging) claim for the primacy of physical descriptions and physical-causal connections in explaining any phenomena including mental phenomena but we will discard that desperate move.

If the trick of a one-to-one matching of physical and mental descriptions could be done it would be a first step towards physical reductionism because the physical theory of nature is the more inclusive theory (forgetting for the moment that the physical level of description is as much a mental production as Leibniz's Monadology). However it is possible to argue that, in fact, there could be no identity theory of the kind to ground a reducibility claim because there are not two streams of events which could be correlated the one with the other in the required way. This argument examines the kind of matching required by physical reductions of conscious acts according to the following portrayal.

conscious	$C_1 \rightarrow C_2 \rightarrow C_3 \rightarrow C_4$
physical	$P_1 \rightarrow P_2 \rightarrow P3 \rightarrow P4$
time	t1 t2 t3 t4

The blocking move is to establish that such a matching is impossible. Consider, for instance, the colour phi phenomenon (Dennett 1991). In this phenomenon a subject experiences a coloured spot moving from point A to point B and changing colour at a certain intermediate point from red to green. In reality the only stimuli arriving in the visual system are a red spot at point A and a green spot at point B. So where do the intervening mental events come from? Whatever story we tell here we do not, and could never, get a set of one to one correlations between brain events and mental events. In fact, when we consider the variety of cases cited by Dennett in his study of different experiments in sensory psychology, it becomes plausible that the conscious story is a gloss or interpretation based on a series of goings on in the brain which have to be woven into some ecologically probable and coherent stream of experience. There is no brain event corresponding to the intermediate points of the colour spot's trajectory, there is no conscious event corresponding to the obliterated first stimulus in a metacontrast phenomenon, and there are no intervening points where the skin is touched by the cutaneous rabbit. The positing of the missing events is a product of the following philosophical thesis — call it Cartesian materialism.

1. There are discreet temporally and spatially located mental states and events such as thoughts, intentions, beliefs and so on.
2. These are based on incorrigible access to perceptually and internally generated inner information states.

3. The actual medium in which these states and events occur is the brain.
4. These states and events are actually brain states and events able in principle to be described by a complete neurophysiology.
5. Mental states and events are, metaphysically speaking, brain events under another description.

The fatal flaw seems to be in 2, where we posit a set of objectively existing but only subjectively accessible inner events or seemings — the realm of "the objectively subjective". These seemings are events that are really somewhere even though, in fact, it just seems as if they are (a description worthy of Lewis Carroll). Once we have dispensed with the reified "seemings" then there is nothing being referred to by the persuasive phrases using the term "states and events" in premises 3, 4, and 5, of the Cartesian materialist thesis. Our account suggests that conscious acts are conceptual "takes" on an ongoing interaction between the subject and the world in which the brain plays an important part but the overall story is told by a person who is using tools provided by (culturally situated) others to describe and intervene in what is happening to him or her. Our account implies that consciousness (simpliciter) is a state description made up of any combination of a diverse range of possible conditions jointly contributed to by the brain and the environment. What distinguishes conscious acts from others is that conscious acts are those in which a whole range of intentional abilities can aim at the state of affairs in which one finds oneself. There is no central theatre in which inner events presenting the way things are for me are displayed for the inner me, there is only the way things are and my intentional characterizations which articulate and enrich that in a myriad ways. In this articulation (Wittgenstein) or enrichment, my language, my interests and my bodily dispositions all take a part and the state that results is called being conscious of, for instance, there being a tension in the air you could cut with a knife. Thus our account of consciousness renders suspect the Cartesian materialist thesis, and reductive theses based on it.

Dennett's theoretical and experimental work has tended towards the view that consciousness does not comprise a series of discrete events temporally located with respect to each other and observed by an inner self. Rather, we have a commentary on a stream of brain activity which seamlessly flows in and around and through different processing areas with little respect for the categories of mental events we so commonly and blithely talk about. The reality of brain function therefore does not support the temptation we experience, in philosophy but not real neuroscience, to talk about discreet brain events. To be conscious of something, on this view, is to have the information caused by that thing hooked up to a wide range of intentional abilities including those which serve language function. As far as the brain is concerned this implies that conscious experience is experience that is not excluded from the higher and more socially conditioned areas of processing space. The ability to 'tell', in the narrow reporting sense, what one is in cognitive contact with is only part of the wider ability to tell what intentional shape a given object has. This requires one to discriminate, discern, explore, and manipulate the environment around one by means of one's full repertoire of noetic or conceptual abilities so as to be able to characterize, in a potentially open-ended way, the nature of a given object. When one can do that one is conscious of what is around one.

The importance of consciousness

The fact that the brain story moves us away from a discrete compartmentalized function performed by, or an inner "Cartesian" location for, consciousness deflates pretentious views about "the function" of consciousness in human life. We are left instead with a revised understanding of the power of the whole system and the internal connection between consciousness and the way that the individual is embedded in an intentionally structured world of experience. This can be mistaken for a deflationary view of consciousness. Wilkes, for instance, acknowledges that science finds consciousness hard to grapple with and could not be expected to do otherwise given that "conscious" is an ordinary language term and lacks systematicity. She concludes: "the presupposition that consciousness is an important, or a real, phenomenon should be dropped"(1984: p. 241). What she means by "real" here is the kind of thing that does some work in our understanding of the psychology or neurobiology of human beings rather than a less distinctively philosophical use of that term.

However, we have argued that consciousness and the intentional objects which form the contents of conscious states are a way of describing and classifying, by appeal to concepts which structure human communication and activity, that range of relationships to the world that we call mental and that embody the secret that spectacularly distinguishes us from the other denizens of the earth. The importance and reality of consciousness is coeval with the importance and reality of intentionality in its human form and the intentional contents it makes available. Other creatures share consciousness with us only to the extent that their activity is appropriately characterized by the use of intentional ascriptions based in human language.

CHAPTER 7

Animal Consciousness

In this chapter we will argue that there are important distinctions between human and animal consciousness. We shall develop the thesis that human conceptualisation is of a sufficiently more developed degree than animal counterparts so as to provide a richness of intentional differentiation unparalleled in animal consciousness.

We have shown that an essential feature of the relation between consciousness and action is the normativity of human action (as contrasted with an individual's merely being disposed to perform an action). This idea has been important in our claims about objects and consciousness (when we see or describe an object we are implicitly aware that there are particular ways that we ought to see or describe this object). The normativity of adult human consciousness is an important issue because it provides the crux of a distinction between "thin" and "thick" representations. *Thin* representations have no implications for the existence of other minds and the ability of the representation to be conveyed to another mind. *Thick* representations have contents which are both accessible to the subject itself and conveyable to other minds. Thin representations do not bear a great deal of scrutiny about their content whereas thick representations present a significant structure which it is necessary to understand in order to appreciate their role in behaviour. Human consciousness involves thick representations while systems of representation possessed by animals are, we will argue, almost always "thin". It is a corollary of the definition that representations involving normative evaluation (or reflective assessment) are thick, and those that without that feature are thin. By considering this we shall explain one the most important distinctions between human and animal consciousness.

If there are animals capable of "thick" representations then we would expect that the most likely candidates would be higher primates. So our discussion of thick and thin representations will include insights from primate language research.

The crux of our distinction will depend upon an application of the Gricean conditions for non-natural meaning. First, an example of insects, evolutionarily far removed from ourselves, which appear to exhibit language use of a complexity that might, in accordance with economy of explanation, be taken to imply a high degree of noetic sophistication. Von Frisch's bees seem to show intelligent communicative behaviour designed to convey to their fellow bees the distance, direction, and quality of sources of food. There is, therefore, a *prima facie* case to regard animals as lowly as bees as having thick representations. We shall argue that this initial appearance does not bear up under scrutiny.

The breadth of views about animal consciousness

In Chapter 1 we defined the "principle of economy of explanation". The idea is that in explaining the behaviour of an organism we should credit it with only those mental abilities that are needed to account for its behaviour. Because what happens in an animal's mind is not something we can make some sort of introspective comparison with, this principle assumes an important position.

Of course it is possible that there is much more going on in animal's minds than we can ascertain from behaviour alone. In Douglas Adam's *Hitchhikers Guide to the Galaxy* Arthur Dent discovers (after the destruction of the Earth) disturbing facts about Earth's species. He discovers that dolphins were the second most intelligent species on the planet: the most intelligent were laboratory mice. All of the operant experiments conducted by psychologists on mice were in fact elaborate experiments on the psychologists conducted by the mice. Laboratory mice had a conscious experience as rich, perhaps richer than their human counterparts.

Although is very unlikely that laboratory mice really are this smart, because we cannot know for sure what it's like to be a mouse doubt continues about what really does happen in their minds. We maintain that explanations of behaviour should only attribute the mental complexity necessary for them to be good explanations (adequate to their explanatory tasks). In fact the attribution of noetic states required to explain clever animal behaviour is a complicated and controversial exercise. The problem is that for most apparently clear examples of higher primate thought complicated behaviourist explanations can be given. (Smith 1996)

The philosophical difficulties involved in knowing what animal consciousness is like is reflected in the broad range of philosophical views about animal consciousness. At one extreme is Donald Davidson who claims that,

1. propositional attitudes are necessary for thought
2. propositional attitudes must make sense within a web of other propositional attitudes
3. animals do not possess the PAs of 2
4. therefore animals do not think.

An example of Davidson's argument is the way in which he responds to Norman Malcom's dog. Malcom saw his dog chasing the neighbour's cat. The cat climbed up an oak tree after making a feint toward a maple tree. The dog barked up the wrong tree seemingly *believing* ⟨the cat is in the maple⟩.

> We identify thoughts, distinguish between them, describe them for what they are, only as they can be located within a dense network of related beliefs. If we really can intelligibly ascribe single beliefs to a dog, we must be able to imagine how we would decide whether the dog has many other beliefs of the kind necessary for making sense of the first. (1985: p. 485)

Implicit in Davidson's insistence that Malcom's dog doesn't think are his beliefs about meaning and its relationship to thought.

At the other end of the spectrum is Fodor who claims that animals and infants clearly do have propositional attitudes: beliefs, desires etc. (1987) They do not have a natural language, hence the contents of their propositional attitudes cannot be natural language based. Therefore he believes that animals and prelinguistic infants have propositional attitudes that are thought in the cognitive language, "mentalese".

One possible response to Fodor is to deny his premise and simply argue that infants and animals do not have beliefs, desires and so on. This is, no doubt how Davidson would respond to Fodor. Carruthers takes a different approach (1996). He accepts that animals and infants have propositional attitudes and that these attitudes are framed in mentalese. However he believes that "conscious thinkings are relations to natural language sentences, whereas non-conscious ones are — or may be — relations to sentences of Mentalese." (p 66) It is clear that this thesis stands or falls with one's belief in mentalese and we have throughout tried to relate the intentionality proper to consciousness to natural language and the kinds of activities which give rise to it.

Another view is held by Richard Jeffrey (1985) who believes that many animals (Malcom's dog included) do have propositional attitudes. They just do not use the same concepts that humans do and this is why the dog's belief ⟨the cat is the maple⟩ does not fit into the network of other propositional attitudes that we would expect a person who had this belief to understand. Like Davidson he does not believe that animals are rational in the same way that human beings are, a view that follows from the fact that rationality of the requisite sort is co-extensive with the network of propositional attitudes that exhibit the rational structure of human thought.

Our view is different from most of these authors. We disagree with Fodor's assertion that because infants and animals do not possess natural language they must therefore think in mentalese. We argued in chapter two that conceptual development in children was best thought of as a gradual progression of conceptual or noetic sophistication in different domains in response to the requirements of the child's environment. We also argued that there is a relationship between sophisticated use of language and sophistication in thought. Infants' thinking is as sophisticated as their mastery of language. Carruthers' suggestion that animals and infants think, but only non-consciously and possibly in mentalese is one that is untenable on the account that we have been developing. Consciousness is a term that admits of degrees. Animals and infants clearly are conscious. The real question is, how conscious are they and in what way? Davidson and Jeffrey are both more congenial on this point, even though they are primarily concerned with the question of the rationality of animals.

We mentioned in our discussion of language and thought that Davidson believes that it is a necessary condition of a thing being a thinking thing that it understands the language of another. We have taken a somewhat less chauvinistic line and espoused the weaker thesis that competence in language is necessary for the kind and richness of thinking characteristic of human beings. Davidson's suggestion does, however, provide the basis for our distinction between thin and thick noetic states. The possibility of understanding the mind of another person, either through language or other means of interpreting the consciousness of another person was one of the key features of consciousness that we identified in chapter one. Thick noetic states are ones that involve, or could by their phenomenal quality, include the awareness of another mind with a consciousness of the relevant contents. Fully developed human consciousness is typically characterised by thick noetic states. Towards the end of this chapter we will consider which animals, if any, can be described as possessing thick noetic states.

The language of the honey bee

Thus far we have claimed that the key feature of human consciousness is the conceptual nature of human thought. We argued in chapter two that language use of a sufficiently complex level is a developmental feature essential in explaining the noetic sophistication of human thought. If we were to discover animals with consciousness exhibiting intentional qualities that also possessed this degree of conceptual sophistication, this would create doubts about whether there is any interesting difference between human and animal consciousness.

We have already mentioned one of the most striking apparent examples of animal language use popularised by the work of Von Frisch. In a seminal paper he describes the "language use of bees". Von Frisch (1965) observed that bees communicated via the senses of smell and touch.[18] This is not to imply that these are the only modalities used by bees, as recent bee experiments have detailed how some species of bees communicate via acoustical means. (Kirchner and Dreller 1993) The sensory modality is secondary in import to the issue at hand, which is whether the bee language involves conceptualisation analogous in some ways to human thought as we have described it.

Von Frisch was careful not to make to any claims about the similarity of bee and human language use. In fact he is clear that the mental operations of human speech are incommensurate with those of the bee. Although it is interesting that he thought the bees language was "more linguistic: than higher primate language use".[19] Given what primate language experiments have shown since then this claim appears not only problematic but false.

Von Frisch's bees conveyed information about the direction, distance and type of food sources by the variation of two dances. Bees aware of the

18. "The "language" of the bees is not a verbal one. It depends on the senses of touch and smell. Their words are rhythmic movements and scents" (Von Frisch 1965: p. 347).

19. "It is evident that the mental principles of communication between bees are quite different from those of the human language" (ibid. p. 348).

communication then might or might not respond by flying to the food source. A bee that detects the presence of a rich new food source close to the hive will convey this information to other bees in the hive by performing a round dance. Round dances give no indication of the direction or distance of the food source relative to the hive. Information about the food source that the responding bees must search for is communicated via the scent of that food source on the bee.

When the food source is more than 50 to 100 metres away from the hive the bees perform a waggle dance instead of the round dance. This dance informs the bees about the type of food source in the same way as with the round dance but the waggle dance is also used to communicate the distance and direction of the food source. The rhythm of the dance and the number of straight runs within the waggle dance convey the distance of the food source. The further the distance to the food source the more the number of straight runs within the dance decreases and the rhythm of the dance decreases. The direction of the food source is communicated via the angle that the bees dance on the vertical honeycomb in the hive. A vertical angle on the honeycomb is a sign that the food source is directly in line with the direction of the sun relative to the hive. For each angle of variance from the vertical the direction of the food source lies in a direction lying in a corresponding angle of variation from the direction of the sun. So if a bee performed a waggle dance at an angle of 60 degrees measured from the vertical this is a sign that the food source is 60 degrees to the right of the sun when setting out from the hive. Bees that will set off for the indicated food source accompany the communicating bee's dance. Bees will continue to perform the waggle dance on their return to the hive as long as the food source does not diminish in quality. Von Frisch noted that when the hive needs a new nest, bees will use the same dances and variations to convey information about possible nesting sites.

We have claimed that it is the organisation of human practical intellect by linguistically mediated thought that makes human and animal consciousness distinct. The resulting conceptual sophistication of human thought and language is supposedly something quite unique to humans. Yet Von Frisch's bees are organising their practical intellect with signs. Fewer straight runs and a slower rhythm mean that the food source is further away. The angle of the waggle dance from the vertical signifies the angle of the food source relative to the sun. It is not immediately obvious why the bees language use is not an example of what we have called noetically sophisticated consciousness.

Whenever we conjecture about the mental representations, or consciousness of animals we make a leap of faith. However it would be extremely unlikely if bees are consciously aware of the communicative function they perform in the same way that you or I would be if I told you how to get to the Thai food takeaway. To attribute such conscious awareness to the honeybee would be to attribute them a degree of mental complexity that is not needed to explain the behaviour. The honeybee's communicative ability need not be something that is consciously accessible to them it need only be a well-formed set of innate responses to features of the patterns evident in bee dances. There need be no torch in the bee mind that shines upon the communicative activity to hold it up to reflective scrutiny and the bee need not have the ability to entertain the thought that the incoming bee might be misleading it.

A good example of the level of explanation sufficient for bee behaviour is the reaction when one bee dies in the hive. When this happens other bees quickly remove the body from the hive. Clearly this behaviour serves an important function within the hive: without it disease would be likely to spread in the hive. Ethologists have discovered that the trigger for this behaviour is oleic acid. Applying oleic acid to the back of a healthy bee will result in the healthy bee being dragged struggling from the hive. (Dennett 1987) Thus when we describe the behaviour of the bees disposing of a dead bee an explanation involving an innate response to oleic acid is going to be adequate. This level of explanation attributes no conscious cognition on the part of the bees and no ability to modify their behaviour in the light of obvious signs of life on the part of the marked bee. When we interpret the bee language we should therefore take account of these limitations. Bees really are just complicated mechanisms that react causally in the presence of this substance and other triggers and whose patterns of stimulus and response have been carefully designed by heredity to optimise the function of the hive.

In previous chapters we have pointed to the normativity requirements that apply to human consciousness (perception, action, language). An essential component of making judgements about our consciousness is that the objects of our attention are potential foci for our conscious attention. As the bees' communicative function is not a potential foci for conscious reflection then the bees do not know what they are doing in the sense of taking normative attitudes to their own representations. These are therefore not thick representations and cannot be used to reapply representationally structured skills to other possible domains of application.

Orders of intentionality

Daniel Dennett, following Brentano, defines intentionality as aboutness (Dennett 1987). Consciousness is directed toward objects, states or operations. In chapter one we argued that a key feature of consciousness, which a theory of intentional and consciousness must take into account, is referential opacity. Suppose I stopped outside a French bakery with a friend, pointed at a tart in the window of a pastry shop and said "Look Guiseppe, apple pie, that would be delicious". Alternatively, deciding that I wanted to impress him with my knowledge of classical French cuisine I might remark to him "*Tarte Normande* takes a few attempts until it can be made perfectly but I must say that looks very good". If Guiseppe turned to me and said "Keep your fancy French food, I would be happy to have some of that apple pie" he would have successfully referred to the pastry and remained unaware that this is the same thing as *Tarte Normande*. Thus when he referred to the pastry his understanding was referentially opaque with respect to the expression that I had used to make the same reference.

Dennett is correct when he describes such events as referentially opaque because "the terms in such clauses are shielded or insulated by a barrier to logical analysis, which normally "sees through" the terms to the world the terms are about." (1987). We can apply these distinctions (between sense and reference) to Vervet monkeys who make various vocalisations apparently intending to denote objects in the world.

The questions that we shall investigate are twofold:

1. What degree of noetic, hence conceptual sophistication do we need to attribute to vervets so as to explain their behaviour? and
2. If they do denote things in the world does their denoting mean they are capable of forming "thick" representations?

Dennett's ingenious account of levels of intentionality provides leverage with which to answer these related questions. Typically when an object becomes the centre of conscious attention we think that *it* is an *x* where the *it* indicates a bare demonstrative reference to the object. We commonly do make attributions to an object in this way without specifying what kind of thing it is. For example you might see an object on the horizon and not be able to make out what it is apart from the fact that it is red. Here you might say "That red thing, what is it?" In such a case the analysis still holds, the object, although unspecified is still the focus of attention and a potential target for warranted conceptual judgements that you cannot currently make.

Believing that the car is a Ferrari is a good example of the intentionality of consciousness. Believings have the aboutness relation necessary for intentionality and also the intentional content that specifies the way in which the object is being thought about. Similarly we could cite instances of desiring, knowing, understanding and proposing. An instance of any one of these intentional acts is an example of what Dennett calls first order intentionality. The distinctions in orders of intentionality are directly relevant to a discussion of thin and thick representations.

> A first-order intentional system has beliefs and desires (etc) but no beliefs and desires about beliefs and desires. Thus all the attributions of a first order system have the logical form of
> (7) x believes that p
> (8) y wants that q (Dennett 1987)

When Pierre wishes that his measles would go away this is an example of first order intentionality. Davidson believes that a thing can only be counted as having beliefs if can think of itself as having beliefs in other words take an attitude to its own states of mind. His reason for thinking this is because a creature that cannot think of itself as having beliefs is incapable of questioning whether what it believes is in fact true. The ability to take a normative attitude towards one's beliefs is on Davidson's (and our) account an essential part of noetic consciousness. This means that Davidson would say we cannot count infants or children who have first order intentionality as really having beliefs. We have already argued that there is a danger of constructing hard and fast distinctions between the different developing capacities of children at different ages. This danger seems to loom in the fairly clear-cut distinctions erected by Davidson.

William Child has adopted a position more convergent with our own in focusing on the objectivity of the judgements made by other intentional systems. He argues that there is no necessary contradiction between believing that first order intentional systems have contentful mental acts so long as we are clear that such a system does not think of "things and events *as* objective events things and events" (1994: p. 19). By "objective" Child means the creature must be able to think about how things *really* are as well as how they seem to it. We have cashed this out in terms of the way that the judgements concerned would map onto the norms prevailing in a shared world of communicative activity.

Human beings often combine two levels of aboutness in their mental operations. This Dennett, again following Brentano, calls second order intentionality. When Pierre wants the pastry shop owner to believe that he is hungry; Olive is worried that the dog will sense her fear; and Van Gogh hoped his audience would understand his work, they all are exhibiting second order intentionality in that they have intentional attitudes not only to things around them but to mental acts (their own and others) which take those things as contents. In chapter one we mentioned Brentano's distinction between primary and secondary objects of consciousness. When I am conscious of the freighter bearing down upon my small yacht the freighter is a primary object of consciousness. When I realise the existential immediacy of this predicament and become conscious of the fact that it is me who is conscious of the freighter bearing down upon me then the freighter is a secondary object of consciousness and the urgency of the situation depends on it being a secondary object of my consciousness.

The idea that there can be orders of intentionality is a very similar idea to that captured by Brentano's use of the apparatus of primary and secondary objects. Brentano was primarily concerned with the necessity of self-consciousness implied by intentional consciousness (a preoccupation later found in Sartre). However the phenomenological move made in being aware of our consciousness of an object is very similar to that we make when we are conscious of the consciousness of others. We have, in fact, argued that the ability to become self-conscious is built on the ability to imitate or catch on to the type of judgement that is being made by others when they respond to our responses.

A third level intentional system is an intentional state that combines three levels of aboutness. For example, a psychiatrist might write a prescription for an anti-psychotic medication while hoping that her patient understands that she is prescribing anti-psychotic drugs because she believes that it is in his (the patient's) best interest. There are three distinct noeses combined in the one mental act. The psychiatrist is aware of herself:

1. writing the script for the anti-psychotic drug;
2. believing that anti-psychotic is best; and
3. wanting her patient to know that she thinks the anti-psychotic drug is best.

It is also possible for a system to have "zero order intentionality". We have mentioned that our strategy was to attribute to an information processing system only the mental complexity necessary to explain its behaviour (a snail's taxis towards dark shady places) according to the principle of economy. In other words we do not need to attribute any mental states in order to explain the snail's behaviour, therefore there is zero order intentionality. The link that Dennett wishes to make to human communication is made through describing Grice's work on speaker's meaning. The question that shall be investigated in the light of Grice's ideas about human communication and Dennett's levels of intentionality concerns whether vervet monkeys' vocalisations have to be ascribed third level intentionality in ordered to be explained.

In his classic paper, Grice provides an account of speaker's meaning which, due to counter examples, ends up being rather complicated. The main point of discussing Grice is to show that human communication often involves grasping three levels of intentionality at one time. So this point is not lost in a series of refinements we shall use the final working of his theory in *Meaning*. Grice's formulation of what is necessary for *A* to mean something by *x* is

> *A* must intend to induce by *x* a belief in an audience, and he must also intend his utterance to be recognised as so intended. (1957: p. 383)

When I say to my fishing partner Rudolph "Autumn is the best time of the year for mayfly imitations" I hope to make him believe that autumn is the best time of year for fishing with this type of dryfly. I also aim for my utterance to be recognised by Rudolph as an attempt to inform him of this fact. This example and Grice's theory of speaker's meaning involve third order intentionality. My utterance to Rudolph involves three orders of aboutness: the belief that I intend Rudolph to acquire; my intention to have Rudolph acquire this belief; and my intention that Rudolph count the fact that I have made this utterance as being evidence that I want him to acquire this belief.

For those unfamiliar with Grice it may not be immediately obvious why the person that an utterance is directed to must recognise that a given utterance is additional evidence for acquiring the relevant belief. Grice argues that the recognition that an utterance (or one presumes, any other semantically contentful communication) does provide additional evidence for A acquiring the belief that p is a necessary condition (secured by convention) for the utterance to mean p. Herod presented Salome with the head of St. John the Baptist on a charger. Herod intended Salome to acquire the belief that "St. John is dead". Furthermore Herod wanted Salome to recognise that he intended her to believe that "St. John is dead". Yet Grice does not think that the presentation of St. John's head (the actual head on the charger) meant "St. John the Baptist is dead", because no convention was involved.

It is important to note at this point that Grice's account has features in common with Davidson's insistence that language users can understand the language use of another person. If the fact that we can recognise the intentions of others was not a feature of language, as speaker's meaning requires, then it would not be possible to understand the language of another person. In our terms, third order intentional systems of this type are ones that utilise thick noetic states and the attribution of such noetic states is part of linguistic meaning.

Do vervet monkeys possess thick noetic states?

There are many instances where animals use features of their environment and or aspects of their behaviour to designate objects or events. We began this chapter by considering the dance of the honeybees. Grice's analysis of speakers' meaning credits human communication with a degree of richness that is commensurate with the phenomenology of language use but incommensurate with the behaviour of bees. In understanding and communicating we are constantly attentive to the reciprocity involved in linguistic acts and the effects of our words on others. As this is such an important feature of our linguistic praxis investigating whether animal communication is similar in kind is a fruitful manner of investigating the richness of animal intelligence and consciousness.

It is also worth stressing that when Grice speaks of "intention" he means to refer to a purpose or aim with which an action is done.

> ...There will be cases where an utterance is accompanied or preceded by a conscious plan, or explicit formulation of intention (eg I declare how I am going to use X, or ask myself how to "get something across"). (p. 385)

As we have already suggested in our analysis of action most instances of intention (as purpose or aim) are likely to be instances of intentionality (aboutness) in that they are directed upon items and states of affairs in the world. Dennett in fact has difficulties with ethologists using his work and being mislead by confusing intentionality as aboutness with intentionality as purposiveness.

> Another shortcoming in my attempt to impart philosophical niceties to students of animal behaviour has emerged from my continuing discussions with

> ethologists: by and large they persist in conflating the philosophical notion (Brentano's notion — the concept of aboutness, in a word) and the more or less everyday notion of intentionality: the capacity to perform intentional actions or frame intention as to act. (1987: p. 271)

Cheney and Seyfarth (1990) agree with Dennett that Gricean meaning is an essential and interesting feature of human communication. They use it in their investigations of vervet monkey vocalisations and offer accounts of vervet behaviours that seem to indicate second or third order intentionality. In the following sections we shall consider a series of behaviours and consider what degree of intentionality we actually need (in accordance with the principle of economy) to attribute to vervets in order to explain their behaviour.

In *How Monkeys See The World* Cheney and Seyfarth (1990) describe their field research with vervet monkeys. The well-known primate language experiments of the 70s and the 80s were primarily conducted on laboratory chimpanzees. The field research is particularly interesting because it tells us something about monkeys' communication in their natural habitat. Thus their research gives says more about how much language monkeys really use rather than detailing the tricks they can learn human communication systems devised in the laboratory.

Cheney and Seyfarth are aware of the warnings of philosophers about attributing mental content to animals. A famous and often misinterpreted example is Wittgenstein's warning in the *Philosophical Investigations* "If a lion could speak we would not understand him". We should take from that remark a plea to consider the entire range of activity in which the language is embedded in trying to understand its content and not assume that the language wears its meaning on its face absent considerations about forms of life. This more holistic or contextual interpretation as well as the principle of economy of explanation both play an important role in the task of observation and inference. We agree with Cheney and Seyfarth that it may be necessary to attribute complex intentional states on to explain the monkeys' behaviour. Of course the holistic considerations, in combination with the principle of economy imply that it may be difficult to get the attributions right (as Wittgenstein remarks).

Vervet monkeys have distinct types of alarm call that they make in response to three kinds of predator: leopard, eagle and snake (Cheney and Seyfarth 1990: p.102). Leopard alarm calls are made in presence of large cats (including leopards). In the presence of a leopard the vervet noticing it makes a loud, barking alarm call. When other vervets on the ground hear this call they run into trees. Hiding in the trees offers vervets their best chance of safety from the leopards.

The eagle alarm call is made in response to the two large species of eagle that prey upon them. The call is a short double-syllable cough. Eagles attack monkeys from the air, swooping upon them. Not surprisingly, the vervets' response to an eagle call is to look skywards or to run into bushes. Both are strategies that make sense from the point of view of the type of attack that is likely.

The snake alarm call is given in response to sightings of snakes of the types that predate upon vervets. The alarm call is what Cheney and Seyfarth describe as a chutter. Snakes hunt vervets in long grass. The best defence for a vervet against a snake therefore is to see where the snake is and avoid it. So the vervet response to a snake alarm call is to stand upright and search the grass around them.

For male and female vervets the alarm call for leopard is quite distinct. The temptation with these alarm calls is to think they denote their objects (leopard, eagle, and snake). For instance, it is tempting to think that the short double syllable cough means "eagle attack" and that when it is successfully used it refers to an eagle attack.

Each alarm call elicits a different response in the monkeys. So it is possible that the monkeys' alarm calls in fact refer to types of escape strategy (make for the trees, stand up and look in the grass, look up). A third possibility is that the alarm calls may express no more than the emotional response produced in the vervets by the presence of a predator. On that account, the vervets' vocalisations are no more than expressions of affect. If the vervets alarm calls are adequately explained as expressions of affect there are implications for the level of intentionality that we need to attribute to the vervets' mental acts of producing them. If the vervets' alarm calls are simply howls of distress at the presence of a predator their calls are not *about* anything. The calls are responses that are adequately explained by invoking the stimulus that has caused them. Thus the alarm calls could be explained as a zero order intentional systems. Of course the fact that the vocalisations themselves may not be intentional does not imply that the perception of a predator is likewise a zero order intentional system.

Cheney and Seyfarth offer a fourth possible explanation. Alarm calls might act as general alerting signals that cause the monkeys to look about them. Once the monkeys had spotted the predator then they would make the appropriate avoidance behaviour. On this theory, unlikely in view of the distinct types of signal, alarm calls would mean something like "predator (type not specified), watch out". To test these hypotheses they concealed a speaker in the bushes and played the alarm calls of one of the members of that vervet group. As they were playing back a tape of the calls the normal conditions of utterance were not present and the response could be interpreted as purely being a result of the call.

If the third or fourth explanation was correct, vervets' should emit general responses — either general alarm or the "what's going on" response — they stop what they are doing, look about, realise the coast is clear and then go back to what they were doing. If the third explanation is correct they posited that varying the intensity and length of the vocalisation should increase the frequency and intensity of the response. They found that altering these variables had no detectable effect upon the monkeys. They found that when vervets were played the leopard alarm call of one of their kin they would perform the leopard escape method. They found that vervets made different avoidance behaviours varying upon the alarm type. Therefore neither the third nor the fourth explanation can be correct, alarm calls are linked to different avoidance behaviours.

If the vervets used the acoustically different calls to denote different predators (explanation 1) or elicit different responses (explanation 2) then the fact that the calls were played in the same context would not affect the different patterns of response. The fact that different calls were followed by different avoidance behaviours corroborated one of these differentiated explanations. When monkeys see an eagle they make an alarm call that causes their companions to look skyward and then seek cover. If an eagle is very close to a group of monkeys (within a few seconds of swooping upon a monkey and picking it up), vervets make the leopard alarm call. The leopard call causes group members to scatter and run for the trees. The behaviour that a leopard call evokes is likely to provide the best means of escaping an eagle attack when it is very close, in that stopping to check the sky could mean that the vervet is stationary, or will not make the trees by the time the eagle swoops upon them. It looks like the warning vervet realises the immediacy of the danger and realises that running for the trees is the best chance for the attacked monkeys. This realisation suggests that vervets' alarm calls correspond to different kinds of escape, although it is still possible that they refer to kinds of predator. Leopards are the biggest threat to vervets. So their reaction to hearing that one is about is likely to be to move fairly swiftly and decisively without any dithering about. The calling vervet might know this and realise that the attacked vervet's best chance of survival will be if it thinks that there is a leopard bearing down on it.

Varying the acoustic quality of the different calls was the only feature necessary and sufficient to explain differences in response. As the third and fourth explanations cannot account for the results of this experiment it seems that either the vervets refer to predators with their alarm calls or the calls refer to the most appropriate method of escape.

This finding raises the possibility that evidence of flexibility in vervets' use of alarm calls would provide evidence for attributing them with an interesting degree of consciousness and intelligence. For instance, were they to use the calls to induce false or inappropriate reactions in their fellows it would mean that they did have something very like thick representations (ones that allowed for the possibility of the thought that others also represented things in a certain way). But the fact that particular behaviours are correlated with particular alarm calls shows nothing more than the monkeys are responding to specific alarm calls and does not necessarily show that the monkeys denote in the same sense that humans might (with flexibility of cognitive engagement). It is therefore possible that the monkeys' response is linked to the alarm calls by a mechanism that that does not involve consciousness of anything.

However, Cheney and Seyfarth observed an uncommon practice that suggested the monkeys vocalisations involved intentionality of at least first order. Wandering male vervets provide an example of flexibility in the vervets' alarm calls. A lone foraging vervet will not respond in the same manner as if they were in a social setting. Cheney and Seyfarth observed a lone vervet that saw an eagle and made the appropriate escape behaviour (hid in the trees), but did not make an alarm call. Here is an instance of the appropriate stimulus being present, but not eliciting the expected response. If vervets alarm calls were in causal relationships with certain stimuli then we would expect the lone vervet to elicit the eagle alarm call whereas here it seems that some sufficient degree of socialisation is necessary to provide the conditions for the warning behaviour.

It is possible that this apparent flexibility in the use of alarm calls does not belie the presence of sophisticated intentional states in vervets. It is possible that there exists a mechanism that creates multi-tracked dispositions such as:

⟨make alarm call 2 (eagle alarm) when eagle is observed, unless either you are the only vervet around in which case just perform the right escape procedure or the danger is high in which case make alarm call 1 (leopard alarm)⟩;

It is tempting to invoke awareness of the denoting function of alarm calls and the purposes that they serve to the lone vervet in order to explain this behaviour. But it is not necessary to do so. As with the flexibility of alarm calls in eagle attacks a similar mechanism can be invoked to explain this flexibility. It may be that vervet is programmed to make alarm calls only in the presence of both predators and other vervets.

What about our claims about thick and thin noetic states? Awareness of the denoting function of language and the possibility of different individuals using the same denoting device would seem to be a necessary condition for having a "thick" representation. If it is not possible to think reflexively about the behaviour that you are performing as a response linked to certain conditions of appropriateness then you can not ask the question "is this what I should be doing?" If it is not possible to ask this question then it is not possible to decide ⟨yes this is the response I should make⟩, or ⟨no this won't work I should think of something else⟩. If an organism cannot ask questions of this kind then it cannot form questions about what it *ought* to do. Thus being able to reflect upon one's denoting means that one is also able to respond normatively to situations. If it could shown that vervets are aware of the denoting function of their alarm call then we would know that their representations were "thick". This would not establish that vervets have intentional states as rich and varied as human beings, but it would show that they are in the same ballpark.

Evidence for deception on the part of animals would provide compelling evidence for awareness by animals of the denoting role of vocalisations. Only if an individual thinks X denotes Y and therefore emitting X will cause A (another animal) to think that Y is present could the animal intelligently reason about what a vocalisation is likely to do to another animal and intend to produce this behaviour by making this vocalisation. An awareness of the link between signs of the type X and situations instancing Y seems to be the minimum basis on which we could plausibly describe an animal as deceptive. The paradise duck is a waterfowl native to New Zealand. During their nesting season they exhibit behaviours that we ordinarily describe as attempts to deceive. When walking along a riverbank toward a pair of nesting ducks they will make loud alarm calls. When the predator enters a zone close to the nest one of the ducks will attempt to lure the predator away from the nest with a broken wing display. Often the deceiving duck will nurse its crippled wing across land in a direction away from its nest. When the duck is satisfied that the predator has been lured a safe distance away from the nest it will miraculously heal and take to the air.

Should we describe this behaviour as an act of deception? When a person deceives another usually there is present third order intentionality. A person makes an utterance (or performs an equivalent behaviour) intending to produce a belief in an other, while knowing that the belief acquired by the other is different from that indicated by the utterance. Its possible that paradise ducks undertake this elaborate cognitive process when making broken wing displays. To say that they do so would credit them with a degree of mental complexity that is not necessary to explain their behaviour and is *prima facie* inconsistent with what we know about the duck's brain and other general facts about neuropsychology. Such a degree of complexity in ducks would lead us to expect that they would be able to apply these sophisticated skills to other areas of their life that in fact they cannot do. It is therefore hard to swallow the idea that the ducks are consciously aware of how a predator would be attracted to a bird with a broken wing and then perform a broken wing display intending for the predator to be fooled.

It is still appropriate to call the duck's behaviour deceptive as long as we are aware of the nature of the attribution. This is the evolved function that this behaviour serves. Yet in an obvious sense it is not deceptive in that it does not imply a conscious intention to exploit the gap between sign and denoted condition. If we decide that it is still appropriate to describe this act as deception this will provide a problem for Dennett's assumption that all instances of purposiveness are intentional instances. The duck is lacking the thick representations or complex intentional states that typically correspond to deception. However a more convincing case can be made for deception by vervet monkeys.

In a few instances where there was inter-group conflict a male vervet gave a leopard alarm call. The call was followed, as expected, by all the vervets hearing the call taking to the trees. In these cases there was no indication that a leopard was in the vicinity. The result of the alarm call was that the conflict between the groups was, temporarily, stopped. Cheney and Seyfarth are aware that this may reflect an affective response to what is an emotionally charged situation. But they think that, although there is clearly a large affective component to the call, this cannot be the sole explanation of the call. The males that made these calls made them in two specific contexts:

> When the group was being driven back towards the centre of its territory and hence was losing the encounter and when a new migrant male was attempting to approach the group. (1990: p.108)

It is tempting to think that this is a deceptive behaviour guided by complex intentional states involving a recognition of the denoting role of the call and its probable effect on others. It appears as if this vervet has realised that the attacking vervets will take the call to denote the threat of a leopard. While the uttering vervet has *intended* that this utterance count as good evidence for the marauding vervets to *believe* there is a leopard, the utterer does not *believe* that the conditions exist which would normally ground the content of their utterance. This vervet's utterance therefore appears to satisfy Grice's conditions for speaker's meaning.

A "killjoy" (Dennett 1987: p. 248) interpretation of this phenomenon is that the vervet's alarm calls are imperatives (as opposed to informative statements). Thus when the uttering vervet makes the alarm call this means something equivalent to "run into the bushes and climb a tree". Dennett discounts this interpretation because there is no reason why the attacking vervets should honour the imperative of one of the vervets they are attacking.

> ...It is not simply a case of the vervet uttering an imperative "get into the trees" in the expectation that all the vervets will obey, since the vervet (being rational — our predictive lever) should not expect a rival band to heed his imperative. Dennett (1987)

Dennett argues that alarm calls are not simply commands to perform a particular means of escape. In effect he is suggesting that vervet alarm calls denote a type of predator and are intended to elicit a certain kind of response which will have the effect of getting the threatened group out of a tight situation.

If Dennett is right what can be said about the nature of the vervet's representation of these events? The deceiving vervet realises that making this false utterance will have a good outcome for his group. It appears that this vervet is capable of reflecting upon the denoting function of his language and its meaning to other vervets. We have suggested that this is a necessary condition for having a "thick" representation. This condition, although a key feature of thick representation does not establish that this vervet is thinking reflexively about the leopard alarm call but it does at least establish that the vervet has some conception of the call and its content as a representation.

Cheney and Seyfarth describe an instance where a group of vervets foraging in long grass heard a snake alarm call. Most of the foraging vervets scanned the ground surrounding them for a snake. One of the vervets did not do so, but continued to forage in the long grass. The same vervet, a few hours later returned to the same area of long grass, but before foraging searched the long grass in the manner that other members of its group did when the snake alarm call was given. The fact that this vervet did not respond to the alarm call when uttered did not mean that it had not heard the call. It appears as if this vervet had decided that others were looking for the snake and the risk was not that great. It if was the case that alarm calls are imperatives then the vervet should have responded by performing the appropriate behaviour. It is hard to explain this vervet's recall of the likely presence of snakes in the area, on the basis of a sign given by another vervet unless the calls are informative in some way. Thus we agree with Dennett's claim that alarm calls are informative and recognised to be so by those who use them. The foraging vervet's behaviour suggests that alarm calls denote to vervet's the existence of particular class of predators. What is even more interesting about this example is that the alarm calls are organising vervet's practical intellect.

A theory of mind?

Philosophers in both the analytic and continental traditions have theorised about our knowledge of other minds. Analytic philosophers tend to talk of 'a theory of mind' and in continental philosophy 'the other' is a term used to indicate the presence of another mind and the implications of that presence for my own situation. While in analytic philosophy the possible non-existence of other minds has been seriously entertained, continental philosophers tend to treat it as an *a priori* recognition of embodied consciousness in the real world. Hegel and Sartre both seem to think that awareness of the other is a primary or fundamental condition that has a basic role to play in the structure of human consciousness. When continental philosophers use this term, what is usually referred to is the phenomenology of the conscious awareness of the presence of another person. A good example of the kind of use this concept is present in

Jean Paul Sartre's play "No Exit". In the chapter "Hell is Other People" Sartre describes three people in hell. They are confined in a small room and none of them can ever leave. Thus each character must be conscious at each and every moment that the other people in the room with her are there. She is conscious of them as people and therefore she is present to them and scrutinised by them; she cannot pretend that they are objects, like the tables and chairs that are also in the room. Her companions in hell are "others" and they inescapably condition her own experience by their presence.

There are some interesting connections between continental use of "the other" and the material we have been discussing thus far. As we have mentioned, Grice's analysis of speaker's meaning necessarily involves the existence of an other. He argues that uttering x with the intention of y counting as evidence for what is attempting to be communicated implies that the speaker conceptualises the listener as another mind.

Furthermore, there is considerable evidence that children begin their epistemic journey as a journey in company with others (Butterworth 1991; Donaldson 1979; Trevarthen 1979). It is therefore overwhelmingly plausible that, as Sartre suggests, the presence of others is a basic feature of adult consciousness. Let us take it as a given that adult human beings ordinarily have a theory of mind and are aware of others to whom that theory applies. The interesting question for a discussion of animal consciousness is do animals have a theory of other minds? More specifically on the basis of Cheney and Seyfarth's observation of vervet language use, do vervets have a concept of other minds? If we could be satisfied that they did then this would advance claims about them having thick noetic states.

Premack and Woodruff argued that chimpanzees have a theory of mind (1978). They claimed that chimps imputed a "purpose" to an actor when solving particular problems. Cheney and Seyfarth's deceiving vervet and the vervet that was "relaxed" about the snake alarm did seem to attribute purposive states to other vervets. Third order intentionality requires that speakers have a theory of mind to the extent that they believe of others that those others have thoughts about their (the speakers) thoughts. If it is the case that the deceiving vervet did in fact make the leopard alarm call in a conscious attempt to convince the attacking vervets that a leopard was near, while knowing that there was no leopard, then we can describe it has operating with third order intentionality in that it thought ⟨they will think I have seen a snake⟩. Vervet monkeys therefore do *appear* to have a theory of mind. From the fact that they have less developed language use than adult human beings it appears that this fact alone even if it has a significant role in language use is not enough to give the richness and variety that we find in human language and therefore in human thought and consciousness.

Daniel Povinelli (1996) notes that chimpanzees in 'theory of mind' experiments performed poorly on tasks that we might expect them to be able to do if they did in fact have a theory of mind. This is the same difficulty that we are faced with in deciding whether vervets have a theory of mind. If the apparent examples of deception and third order intentionality do suggest that vervets have a theory of mind why do we see them using it more often and in other domains? One possible way is to suggest that chimpanzees and vervets have a 'weak theory of mind' or one that is limited to vary circumscribed domains of activity but then this seems hardly to come up to the kind of thing we mean by the very general human abilities to use such thinking.

Povinelli says that this would in effect mean that

> chimpanzee behaviour is largely governed by learned or evolved social algorithms but that their representational code can compress less information about social information, and hence ultimately their (presumably) image-based representational system for encoding mental states is less efficient than the additional linguistic-based system of humans. This alternative could make good biological sense if we viewed some human psychological innovations like language as providing a mechanism which allowed for more complex representations of mental states. (p. 322)

We have already argued that the sophistication of human intentionality and hence the thickness of our noetic states is essentially connected with our linguistic capacity and the complex social institutions that language potentiates. Povinelli's suggestion is that even though chimpanzees are social animals, meaning that their behaviours do involve reciprocity and complex interactions strongly suggestive of an active conceptualisation of 'other' chimps, their social organisation is rudimentary and does not allow for the proliferation of complex meaning that is possible in human society. He conjectures that this poverty is due to the way in which they 'think' about this social information using imagistic techniques rather than articulated linguistic devices. The thought that chimp thinking only exhibits a theory of mind in an infrequent or weaker way than is the case for human consciousness adds little to these remarks.

Andrew Whiten (1996) also believes that there are grades of "mind reading". He reviews four candidate bases on which I might become genuinely informative to talk of a non-verbal creature being a mentalist in the sense of thinking about the mental life of other creatures. The Paradise Duck's broken wing displays can be thought of as at the lowest level of 'mind-reading'.

> Animals can, in principle, forecast the behaviour of other animals, because sequences of behaviour follow statistical rules. Ethologists discover the rules systematically by recording long sequences of behaviour and the analysing them statistically, for example by transition matrices, and in the same way an animal can behave as if it is predicting another individual's future behaviour. (Whiten 1996: p. 280)

This suggestion explains how it is possible to describe the duck's behaviour as deceptive without implying that the ducks have thick noetic states and intend to deceive. However this low level mind-reading is not adequate to explain the more innovative deceptive behaviours that vervet monkeys occasionally perform, largely because this level of mind-reading doesn't necessarily require anything greater than first order intentionality. Although it is not possible to rule out clever behaviourist interpretations of vervet's deceptive behaviours (and further research may throw more light on these behaviours) the evidence does seem sufficient to describe the vervets as possessing at least a kind of limited third order intentionality as a theory of mind.

We started this chapter with examples of the breadth of views about animal consciousness and have now considerably narrowed the range of diverse views that look plausible.

The communications of Von Frisch's bees can easily be distinguished from human language because the bees representations possess zero order intentionality. Adequate explanations of their behaviour can be given purely as responses to environmental input, which, when coupled with the absence of any cerebral cortex suggests that we ought to describe the bees as not conscious of their communicative abilities.

There is evidence that vervets' alarm calls are genuinely informative statements. This evidence is, unfortunately, largely anecdotal. Therefore it would be imprudent to claim that vervets representations are "thick". However, if one accepts the interpretation given of the "deceptive" vervet and the "relaxed" vervet it seems vervets do, at least occasionally, respond normatively to their representations and vocalisations and show third order intentionality thereby seeming to possess a (somewhat limited) theory of mind.

Vervets and probably other higher primates do not possess thick noetic states with the nuances and reflective features of human thought. As one commentator has suggested compelling evidence for the existence of conscious complexity of this sort would, as Davidson suggested, have to come from sophisticated language use. Do vervets have a theory of mind? We believe so, but it is one that is, as one might expect, as constrained as their communication and co-operative life together. To get to the level of formulating theories of knowledge and consciousness seems to require the ability to manipulate linguistically mediated noetic states of a sophistication undreamed of in the world of any vervet Horatio.

Thus we have argued that the attribution of conscious content is difficult in animals and is, as Edelman suggested, relativised to human psychology. Animals are clearly conscious but it is hard to say just what they are conscious of if we want to isolate contents of consciousness and not just the objects in the world that seem to be involved. To differentiate the contents of animal consciousness at the level of sense or content we need to have a very extensive grasp of the articulation in animal intentionality, knowledge that is not evident from scattered observations in artificial settings.

CHAPTER 8

Anomalies of consciousness

There are a number of states which seem clearly to belong to the realm of mind but in which the identification of intentional objects of which the subject has a conceptual and potentially reflective grasp seems problematic. These are prima facie anomalies for the theory of consciousness and intentionality that we have outlined. The problems arise in relation to moods, the unconscious, hallucinations and delusions, self deception brain bisection and Dissociative Identity Disorder (multiple personality disorder). It is interesting to see how the present theory will cope with the difficulties presented by this rich phenomenological field. The first area into which we ought to look is the concept of mood. The thoughts that allow us to understand this phenomenon will then allow us to explore the idea of the unconscious. The relationship between normal consciousness, delusions, and hallucinations is also important and will be illuminated by the intentionality of conscious content.

Examples where we are tempted to say that the person is both conscious and unconscious of things at the same time are found both in bad faith and self-deception. The first clue we should follow in this brief study of anomalies in consciousness is the fact that the conditions included are usually human conditions; we do not wonder about split personality in dogs, or the unconscious of a parrot. It therefore seems as if Jean Paul Sartre is right when he puts the integration and guiding co-ordination of human consciousness as the fact that allows us to study the types of disintegration that can occur in the mind (1957).

We have argued for the central importance of the realisation that consciousness is an integrative, conceptualizing activity which constitutes intentional content to which a subject react in a variety of ways. This integrity allows us to be more-or-less smoothly co-ordinated intentional beings with a rich set of strategies for dealing with the world around us in concert with our fellows. This last aspect of consciousness, the "con" of *conscio*, is important in the account we will develop. We are interested in the anomalies of consciousness, in which the usual integrity of this intentional activity does not seem to hold, because of the way such anomalies throw into relief the subtle and pervasive inter-relationship of intentionality, consciousness, and the social context within which a subject lives. We can further demonstrate the importance of giving a fully informed reading of the nature of human intentionality as an interpersonal product by showing how disruptions of the interpersonal and discursive features of consciousness reveal themselves in such anomalies.

Moods

Moods are not really anomalies of the human mind but they do pose a problem for the present theory because they are relatively devoid of content. This special feature of moods has led some philosophers to suggest that moods may not exhibit intentionality.

John Searle (1983) argues that only some and not all conscious states are intentional. He has in mind some forms of nervousness, elation and undirected anxiety. It is because these states may not be about anything that Searle thinks they cease to be intentional. Intentionality as we have argued involves an aboutness relation between a thinker and *noesis*. He offers the following conditions to help us determine whether or not a state is intentional.

> If a state S is intentional then there must be an answer to such questions as What is S about? What is S of? What is it an S that? (1983: p. 2)

The distinction is not just between types of mental state which are intentional or not intentional as there are states whose intentionality is indeterminate.

> ...Just as there are forms of elation, depression and anxiety where one is simply elated, depressed, or anxious without being elated, depressed, or anxious about anything, so, also, there are forms of these states where one is elated that such and such has occurred or depressed and anxious at the prospect of such and such. Undirected anxiety, depression, and elation are not Intentional, the directed cases are Intentional. (1983: p. 2)

In order to be satisfied with Searle's conclusion it is necessary to consider whether there are examples of undirected anxiety, depression or elation.

> Jean is mildly depressed. His depression came upon him slowly and he has not realised that over a period of several weeks he has gradually been getting lower. Jean's depression is such that he exhibits a number of the behavioural features that we would associate with depression. Others notice that he is emotionally flat, while he himself notices that his appetite has diminished and that has trouble sleeping. However Jean does not come to identify these symptoms with the fact that he is depressed.

There are at least three ways in which Jean could be conscious of his depression. If a friend of Jean's pointed out to him that his behaviour is consistent with that of a person suffering from depression then he might have the realisation that he is depressed. Once Jean has this insight then the distinct ways in which he could be conscious of his depression become important. Jean could realize that he, in fact, feels depressed. This mode of thought could involve him being conscious of depressed feelings so that he himself in his depressed state becomes an object or topic of his consciousness. Searle would claim that in order for such a conscious state to be an intentional state there must be an intentional object to which this conscious state is directed but here the argument would be that he, Jean (characterized as feeling a certain way), was the object at which thought was directed. Jean has gradually become generally depressed and not for any specifiable reason but when Jean thinks about the fact that *he* is depressed the object to which the depression is directed is himself being in a certain state.

The second possible way in which Jean's depression might be intentional can occur even when he is not thinking explicitly about his depression. Before Jean's friend pointed out to him that he was in fact depressed Jean would have tended to attach a different sort of significance to anything with which he interacted. People with depression tend to apprehend all things around them with an attitude of apathy or blackness. It is this aspectual coloration that leads those around Jean to think that he may be depressed.

The third possible way in which Jean's depression could be intentional is when the depression itself becomes the object of an intentional mental act. When Jean decides that he has had enough of his depression and has thoughts such as ⟨my depression is causing me problems⟩ or ⟨Prozac will help me with my depression⟩ his depression becomes the intentional object for a number of thoughts.

Therefore mood state, M, is intentional when

i. M is about an intentional object O, or

ii. M has an aspectual influence upon a series of intentional objects MIO (moodily-affected intentional objects), or
iii. M itself is the object of an intentional act.

The intentional object for Jean's reflections upon his depression (possibility i) is the cognitive category which we all use when thinking about ourselves. If it is not the case that a mood state satisfies conditions i, ii or iii then it is not conscious mental content. All mood states that satisfy i, ii or iii are directed mental acts. Therefore Searle's claim that there can be conscious mood states that are not intentional is false.

We can illuminate further the nature of moods as distinct from other bodily states if we consider two situations. In the first the subject, call him Herman, is non-specifically restless and keeps fretting and fidgeting. If asked, Herman would say, "I don't know what the problem is, I just can't keep still."

The other situation involves Imran who is showing similar behaviour but when asked says "Something is worrying me, but I can't put my finger on it, it's just there nagging away. If only I could think what it was I am sure I could sort it out."

The first we might call agitation and the second anxiety. The difference seems to be that Herman feels that a bodily state is causing his agitation and does not connect this with any cause of psychic dis-ease (or even one which is at present unknown). He is not looking for an intentional object or mental state at the root of his bodily state and is prepared to acknowledge that although the state of agitation itself is an intentional object for him, whatever is causing that state is probably not. Therefore, although we might want to say that he is undergoing a purely bodily state he would fulfil two of our conditions for the mental status of moods if either:

a. he thought of the state he was in as something affecting all his other conscious life (condition ii); or
b. he thought "What a funny state I'm in" and therefore made the state itself into an intentional object (condition iii).

Either of these conditions may or may not come to hold and, depending on whether they do, we would then designate his condition a mood (anxiety or similar) or a bodily disturbance (restlessness or agitation).

By contrast, Imran knows, or at least believes, that there is some psychic or conceptualisable origin for his mental dis-ease. He is trying to identify it because he recognizes that a cognitive reconfiguration of the situation might well help. In either case changing the state of responsiveness of the body will affect what the person feels but Herman would have no reason to attack the problem in a cognitive way whereas Imran would. Herman would most plausibly use a physical or chemical agent and thereby attack the source of the problem in a way that fitted with his conception of it (as a disturbance of his body). In fact Imran might also be advised to do exactly the same thing although he would then need some justification (such as the thought that the brain does strange things under the influence of certain chemical agents) to think that the physical intervention would address the root of the problem. This is quite compatible with the idea of a mood disorder such as depression where all one's thoughts seem to inherit a kind of blackness or bleakness quite apart from their content such that if that negative "colour" or "flavour" could be removed then the person's state of mind would be improved. The sufferer might feel that the world itself has gone black but this is consistent with our condition i for the mental status of moods (the thesis that it is because the physical states in question infect states which take intentional objects that they are mood disorders rather than just alterations of bodily functioning). Thus we might say that the contents of a state of altered mood are determined by the concurrent intentional states such as beliefs, desires, and so on to which the moods are attached.

It therefore seems plausible that moods are properly so classified on one of the three counts we have outlined — they directly affect mental content, they take the person and that person's states as intentional objects, or they themselves, as moods become a topic for thought. This disjunctive ground of categorization allows a principled grouping of mood as distinct from other (purely bodily) affectations of human beings.

For any broadly Aristotelian approach to the mind the states which we call mental states are relations between the body and the world mediated by conceptual content. On such an account, mental or conscious states and bodily states would have a great deal in common but only mental acts, states, and events would be characterized by intentional content. The need for content ascriptions to be invoked when the effect of certain states and their role in the life of the person is being considered is the basis on which some of the many things which happen to us come to be seen as mental states. Among those states whose operation critically depends on mental content some are then considered to be conscious and some are not. We have already discussed states in which the person as a whole is less than fully conscious as a result of dysfunctions of the brain. In such circumstances the very existence of contentful states with an intentional role in the behaviour of the person is in doubt. We must now consider states in which ascriptions of content are routinely made but the contents are not consciously entertained or reflected upon by the person concerned. Mental states, acts, and events of this type form the dynamic unconscious which is said to influence behaviour in virtue of its intentional content even though the person concerned does not have conscious access to that content or the mental acts in which it operates. This prompts a number of further questions which concern the principled basis on which a distinction between conscious and subconscious intentional acts might be made, the manner in which intentional content is fixed for states of the latter type, and the posit that such states cause changes in consciousness and behaviour explicable by appeal to their content.

The unconscious

The idea of the unconscious is primarily attributable to the work of Freud. It was he who was prepared to depart from the Cartesian idea that the mind was co-extensive with the realm of introspective awareness. For Freud the origins of human thought and behaviour were not only those intentional phenomena to which a person had access but might also include contentful phenomena which were hidden from consciousness. The material in the unconscious was important for Freud because it could be invoked to explain what people tend to do when they act in ways at variance with their consciously avowed intentions and motives. It could therefore explain emotional reactions and attitudes connected to present and past experience in ways not explicable by appealing only to the conscious thoughts and reasoning of the person. Freud believed that some of these manifestations betrayed the presence of repressed memories and emotional conflicts located in a discrete mental domain of unconscious forces.

In the unconscious the links between mental states and events are served by the *primary process* that is a loose and promiscuous domain of associations and causal influences not mediated by rational constraints. The primary process allows connections to form that obey no principle of implication or rational order. The associations formed may be on the basis of imagistic resemblances (the flames of a sitting room fire and the breath of dragons), chance and arbitrary similarities in the sounds of the signifiers used (water and daughter), connections in meaning (paint and colour), or any other chance or meaningful way of eliciting one item of mental content by means of exhibiting another. The domain of reason and reflection — the conscious ego — does not allow this profligacy and exerts some sort of integrative control over the conscious lived experience of the subject but the fact that the conscious ego is a cumulative set of mental acts realised by the elaboration of functions initially developed in a more primitive neural and intentional substrate means that the unconscious compartment can have significant influence on conscious life. This is in part because its trains of intentional acts might be unconstrained and not well integrated into any harmonious narrative.

According to Freud, an important subset of intentional and contentful mental acts are confined to the unconscious by repression. Repression happens when the contents are associated with events too disturbing to be dealt with by the ego and therefore not able to be included in the conscious integrated thought life that makes up the "presented face" of the mind. Freud posited that, from the time a memory or feeling is being formed, a process of censorship is at work that may cause that memory to be repressed. If this happens there is then a barrier to be overcome which becomes evident in a person's resistance to talking about or making explicit to consciousness the repressed material. The repressed material, imbued with a certain amount of nervous energy attempting to find a route to discharge itself, seeks expression, just as a build up of hydraulic pressure seeks release. This discharge or expression, despite the fact that it is potentiated by the effects of the intentional content involved, occurs in ways that do not straightforwardly reflect its intentional content because the direct articulation and expression of the intentional content also contains the reason for the repression. For instance, consider the following hypothetical case based on the posited oedipal attraction between a male child and its mother.

> Ian, as a child, feels a sexual attraction for his mother. He also has some awareness that the desired relationship is proscribed and must not be indulged. Perhaps there is a traumatic event in which his father finds Ian being cuddled by and kissing his mother and Ian breaks guiltily away, condemned by his own thoughts.

One might expect this event to lead to the repression of oedipal desires that would then express themselves in overtly oedipal dreams (when the ego is disabled and off-guard because one is asleep). But it may be that the memory is too painful for such an obvious form of expression, even though it would happen at a time when the ego defences were disabled (in sleep). Imagine that Ian begins to play elaborate games in which he is trying to rescue a queen who has been captured by a large dragon. He is pursued by the dragon who is intent on destroying him but in every game, he fights the dragon and kills it. Perhaps as he becomes an adult, Ian develops an almost self-destructive penchant for taking the side of the underdog. He always aligns himself with the weak and has an unerring nose for those who are powerful and whom he might defy. However he always fails when he looks set to achieve a senior position for which he might be well suited on other grounds. Under therapy it is revealed that Ian's career problems are attributable to a failure to ever overcome the Oedipal resentment and self-condemnation that was thrown into emotional condensation by the "father caught us" incident with its associated phantasies of forbidden oedipal love.

Here the picture of the unconscious is shown in its true colours. There are intentional states and there is a narrative but it is not straightforwardly connected to the actual objects of which a thinker might become conscious in the normal course of experience. Concepts are used but they bear only symbolic or associational links to many of the things being thought about and motivating the trains of thought and experience. Notice, as MacIntyre points out, that there is a mixture of observation and conjecture here loosely knitted together by theory (MacIntyre, 1958). In a real psychoanalytic case report there would be observations about the points at which the patient resisted the line of conversation by changing topics, or becoming silent. There would also be associative material based on the therapist choosing certain words to say to the patient and exploring the links that appear between them. Imagine, for instance, that one of Ian's sessions has the following free association material:

Therapist: "dragon" Ian: big, dangerous, powerful, fire …
Therapist: "father" Ian: work, big … he lights the fire.
Therapist: "queen" Ian: beautiful, holy, rich and powerful, king.
Therapist: "King" Ian: master, father, eagle, powerful,

In these deliberately constructed word sets the convergences are suggestive but the therapist may find the material subtle, difficult to penetrate, and well disguised, so that the theory has to play an important part in driving the search for links and the interpretations that reveal them. In this process the therapist looks for possible connections which provide some grounds for a narrative based on the content-types appearing in stories of jealousy, sovereignty, forbidden sex, and so on.

The ultimate resolution of a case depends on the therapist finding a narrative or synthesis that allows the patient to redescribe his or her life and acknowledge areas of tension and difficulty. To overcome these tensions, they might be related by the therapist to unresolved childhood tensions and real or imagined trauma. According to the theory such links allow the unconscious material to come into the revealing light of the ego functions where it can be reflectively integrated into a new conscious understanding of self. It is acknowledged that some of the areas of psychic tension and emotional disturbance might only be resolved by the crucial emotional interactions being re-enacted with the therapist through transference.

Notice the intentionality operative at many levels in this process. Certain inexplicable and apparently irrational events and feelings in the person's life are conceptualised as arising from unconscious causes. It is presumed both that their existence in the mind is real, in that it has a causal influence on behaviour, and that they have intentional content related to objects, events, and feelings that have occurred in the person's experience. The intentional connections between these events are then reconstructed in a way that makes sense. If a father were to be thought of as, *inter alia*, a big, powerful, fire-associated being and a dragon has the same conceptual features then it is concluded that there is a link between the two. If the attitude of the child to the mother, not fully explicit but in some sense present in the incident concerned would provide a reason to feel guilt or anticipate threat from the father, then father and threat or danger are linked again through their intentional contents. This sets up the framework of the subsequent analysis and therapy.

Although we have discussed the case of Ian in a Freudian framework, most of the remarks can be generalised beyond that specific framework as the form of both theory and therapy is the same for many different types of psychoanalysis or psycho-dynamically oriented approaches. The patient is distressed by certain incomprehensible things in his or her life. The therapist finds a way to explain these by pulling together what the patient complains about and other features of the life story in a way that makes sense of the problems the patient is experiencing. In doing this many of the patient's attitudes, beliefs, unspoken desires, and so on are explored and discussed with the therapist who gives permission for the patient to admit to thoughts and feelings that are normally excluded from, or not legitimated in, everyday discourse. The patient is encouraged to be open about these forbidden areas of mental life without worrying about the normative judgements that would normally apply. As is to be expected, the opportunity to talk about areas of tension and discomfort in their relationships brings reflection and broader considerations to bear. This all happens within a relationship which is supportive and in which an emotionally charged interplay between patient and therapist is going on. The patient is encouraged to achieve more integration of the various strands of mental life that are being revealed and thereby comes to a greater peace within himself.

This form of therapy actually betrays some of the commitments of the theory to which it is so inseparably bound, at least in its traditional formulations. The first commitment is to the idea that mental states and events causally interact in virtue of their content and by so doing configure the thought and behaviour of the individual concerned in ways that may or may not match the conscious thinking of the person concerned. The way states of mind do act upon each other and within the mind is given by a specification of their intentional content but the reflective aspects of those trains of thought that feature in the conscious mind are not necessarily fully engaged in the process. Whether or not reason and reflection are engaged depends to some extent on the amount of attention and effort used to detect inconsistencies and leaps of thought or association and submit the resulting trains of thought to reflective scrutiny. Reflection is, however, only part of the process and the emotional work done with the therapist plays a deep and significant part in any healing that occurs. The fact that the unconscious is not supposed to be accessible in that way means that the same rules do not apply and acts attributable to unconscious forces are to some extent excusable to self and others. The challenge for the present account is to spell out what might be going on in the mind such that we are led to find plausible a dynamic unconscious which can operate with intentional content but outside of the reflective norms that are part of the mastery of the rule-governed use of intentional abilities. This is an important thesis in our understanding of the conscious agent.

We have remarked that the reflective norms which apply to concepts and their use entail that any given judgment can potentially be interrogated by the thinker who can ask, "Is it really….", "Does it satisfy the conditions….", and so on (although these normative attitudes may not be explicit or articulated). It is this possibility that secures the place of the thinker in the conscious narrative as its author and regulator. The psychodynamic thesis is that mental states and events *qua* mental or intentional have causal relations which are not regulated by the norms pervading the conscious mind. The corollary is that these states of mind motivate us or cause behaviour that is not under conscious control or rational reflective scrutiny. Thus if we accept Freud's view of the causal effects of unconscious states and their irrational interactions we undercut the deliberative or at least voluntary and principled regulation of thought and action which we have argued is a feature secured by the internal relation between conceptual content and rule following. However, this thesis is not without its own problems.

There is a quite insecure basis for content ascriptions in the case of subconscious states in that the normal criteria such as avowability, speech acts, expressed attitudes, and reasons for action and other conscious mental acts, have only an indirect relationship to the content of the subconscious states supposedly causing them. This means the way we normally read people by drawing on a fairly straightforward set of abilities to understand others is not applicable in the exercise of discerning the content of subconscious or unconscious states. Given the doubts which arise even in the normal case (the content of conscious mental acts) we must conclude that there is significant indeterminacy attached to any content ascriptions involved in knowledge about the unconscious mind. This puts a great deal of weight on the correlations between real (but unconscious) contents and the manifestations that reveal those contents (for instance in therapy). But here there is a further problem. There is a close circle of theory and observation evident in psychodynamic writing. First, it is assumed that there is only one way to account for conscious conflict and that must be cashed out in terms of formed subconscious content forming complexes that influence the ego. This content is then searched for and an account in terms of the variables permitted to appear in psychodynamic explanations is posited. Because this relates to material that may be suppressed, confirmation from the conscious subject of the alleged mental states is not required or even expected. In the meantime a number of potential points of emotional distress are canvassed in a supportive environment in which a surrogate father or mother or sister or brother figure is provided. It is likely that some story involving sexuality and ambivalence about some of the deepest and longstanding relationships in our life may be able to be told of many of us, given that troubles in those same areas of the psyche are so prevalent. Therefore it is unsurprising that a proportion of people will gain positive help from such an encounter. However, the concomitant is that in many cases the theory will be self-fulfilling because the mythology that it weaves around the individual's problems and discontents will be thought to be confirmed when such help eventuates.

There is also a conceptual problem identified by MacIntyre in relation to the ego in psychic conflict. The aim of psychoanalysis is to restore the mental integrity of the psychically disturbed person by enabling the ego to regain its integrating role and submit the processes operating in the mind to conscious control. This project requires that reason be capable of taking the key role in the transactions occurring in the psyche. This is inconsistent with the view that causation operates fairly uniformly from the bottom up and that it is the psychic economics or libidinous hydraulics of the unconscious that determine our behaviour. The inconsistency between the determinism of unconscious causation and the (conscious) agent's role in intentional mental acts is subject to sharp criticism by MacIntyre:

> 'cure' for Freud means more than 'the mitigation of neurotic symptoms' which is what it tends to mean for those who apply physical methods in psychiatry. To be cured is to have become reasonable, aware of the true nature of one's situation, able to cope with it instead of being overcome by it. But curiously this whole distinction, lacking which the whole project of psychoanalysis would be meaningless, is obliterated by the determinism of Freud's general theory. (p. 90)

The distinction is obliterated because Freud believes that irrational configurations of psychic energy drive conscious thought and therefore drive the rationalisations that epiphenomenally appear and lend to our thoughts a semblance of forming coherent trains of reason and action.

> The psychoanalyst as therapist contrasts compulsive and unfree neurotic behaviour with normal free choice; but as theorist his conception of unconscious causation leads him to deny this contrast by seeing both as unfree. (p. 91)

These passages amount to what MacIntyre calls "intolerable paradoxes" and suggest that we might do slightly better by elaborating some of the points we have already made about consciousness and thought. They are not perhaps as devastating as one might be tempted to suppose. A minor concession by psychodynamic theory would allow relations in the psyche to go two ways and have the ego influencing the unconscious and its complexes to some extent that might vary from cases to case and occasion to occasion. This would defuse to some extent the strong Freudian dogma of repression as well as the sharp divides in the psyche and it would allow psycho-analytic theory to acknowledge the role of discourse in the intentional content appealed to by most dynamic explanations. However such a concession should cause us to reconceptualise the kind of material that could plausibly form the activity we call unconscious and also drift in a Lacanian direction in relation to the importance of language not only to the ego but also to the unconscious mind.

Degrees of self knowledge and unconscious content

We have outlined an account of the mind in which there is a close relation between intentional content and consciousness. Freudian theory posits unconscious states and events that have intentional contents which explain certain of our mental acts, reactions, and attitudes. The ways in which these states interact is also determined by their contents and they influence a person's behaviour in ways over which the person does not have conscious control. While this is congenial to our view that rational control goes along with consciousness we need to say something more about the intentional content of these features of a person's mental life that are, according to the theory, contentful but without being subject to the explicit normative judgements that is implicit in the conceptual contents that structure consciousness. What is more we do not want to create the idea that all less-than-conscious mental acts are tied to some such notion as the dynamic unconscious.

Notice that things happen to us that may not be fully conceptualised because they are not attended to. This lack of explicit articulation or conceptualisation of what happens to a person may result from inadequate conceptual skills but the Freudian dynamic unconscious is intertwined with motivations and conflicts between them. Freud would consider material not attended to as merely being preconscious in its realisation. Many of us believe that some such material is in part operating to explain certain features of behaviour. In order to subject that belief to philosophical scrutiny, we ought first to attend to the less contentious forms of subconscious cognitive content and then notice the shift to a more dynamically structured situation.

> Owen might be driving home and pass a row of shops but not take any particular notice as to whether there is a wine shop there. When he gets home his wife says she would love a glass of wine. He has a vague impression of there being a wine shop present and of reading an advertisement that one was due to open in the shopping centre concerned but he is not sure. When he goes

> back to check he finds a wine shop just where he thought it was with a sign saying "Wine — new shop, new bargains".

Now imagine another situation:

> Peter is lonely and feeling somewhat rejected because things are not well at home and offers to have lunch with Penny, a woman at the office. He pulls out all his charm and acts were he to think about it (which he doesn't) very flirtatiously. This happens several times and the two begin to share quite personal details about their life stories and their hopes and fears. Peter does not think of this as the beginning of an affair and reacts quite sharply when one of his friends remarks that he seems to be "making quite a play for Penny". Peter later reflects on his behaviour and becomes aware of its amorous significance and the possible implications for his marriage.

In these two cases we have a failure to conceptualise certain features of situations because they do not accord with what the thinker is currently intending to do at a conscious level. In each case the material is partially available but not fully available to the subject for conscious consideration and reflection.

In Owen's case the material (the perception of the wine shop) is incidental to his current project until something happens which gives it significance for him. This conceptual relation between conscious project and significance is a key feature of existential phenomenology that draws attention to what is in the foreground by contrast with the background of experience. The mind clearly does have an economy which sometimes foregrounds and sometimes backgrounds a given percept or feeling.

Peter's flirtation is an altogether more complex tract of mental activity. It is, in some sense, motivated by his current feelings of rejection and loneliness, but it is not fully articulated or purposive. Here we could interpret what is going on in several ways. We could say that Peter's behaviour is caused by his emotional state but is not done for consciously articulated reasons in which his loneliness and feelings of rejection are foregrounded. Therefore his "flirtation" does not represent a conscious response to those facts about his life and is, to some extent, genuinely subconscious. We might suspect that Peter does not realize or conceptualise what he is doing because he does not want to face up to the emotional commitments and complications that could arise from his behaviour. However, even if we attribute some awareness of the reason for his flirtatious behaviour we cannot say that he has an intention of playing with the possibility of an affair and his behaviour does seem, in part at least, to be unconsciously driven.

In this case the conflict in motivation is, as it were, nearer the surface and our description of it should reflect its proximity to the reflectively endorsed activity of the ego. To capture these distinctions we need to refine the language of the mind such that we can contemplate the possibility that the causes of behaviour might fall into several categories. Some may be straightforwardly conscious; others conscious but temporarily backgrounded perhaps for reasons to do with conscious determinations and attitudes; others unconscious because conceptualised and then repressed; and yet others unconscious, unconceptualised, but causally effective. This last category might then be psychologically effective without any clear relation to its intentional content or influence behaviour in ways that reflect intentional content (as is posited by the Freudian dynamic unconscious).

To arrive at these distinctions we must picture both Owen and Peter as mature concept users. Each is able to form a clear conception of what he is doing when he turns his attention to it. In other cases this may not be so. That may be because the thinker concerned, while mature, is in an unfamiliar domain or because the thinker is immature and perhaps just learning the concepts needed to articulate what it is she is experiencing. Interacting with this competency variable is a motivational variable to do with the content that the thinker finds acceptable to bring to the forefront of her thought and experience. Thus a thinker may have diminished consciousness of what is affecting her *either* because she has not got the skills to attend to and understand what her experience contains *or*, despite having the skills she does not apply the concepts required to make the relevant features of the experience thematic. The second possibility can occur because of simple inattentiveness or because of a motivated deflection of the mind from performing the relevant mental acts (the dynamic possibility). The cases differ. In each of them the individual does not do the cognitive work to mould the critical clues and signals into a coherent conscious narrative of the current situation but this is explained in very different ways. The former possibility is just the naivete of childhood, innocence, or ignorance. It strengthens our general point about consciousness and conceptualisation and is well illustrated by the following story.

> A little girl called Lizzie who was characteristically active, inquisitive, and easily bored was seven when she visited the Louvre with her parents. She had gone ahead of them and seen all she wanted and was agitating to go while her parents were examining and appreciating the pictures. She rushed up to them

> from one of her many forays ahead and told them to hurry along. They said they had not yet seen the Mona Lisa. "Oh," she said, "I have. It's just a little brown picture with a whole lot of people around it; it's not all that good."

Her ignorance of the importance of the "Mona Lisa" through a lack of conceptual development in the relevant domain is typical of the disarming transparency and naivety of the mind of the child. We have discussed the development of noetic content in relation to shared actual world situations and this exemplifies that process. Owen and Peter are at the other end of the spectrum. Both have the cognitive equipment but do not use it to structure or articulate what they are experiencing until clarification of the intentional content is, in one way or another, forced upon them.

Owen's case is a simple matter of selection of foreground themes in consciousness on the basis of current plans and activities. Peter's is different in that he is actively suppressing certain content. This suggests that there might be forces that cause a person to act thus and so without entering into any actual train of reasoning. Or, to step nearer to ordinary conscious thought there might be facts (Peter's felt loneliness and rejection) that, in an inchoate way, motivate him, potentiate or hint at certain thoughts and fancies, or lurk in the shadows of the mind prompting a certain kind of behaviour, but are not explicitly reflected upon or incorporated into any action plan. This sort of analysis can be conducted without us having to posit a Freudian unconscious with determinate content but somehow sealed off from the processes of the ego or conscious self. Once we have loosened the grip of that dichotomy on our thinking about the mind we can move on to more problematic cases.

The more challenging and interesting problems for a theory of the unconscious are those that arise from an admixture of innocence or cognitive immaturity and emotional turmoil. In these situations the mind is deflected from a task it is barely able to perform. We will not explore in any depth the problems of child abuse where the mix of cognitive immaturity and emotional confusion are rife and sinister. We will, however, focus on just such an emotionally charged example to indicate some of the implications of our view for the treatment of unconscious mental content.

> Imagine the case of a child, Marie, whose parents are heading towards divorce. Both parents are emotionally disturbed by what is happening and the children, whom they love, get caught in the crossfire. The children do not really understand what is going on in a way they may later come to be capable of and they desperately want their family to be happy. They see the signs of anger, confusion, rejection, and desperation in their parents' behaviour and

> cannot make explicit the fact that the family is doomed. They hear inadvertent remarks like: "You kids are driving me insane!"; "You are always in the way creating trouble"; "I can't put up with you messy children any more"; and so on. It is natural for Marie to conclude that something awful is happening and that she and her siblings are partly responsible for it. The conceptualisation of what is happening here will be inchoate, poorly developed, confusing and frightening for the children because they have neither the experience, nor the conceptual sophistication, nor the emotional stability to be able to take cognisance of what is going on and come to a conscious, balanced assessment of the situation.

As a result of this unhappy and complex state of affairs a child like Marie may develop all sorts of feelings of guilt, betrayal, and anger at those who have caused her such pain, further guilt at feeling anger against her parents, pity for them and her siblings, a deep need to go on respecting them so as to have someone to look up to, and so on. How can she articulate these, reflect on them and give her mental life and particularly its emotional and moral aspects some stability or coherence? In many ways Marie cannot even name or conceptualise what she is being torn apart by and therefore does not really know what she is feeling.

If the therapeutic form that we have described as common to most psychodynamic approaches is applied in Marie's case many memories, thoughts and feelings will "emerge"; that is they will come into consciousness be named or given intentional content, and reflected upon. But the process of rehearsing these things and of thinking about them or learning to do so is bound to be painful and accompanied by a great deal of hesitation and emotional turmoil. We can see how this process and the psychic disturbances that it causes would give rise to the view that the requisite moments of mental life, past and present, are there in a reservoir, perhaps called unconscious memory, and the conscious part of self experiences conflict and resistance in bringing them to light. Our view suggests a less reified interpretation of the mental activity involved. On our view the person, who is distressed by such psychic forces is in need of some context within which a story can be articulated that does justice to the lived situation. Marie's normal social context is too fraught, the child's ego too fragile, and the situation too disturbing for her story to be clothed in its fully discursive garments. She has, in fact, to be enabled to do the work of weaving those garments despite the fact that the context that would normally impart the requisite discursive skills to her is causing her distress and disorientation. She needs a framework of conceptualisation in which to make sense of the experiences she has had but the normal framework — created by loving and supportive relationships with competent concept users — is, for Marie, falling apart. Therefore a new framework or context must be given her. This new framework must be sensitive so that she is given space in which to begin to express her fragmented narrative but also assured of her own place in that narrative. Such a framework is often not provided until the person, as a wounded or disturbed adult, enters therapy.

The therapist has to offer an interpretation or, we might say, an acceptable narrative of the problematic passages of the person's life. The patient or client has to accept some of these conceptualisations by using the offered discourse as a way of developing her own narrative into one that she can live. In living and conceptualizing or making contentful the narrative of her formation as a disturbed person, the client becomes conscious of her self and her wounds. The content that emerges is not, on our account, already formed and waiting to be recovered but it is formed as it becomes conscious. This is not however a creation of oneself *ex nihilo*. Clearly the resulting account of a person's life is a joint narrative which has incorporated conceptual structures from the therapist and a series of impingements on the patient which have accumulated over time. This joint narrative fixes the content of the life by putting in discursive form poorly understood features of the experience of the patient.

Wittgenstein makes a telling point about the subtle interplay of discourse and content in a remembered life experience.

> William James, in order to shew that thought is possible without speech, quotes the recollection of a deaf-mute, Mr. Ballard, who wrote that in his early youth, even before he could speak, he had had thoughts about God and the world. -What can he have meant? — Ballard writes: "It was during those delightful rides, some two or three years before my initiation into the rudiments of written language, that I began to ask myself the question: how came the world into being?" — Are you sure — one would like to ask — that this is the correct translation of your wordless thought into words? (1989: p. 342)

Whatever one's reaction to this case (there does seem to be a certain primitiveness about the idea of coming into being and the idea of the world as a whole), Wittgenstein's point is well taken. We cannot answer his question about the proper rendition of wordless thoughts with any clarity even in those cases like Owen's where a mature concept-user does not articulate a clear narrative about ambiguous behaviour. Therefore, where we are dealing with the kinds of things Freud and others refer to as repressed memories, the situation is much worse for all the reasons outlined. Just this kind of ambiguous and chameleon-like mental activity is highly sensitive to the norms of discourse prevailing in the context where it is being articulated and to the motives and subjective orientations of the potential narrator. It is, characteristically, indeterminate in its intentional content, although nonetheless potent in its psychic effects until it is shaped, and therefore moderated, by the discursive or conceptual activity that happens when the business of conceptualizing or becoming conscious of the content of one's life experiences is undertaken with some application and earnestness. This view is, in fact, very close to that of Lacan who argues that the subject must give form to the contents of the unconscious which represent gaps or unsignified silences in one's life history.

Hallucinations and delusions

The dynamic unconscious faces us with the possibility that some of the contents of the psyche that evade conscious scrutiny do so for reasons potentially inaccessible to the subject. In terms of Jaspers' distinction between meaningful and causal connections, these influences are meaningful (and to some extent causal because of their meaning) but the idea of psychotic content raises the possibility that some content may evade the organising work of the ego and its norms because it is disordered by meaningless forces. We can posit that the bizarre connections evident in psychotic thought occur in exactly the way that Freud thought all rational conscious thought was formed, by putting a rational gloss on material operating according to the primary process. In the case of psychosis we must consider that some of the content dominating the mind might be totally epiphenomenal in relation to a meaningless turmoil that has the mind in its grip. However in psychosis the thought content is accepted as veridical by the subject despite the fact that it would not stand up to normal rational scrutiny. The psychotic is unable to distinguish reliably between trains of thought that are irrational and illusory and those trains that reveal the course and meaning of actual events in the world. The result of this confusion is, of course, fear and insecurity, the feeling that life has become generally unpredictable and threatening, and the conviction that one's integrity as a living thinking being is in jeopardy. But it is wrong to reify this psychotic content as having the same qualitative nature as normal waking or non-psychotic experience.

Irrational content of the type found in psychosis is subject to the same sceptical doubts as the supposed intentional contents of the dynamic unconscious. There is, in such content, a lack of the normal going over by, or being subject to, the reflective self scrutiny that we all, to a greater or lesser extent exercise in relation to our lived experience. This might be expected to give rise to those features characteristic of psychotic thought.

Connections reminiscent of the primary process are also characteristic of psychotic thought. Clang associations, imagistic thinking, a failure to assess the reasonableness of the connections being accepted, and emotively loaded self-references are all in evidence and can lead the subject in directions that seem fantastical and completely at odds with a realistic appraisal of his or her situation.

There are other ways in which the cognitive problems of psychosis are evident. Impulsivity is to be expected whenever reason does not intervene to plan and control action according to well-integrated action structures. In psychosis this shows itself as impulsivity of thought, evidenced by pressure of thought and speech, and also impulsive extravagant and unrealistic actions.

Promiscuous associations and an exaggerated readiness to form associations, particularly evident in semantic priming tasks, are also characteristic and seem to indicate a cognitive network that is working overtime (or in turbo-drive mode) in an indiscriminate way.

Hallucinations and delusions are both varieties of abnormal consciousness that arise in this rather frenetic cognitive milieu; the first involves disordered perception and the second disordered belief formation both of which indicate defects of basic skills in the operation of the mind. The present analysis of consciousness reveals that such defects are only likely to occur where there are quite fundamental problems of intentionality and the normal techniques of formation of rule-governed conceptual content. This is, in fact, what is observed in clinical practice where hallucinations and delusions are major criteria for the diagnosis of psychoses, the more serious types of mental disorder. More importantly we will show that even in these highly abnormal mental phenomena the intentionality of consciousness is central in understanding their contents and mental roles.

Hallucination: False perception

It is a common theme in phenomenological analyses of the mind and conscious experience that there is a difference in mode of consciousness between imagination and perception. This difference in mode affects deeply the gestalt of a conscious event such that the thinker is not likely to make a mistake on the basic issue as to whether a particular presentation is a percept or an imaginary content. On our present account such a judgment would touch on the absolutely basic skill of convergence in judgments about "objectivity" or 'intersubjective reality'. Because this skill is so basic, its disruption would plausibly constitute a fundamental threat to the conscious thinker and the order discernible in his mental world. Added to this basic feature distinguishing perception from imagination there are other features of the imaginary conscious experience which distinguish it from the perceptual experience. Consider, for instance, the following:

Imagine a soldier walking towards you.

Now, ask yourself what colour his eyes were. Often one cannot answer such a question and then one of two things happens; either we realize that we now have to do a bit more creative mental work or we pronounce the question unanswerable. In either event if we were restricted to commenting on our original imagined soldier we would be caught in the following trap.

Q. You imagined a soldier? A. yes
Q. He had eyes? A. yes
Q. He was your creation? A. yes
Q. Therefore you created his eyes? A. Yes
Q. All eyes are coloured? A. Yes
Q. Therefore you must know what colour they were.

This brings out the fundamental phenomenological difference posed by the fact that an imagined intentional object is a mental creation and reminds us that we are normally in no doubt about that fact (so that a theory which presents us with identical images but different causal histories as the proper account of imagination and perception must be wrong). We can, of course, be mistaken about the intentional objects of consciousness when we are in an altered state of consciousness such as dreaming but that should not distract us from the main point.

This realisation brings us face to face with the real situation in hallucinatory disorders of thought. They are indicators that a basic feature of our nature as thinkers — Kant's *sensus communis* — is deeply disturbed in psychosis (Spitzer 1990). So basic is this feature to our nature as thinkers that hallucinations are symptoms of a profound disorder. This is evident both to the patient and to others although at times the disturbance of the conscious self is such that the patient may temporarily lose sight of the fact that the disorder exists. What is more, this disorder, we could say, is existence threatening in as much as our essential nature is to be conscious mental subjects. The very phenomenon of hallucinatory experience is therefore only mistakenly thought to be of use in supporting the argument in many standard empiricist accounts that there are contents of experience qualitatively the same in hallucination, imagination, and normal perception. Nothing, as those of us who have dealt with hallucination know, could be further from the truth. The disruption of conscious mental life that produces psychotic hallucinations strikes at the essence of oneself and one's integrity as a thinker.

Delusion: False belief

In DSM IIIR, a delusion is defined as

> A false personal belief based on incorrect inference about external reality and firmly sustained in spite of what almost everyone else believes and in spite of … obvious proof or evidence to the contrary. (APA, 1980)

There are also delusions involving an "extreme value judgment" which must be "so extreme as to defy credibility" and the delusions might be evident in trains of thought in which the *sensus communis* is entirely lacking such as the following thought.

> I looked at my son in bed and thought, 'How beautiful you are; how sad it will be for you to grow and change.' So I decided to put the pillow over his face so he would never wake up and would stay that way forever.

Delusions are not just false beliefs; some might be true, for instance Gerhardt's delusion that his wife hates him. What is more, the example above shows that delusional thinking is not just irrational in a narrow logical sense. Still other delusions are impossible to assess as being either true or false. If a patient believes that God is right now sitting in judgment on him for his past deeds then it is crass to categorize this as simply false because "religious beliefs are neither true nor false, at least in the scientific meaning of the words"(Spitzer, 1990). But the problems do not stop with delusions in psychotic patients not necessarily being false beliefs and out of touch with real life events, so that the individuals concerned are locked into a psychotic world. For instance, delusions are not completely insulated from real life because some patients are influenced by evidence that counts against their delusions. However, the normal constraints on evidential support and confirmation do not seem to apply and the patient may well find some pseudo-rational explanation for conflicts between their beliefs and presented evidence. Thus, even though a delusional belief is sensitive in an odd way to presented conflicting evidence it is not susceptible to the reality testing that a rational and mature subject would normally impose.

In fact delusions show all the characteristics of primary process thinking and their emotive loading is further support for that conceptualisation. When we survey delusions, hallucinations, and disorders of thought form, psychotic thought shows the hallmarks of a cognitive system which has abandoned its normative commitments in relation of belief and knowledge, which is, in short, no longer able to exercise the skills needed to obey the rules governing intentional content and "get it right" when called to form beliefs about the real world.

An extreme manifestation of this problem is the ability of deluded patients to believe in impossible things such as "existing in the past as well as the present ... having inside one's body something larger than oneself (e.g. a nuclear power station); being in two places at one time" and so on. Such patients may even give reasons for their beliefs but, in so doing, they obey none of the canons of common-sense scrutiny of beliefs and inference. The system of intentional contents which has an order tailored to the way things happen in the real world and the real possibilities and probabilities affecting objects and their properties has gone awry in psychotic thought and therefore the determination of the actual content of the states involved is insecure. And here the patient is no better placed than the observer in trying to make sense out of what is happening to him (bring *noetic* order to the *hyle* of experience).

As we found with hallucination, delusional thought should alert us to a deep disorder in the mind. We are essentially members of a kingdom of rational and discursive beings. Our skills of thought are rooted in communication and convergence in judgements and our trains of thought reflect the fundamental role of those skills in organising our experience of and action in the world. Therefore delusion is not just false belief nor is it an immoderate evaluation of a situation, it is a symptomatic of an intentional system in deep disarray. That disarray is manifest in subtle and manifold ways that are reflected in the form and content of thought. The most characteristic malfunction in thought is the tendency to take a "Cartesian attitude" in which the contents of mind are immediately and incorrigibly known. In this state judgments that would normally be subject to established epistemic or evaluative procedures are not subjected to them (Spitzer 1990: p. 389). The intentionality of consciousness, focusing as it does on the relation between the mind and what is outside the mind, emphasizes the other-involving or external nature of the relevant evaluative procedures.

One suspects that common delusions such as those of control (in which the person believes that their thoughts are being controlled by some external agency), thought insertion (where the subject thinks that thoughts are being inserted into his train of thought), or broadcast thought (where the person believes that everybody knows what she is thinking) are, in fact, suspicions which commonsense dismisses as absurd but which, in the insane patient have become disengaged from the normal processes of establishing epistemic warrants. It is instructive that many delusory systems, such as those already mentioned (involving thought insertion, thought broadcast, possession of the mind and will by another and so on) revolve around a failure or major disruption of the person's integrity as a mental agent distinct from and yet existing among others. Thus, in psychotic thinking, the nature of the self as a subject of externally directed or intentional thought and action that is integrated and under one's own control is cast in doubt.

When we consider the nature of belief formation to be an active set of techniques based on rule-governed use of concepts, then it is clear that the psychiatrically disordered patient has, in greater or lesser measure, a defect of the validating, balancing, self-reflective skills which normally control our perception, conceptualisation, evaluations of experience, inferences, and modification of behaviour. Each of these involves the application and manipulation of concepts, an intentional activity crucially linked to the formative role played by others in the development of a thinker. The fact that the essence of existence is, for a human being, to be a being among others makes such a disruption deeply threatening. It's threat is immediately understandable on the basis of our claim that mental life rests on a foundation in which we master the skills of judgement that others use in relation to the objects around us. The psychotic is therefore both unskilled and adrift in a strange sea. It is no wonder that she experiences existential threat.

Irrationality: Bad faith, self deception

In each of these phenomena, consciousness loses its rational connectedness to the extent that the subject does not seem fully conscious of his own desires and intentions and acts in irrational ways. We have seen this to some extent in the case of Peter who did not articulate and therefore could neither reflect upon nor reason about what he was implicitly doing in relation to his wife and Penny. The relation between consciousness and intentional content is even clearer in the following case.

> Anne knows that Jeremy has a reputation for promiscuity and the seduction of relatively inexperienced young women. She is herself inexperienced but persuades herself that she is too sensible to be taken in by Jeremy and believes that the time he is spending with her is because of their shared academic interests. She persists in this belief even when some of their "study evenings" are extended to include a bite to eat and a glass of wine. One thing leads to another and Anne, having succumbed to Jeremy's charm firmly maintains that her affair with him is different from other affairs he has had because he has told her that he has never met anyone like her. Some months later she finds him at a mutual woman friend's house one morning and breaks up with him. She then tells her friends that she cannot believe that she was so taken in.

As one considers this narrative it follows a predictable course, a fact that was quite plausibly realised by Anne's friends much before it was realised by Anne herself. It therefore shares features with Peter's narrative above. Again we need to remind ourselves that the formation of the integrated narrative that is our consciously experienced life is a project in which we must exercise considerable discursive skills. Church discusses irrationality in terms of presentations which are subject to the reflective scrutiny of the rational mind and those which are not (Church 1987). The former are the object of normal epistemic and self reflective skills and the latter are not and can therefore give rise to irrational thought and action. On our account this tends to reify the contents of the unconscious to the point where they look too similar to conscious thoughts and attitudes. We believe there is room for the idea that the stirrings and inclinations in the mind are not fully and clearly formed until the concept using subject has taken them in hand and there is a conscious story to be told.

In the case of Anne and Peter we see self deception, bad faith, and weakness of the will all operating. The self-deception consists in the fact that neither Anne nor Peter clearly articulates what is going on in the face of evidence that most people would take as indicating certain conclusions. Peter should see that his behaviour comprises a course of action which most people would take as the initial moves in "*une affaire d'amour*" but he himself does not conceptualise nor reflect upon this interpretation of his behaviour. Anne is similar, she does not correctly deploy concepts of seduction and promiscuity, in the way required to gain a clear view of what is going on and ends up in an affair that everybody else saw coming long before she did. She cannot claim that Jeremy misled her and she cannot claim that she knew nothing of his characteristic conduct with the opposite sex. She is not ignorant or deceived in the normal sense but she has deceived herself and not faced up to the obvious implications of his character and their liaison. The explanation can only be that she has not brought the skills of reflective scrutiny and common knowledge (used by all her friends) into proper engagement with he current experience.

In these cases the skills of reflective construction of a self narrative that are disordered in psychosis are not used for other reasons to do with unspoken wishes, fancies, and feelings. The result is a course of events clear to all but the main protagonist. We do not need to appeal to a dark unconscious to explain this but only to the fact that we vary in our discursive skills of self construction and in our motivation to use them to full advantage. The same conception of the conscious self, as an intentional project, in both senses of the term intentional, can help us to understand the splitting of the self.

Splitting the self

Multiple personality[18] is the subject of a great deal of controversy in the current literature. It is a condition in which a person claims to have experiences as several distinct personalities each of which have their own memories, emotions and beliefs but each of which is discontinuous with the others. Each of these personalities usually has its own name and manifests a different kind of character to the others in the set. The mental acts of a given personality may or may not be accessible to other personalities and the episodic memories of the person are only accessible to some of the personalities. Typically the syndrome arises in a child who has been abused and, in most cases, at least one

18. Or more accurately "Dissociative Identity Disorder", as it is defined in DSM-IV.

of the personalities is immature or arrested at some stage of childhood. The most famous case is probably that of Eve who had an upright, staid and modest persona as Eve White, a playful, promiscuous and impulsive persona as Eve Black and a third somewhat emotionally barren persona as Jane. She finally achieved a more integrated personality in which the various sides of her were in some kind of balance or harmony and began a life course in which he various inadequacies as Eve White were left behind her. The DSM-IV casebook includes the following example of Dissociative Identity Disorder.

> Mary Kendall is a 35-year-old social worker who was referred to a psychiatrist for treatment of chronic pain caused by a reflex sympathetic dystrophy in her right forearm and hand. She had a complex medical history that included asthma, migraine headaches, diabetes melitis, and obesity. She was found to be highly hypnotisable, and quickly learned to control her pain with self-hypnosis.
>
> Mary was quite competent in her work, but had a rather arid personal life. She had been married briefly and divorced 10 years earlier, and she had little interest in remarrying. She spent most of her free time volunteering in a hospice.
>
> As a thorough psychiatric evaluation continued, she reported the strange observation that on many occasions when she returned home from work the gas tank of her car was nearly full, yet when she got into the car to go to work the next day, it was half empty. She began to keep track of the odometer, and discovered that on many nights 50 to 100 miles would be put on the car overnight, although she had no memory of driving it anywhere. Further questioning revealed that she had gaps in her memory for large parts of her childhood.
>
> Because of the large gaps in her memory, the physician suspected a dissociative disorder, but it was only after several months of hypnotic treatment for pain control that the explanation for the lost time emerged. During a hypnotic induction, the physician again asked about the lost time. Suddenly a different voice responded, "It's about time you knew about me." The (alter) personality with a slightly different name, Marian, now spoke and described the drives she took at night, which were retreats to the nearby hills and seashore to "work out problems." As the psychiatrist got to know Marian over time, it was apparent that she was as abrupt and hostile as Mary was compliant and concerned about others. Marian considered Mary to be rather pathetic and far too interested in pleasing, and said that "worrying about anyone but yourself is a waste of time."
>
> In the course of therapy, some six other personalities emerged, roughly organised along the lines of a dependent/aggressive continuum. Considerable

> tension and disagreement emerged among these personalities, each of which was rather two-dimensional. Competition for control of time "out" was frequent, and Marian would provoke situations that frightened the others, including one who identified herself as a 6-year-old child. The subjective experience of distinctness among some of the personality states was underscored when a rather hostile alter personality made a suicide threat. The therapist insisted on discussing this with other personalities, and she objected that to do so would be a "violation of doctor-patient confidentiality."
>
> The memories that emerged with these dissociated personalities included recollections of physical and sexual abuse at the hands of her father and others, and considerable guilt about not having protected other children in the family from such abuse. Mary recalled her mother as being infrequently abusive, but quite dependent, and forcing Mary to cook and clean from a very early age.
>
> After 4 years of psychotherapy, Mary gradually integrated portions of these personality states. Two similar personalities merged, although she remained partially dissociated. The personality states were aware of one another, and continued to "fight" with each other periodically. (Spitzer 1994: p. 57)

In our view Mary's personalities could be produced by the poor articulation of disturbing memories and conflicted childhood roles. In a situation of this type the child fragments their personality in the attempt to prevent emotional and attitudinal chaos. The person who undergoes the dissociative change is, according to this theory, led to select from their lived experience those events, features of relationships, and attitudes which can be integrated into the conscious auto-biographical narrative without the threat of overwhelming emotional disruption. The resulting disturbance of self is akin to that achieved when a normal person adopts different roles suited to different situations but this is magnified far beyond anything that could occur as a conscious adaptive strategy. The person comes to look like a succession of selves each accommodating some psychic material that, with the co-conscious material, can form a livable package. The work of integration and resolution of conflicting tendencies and memories cannot be done and so the telling of different stories becomes the only way to serve the competing drives towards completeness of autobiography and harmony of mental life.

Again the discursive and intentional skills required to construct a self-narrative come to the fore and again we see that this is not an automatic given of living as an embodied human subject but rather a task which the subject can do more or less well. The dissociative turn as a move to compensate for the inability to do the integrating autobiographical task is a desperate measure and clearly not taken by all those who experience abuse and disconcerting psychic distress. For those who do take this turn, the resulting manifestations are both dramatic and puzzling. Once we see the creation of an integrated conscious self as an achievement or a project, then the formation of more than one stream of experience by a person struggling to come to grips with the contradictions in their life is understandable.

The idea of selfhood or identity being a narrative formed within frameworks is useful when trying to unpack the phenomenology of some mental disorders. But it may mean that some of the more dramatic "cases" have to be judged in the light of the context in which they arise. Perhaps with the psychotherapist's help Mary came to develop different personalities to cope with her fragmented memories. If we assume that Mary's multiple personalities are produced in the process of psychotherapy then an analysis of a self constructed via narratives in accordance with frameworks provides a useful phenomenological approach. Presumably as a result of trauma during childhood, Mary's memories have become dissociated. Sexual abuse as a child presents difficult and contradictory messages for the child to resolve. Mary was sexually abused by her father and would have realised that what happened to her was seriously wrong, yet at the same time would experience the trust and love that children have for their parents. The difficulty in resolving these two experiences may have caused Mary's memories to become fragmented or dissociated. The dissociation of Mary's memories may therefore be a response to the difficulty of integrating these conflicting messages into a coherent narrative. During the process of psychotherapy it may be that Mary could no longer fail to acknowledge the troubling aspects of her past.

Mary's personalities were organised along an aggressive passive continuum. A narrative structure is the means by which a self can become integrated. If the self is a narrative structure then different selves will have different narrative structures. A self (or personality) at the aggressive end of the continuum may be able to construct a meaningful narrative from the memories which had previously been dissociated or fragmented. This strategy may have enabled Mary to still disown the unpleasant aspects of her past, when the memories could no longer be ignored.

This explanation suggests that the development of Mary's personalities is an adaptive strategy of some sort. It is important to realise that the ability to integrate our past experiences into a single narrative is an important aspect of what we ordinarily consider to be normal human development. Furthermore, from the case as presented, Mary's personalities are not existing in a state of harmony. During psychotherapy Mary's mental life was one of constant turmoil and competition. The state that Mary is in when she experiences multiple personalities is not one which we would wish upon any person. For Mary's future well-being it seems imperative that she can reconstruct a personal narrative or sense of self that incorporates her past experiences.

Conclusion

The anomalies of consciousness are varied and include phenomena like moods, the unconscious mind, psychosis, and irrationality. In each of these phenomena the intentional contents characteristic of conscious mental acts do not seem to be able unproblematically to be ascribed to the person concerned. In the case of moods this is because the intentional content seems incidental to the pervading alteration in the affective orientation of the mind. We have argued that even though this is true the intentional content that is affected by the mood is what qualifies it as a mood or mental state rather than a merely bodily state. In the other cases the straightforward intentional attributions fail because of failures in the mind with respect to the implications and connectedness of the contents in question. We have argued that these are best explained if we focus on the intentional, or object-directed, skills which normally organise conscious mental acts and bring to the foreground the conditions which, in each case, obstruct the work of the thinker in bringing those skills to bear on the contents of the mind. Therefore our analysis of these states confirms the connection between consciousness and intentionality that we have defended from the outset.

Consciousness and intentionality
Some conclusions

We have explored at some length the relationship between consciousness and intentionality in the phenomenological sense according to which a state is intentional if it is about a state of affairs beyond itself or is directed upon something other than itself. We have noted that consciousness is a state of readiness made up of many contributing mental acts in which the subject is conscious of this or that in the environment or within himself. We have also noted the use of the term intentional in the psychological literature to refer to purposive activity and argued that our purposes are typically framed in terms of what we hope to achieve in the world so that there is a prima facie relationship between intentional contents in the phenomenological sense and purposes. We have then asked about the constitution of the object or objects that form the contents of a conscious thought.

The contents of a thought are not objects as physical things but they are closely related to objects and features of the world as conceptualised by the subject. When I am conscious, say of a trout in a stream I am conscious of it as something, perhaps a shadow in the water, perhaps a trick of the light or perhaps a trout. Each of these specifications yields a different thought but they may all be directed at the same object — the trout in the stream. Therefore we can say that the relation between consciousness and the world goes via content articulated by concepts. But the fact that what we see is captured by the concepts we apply to the things we encounter should not fool us into thinking that there is a mental object that we see and that therefore the mind is only indirectly related to the world. The mind is directly related to the world but its mode of relating to the world is by using concepts to try and put a certain form on what it comes in contact with.

Concepts are governed by rules. When I think of something as green or square or having a romantic quality there are right and wrong ways of using those concepts. My understanding of the contents involved is determined by how well I have mastered the rules. The rules tell me what kinds of conditions warrant my use of a given concept and how to connect that concept with others that I might use. For instance, if I think that a thing has romantic properties then it leads to the inference that it stirs my emotions or engages me with the sense of wonder I feel in the presence of unspoilt nature rather than making me think of something highly ordered and formally structured. I could apply the term romantic to a sunset or a symphony but not to a ledger book or the specifications of a blast furnace (although the human mind is both flexible and idiosyncratic despite making use of common rules and somebody could conceivably take delight in a well ordered set of figures or the idea of raw power in a blast furnace). The rules governing concepts are the scaffolding on which we build our thoughts just as the rules of chess are the scaffolding on which we build strategies. They are informal rules that enable a subject to do things in thought and action on the basis of mastering the structure that articulates our adaptive skills.

We have also argued that the concepts we use are related to significant terms in a thinker's natural language. There is, we argue a two way relationship between thought and language such that our acts of engaging with the things around us are articulated by the semantics of the language we are immersed in from birth. This is to be expected because we are a species who has a large number of tricks to help us adapt to the world and these tricks are conveyed by language. Those tricks are the ways of thinking of things that the mind is constantly using to explore the significance of what is around it. Thus consciousness and language go hand in hand and by adult life many of our ways of thinking of things have been shaped by the rules that others teach us through the use of language.

Consciousness engages with objects and their properties. We have noted that the objects of thought are conceptually specified by means of an interaction between the cognitive or conceptual system and the world. This interaction is articulated by concepts but when those concepts yield conceptions of objects it is important that the conceptions that are formed track the objects concerned. The idea of tracking is related to visual tracking but is a much broader concept in that to track an object or individual in the normal course of life in this world you need more than perception. Think, for instance of a person you meet today and then again in two days time. You must recognise and re-identify that person and, if you are uncertain if it is the same person you may ask many questions. Do they strike me as being the same? Could the person I met two days ago show up here today given the other things I know about them? Is this person dressed in the way I might expect the person I met to dress? Is this person in a setting that I would expect to find them in? The list could go on.

To consciously register an object and then track that object we use a great number of conceptual skills but in the end those skills must serve the same purpose, to allow us to identify and reidentify the objects we encounter so as to relate our activity successfully to those objects. Thus the object itself is an essential part of the content of our thought however we understand our relation to it. Again it is important not to interpose a mental item, the idea of an object, between the mind and the world.

Human action is the target of psychological explanation and it is structured by mental content. We are always describing and explaining what people do by using psychological concepts as in "he was trying to open the door", "she thought she had put her glasses down on the table and was looking for them", "he was afraid of the dog and ran away", "he is trying not to show that he is deeply hurt", "he is walking out of the room" and so on. Each of these conveys a sense of what the person intends to do in relation to the environment. Each requires us to see the bodily movements in terms of some project or purpose that the agent is pursuing. When we describe things in this way we try and capture the identity structure or concepts (⟨door⟩, ⟨glasses⟩, ⟨looking⟩, ⟨hurt⟩, ⟨out⟩, and so on) that yield an understanding of the action as an action under some kind of conscious direction. What is more we can best appreciate the morphology of a person's behaviour if we track in detail what they are conscious of at a given point in time (he is driving the car but just at the moment he is trying to make out what the road sign says so he is not driving very well because his attention is distracted). Again conscious content is the key to understanding.

Our concepts are highly subject to the social structures and norms that surround us. The way we think of things, the patterns we see in events, the kinds of properties that we learn to detect in our conscious dealings with the world are all influenced by our socio-cultural milieu. Our consciousness of ourselves as beings of a certain type with certain goals that ought to be pursued and projects that ought to be carried out is highly sensitive to these facts. We could express this by saying that the moral structure of the meanings that exist in our culture has an important influence on us but it would be wrong to think of that according to any narrow or stereotyped conception of morality.

The meanings of my actions emerges from and affects the kind of person I am and as a result I take on a certain identity which makes me unique. Although my identity is constrained by the culture in which I live it is not determined by that culture and it can be as individual as I make it.

Our brain gets its microprocessing shape from our semantic environment. The brain develops in its processing structure throughout life and is affected by the ways in which it is presented with information. We have argued that the way information reaches consciousness is intimately tied to the way in which a socio-cultural context creates and articulates meaning and the rules that determine meanings. The brain deals with the world in terms of content and the meanings that surround us shape that content and therefore the brain reflects those meanings. Thus it is wrong to say that we can understand what the brain does in terms of a physical or causal transaction between the brain and world. The forms that are imposed on the information resulting from that physical transaction are the basis of conscious contents. The arguments we have enunciated make it clear that the way we detect and respond to objects and features in the environment is a function of a reality that can only be understood by appeal to levels of explanation other than biological explanation. We can see this suprabiological and supraindividual explanation operating when we try to understand the events that occur in the brain in terms of the way they explain our actions, the way we construct categories to group the items appearing in our experience, and the way we as organisms evolve adaptive strategies to help us deal with the world around us. Without appreciating the influence of concept and the groupings of stimuli that result from our social stereotypes and categories we cannot begin to understand the differences between the adaptive strategies used by different human brains (say an English brain, versus a Japanese brain, versus a !kung brain) and without understanding that we cannot understand the actions of the respective bodies in which those brains are housed because brain and body are inseparable.

Anomalies of consciousness arise when the intentional relationship is not working well. An anomaly peculiar to the intentional view of consciousness is apparently contentless moods but we have analysed these in terms of their essential relation to psychic contents in order to count as moods and the possibility that the mood state itself, or oneself as a being in that mood state might become an object for consciousness. We have also examined hallucinations and other phenomena where there is a disordered state of consciousness and shown that in these something goes badly wrong with the intentional relations between the subject and the world.

The unconscious is a challenge to those who believe that intentional content and consciousness go hand-in-hand and we have devoted some attention to the reasons why we believe in unconscious contents and the certainty with which they can be discerned in oneself or others. There is a great deal of room for scepticism about the view that we can have determinate unconscious contents and many of the phenomena appealed to as evidence do not straightforwardly support that view and therefore do not conclusively undermine our thesis.

Animals are conscious but the contents of their conscious experience are difficult to assess. Animal consciousness displays varying levels of sophistication of intentional content and it emerges that the more secure we are in our attributions of intentional content the more certain we are that the animal is conscious rather than merely displaying a more primitive set of abilities to detect and respond to things in its environment.

We take ourselves to have made a strong case for Brentano's claim that consciousness and intentionality are internally or conceptually linked to one another. We have tested this thesis in a number of areas where we are philosophically interested in consciousness and its contents and found that the thesis is vindicated and assists in the philosophical task of elucidating the mind and its essential features. Consciousness as an intentional phenomenon is central to the phenomenological project but not exclusive to it and the modes of argumentation in the present account have as much in common with analytic or Anglo-American philosophy as with the continental tradition. We believe that it is a healthy sign that the two relatively distinct traditions can be melded in a fruitful way and have a great deal of respect for the deliverances of both.

Glossary

Please note, this glossary is designed to aid the reader who is unsure about how we intend certain key terms to be understood. The definitions that we offer relate to the specific way these terms are used in *Consciousness and Intentionality*.

Cartesianism: the view that mental states are private, internal and therefore not accessible to other minds

complexes: the Vygotskian category for grouping objects in accordance with properties of the object but failing to utilise the conditions of application that are ordinarily expected for concept use

co-referentiality: referential opacity, the possibility that a thoughts or expressions may refer to one object while the thinker thinks they mean two distinct objects

hyle: pre-conceptual mental content

identity structure: the description that identifies an action as being of a certain kind

intentionality: the object directedness that is a characteristic of conscious states

internalist: a view that implies the meaning of expressions is given by private mental states.

intrapersonal: an internal organisation of the person, as opposed to interpersonal which means between persons.

modo oblique: an indirect or secondary intentional object of perception, thought or expression

modo recto: a direct or primary intentional object of perception, thought or expression

noema: the ideal mental content that mediates or makes a noesis of a specific kind with specific properties.

noemata: the plural of noema

noematic: pertaining to a noema or noemata

noesis: the process of being conscious

noeses: the plural of noesis, i.e. more than one process of conscious activity.

noetic: pertaining to noesis

normativity: the attribution of involving rules of correct use.

Noumena: things in themselves, objects outside of or independently of our conceptualisation of them, in Kant's sense

phenomenologist: one who attends in a methodical way to the description of experience as it presents in the first person.

physicalist: a view that or person who implies or states that human behaviour can be adequately explained using predicates derived from the natural sciences. As opposed to those who believe that such explanations can and should make reference to intentional predicates.

self consciousness: the mode of consciousness obtained when an individual's person is primary object of consciousness.

References

Adams, Douglas. 1991. *The Hitchhiker's Guide to the Galaxy*. London: Heinemann.
Armstrong, A. M. *The Nature of Mind and Other Essays*. Ithaca, NY: Cornell University Press, 1980.
American Psychiatric Association. 1980. *Diagnostic and Statistical Manual of Mental Disorders: DSM-III*. 3 ed. Washington, D.C.: American Psychiatric Association.
American Psychiatric Association. 1994. *Diagnostic and Statistical Manual of Mental Disorders*. 4 ed. Washington, D.C.: American Psychiatric Association.
Ayer, A. J. 1979. "Construction of our theory of the physical world." In *Philosophy As It Is*, edited by Honderich and Burnyeat. Middlesex: Penguin.
Bratman, M. 1996. "Planning and Temptation." In *Mind and Morals*, edited by L. May, M. Friedman and A. Clark. Cambridge: MIT press.
Brentano, Franz. 1966. *The True and the Evident*. Translated by Roderick Chisholm. Edited by Oskar Kraus. London: Routledge and Kegan Paul.
Brentano, Franz. 1995. *Psychology From an Empirical Standpoint*. Wiltshire: Routledge and Kegan Paul.
Brentano, Franz. [1874] 1981. *Sensory and Noetic Conscious: Psychology from an Empirical Standpoint III*. Translated by Magarete Schattle and Linda McAlister. Edited by Ted Honderich, *International Library of Philosophy and Scientific Method*. London: Routledge and Kegan Paul.
Bruner, J. 1985. "Vygotsky: a historical and conceptual perspective." In *Culture Communication and Cognition*, edited by J Wertsch. Cambridge: Cambridge University Press.
Butterworth, G. 1991. "What minds have in common is space: spatial mechanisms serving joint visual attention in infancy." *British Journal of Developmental Psychology* 9 (1991): 56–72.
Campbell, J. 1984. "The possession of concepts." *The Proceedings of the Aristotelian Society* 85.
Campbell, A., Charlesworth, M., Gillett, G., and Jones, G. 1997. *Medical Ethics*. Melbourne: Oxford University Press.
Carey, Susan. 1985. *Conceptual Change in Childhood*. Cambridge, Mass: MIT Press.
Carruthers, Peter. 1996. *Language, Thought and Consciousness: An Essay in Philosophical psychology*. Cambridge: Cambridge University Press.
Cheney, Dorothy L., and Seyfarth, Robert M. 1990. *How Monkeys See the World*. Chicago and London: University of Chicago Press.
Child, William. 1994. *Causality Interpretation and the Mind*. Oxford: Clarendon Press.
Church, J. 1987. "Reasonable irrationality." *Mind* 96 (1987): 354–366.
Cole, M. 1985. "The zone of proximal development: where culture and cognition create

each other." In *Culture, Communication and Cognition*, edited by J Wertsch. Cambridge: Cambridge University Press.

Davidson, Donald. 1980. *Essays on Actions and Events*. Oxford: Clarendon Press.

Davidson, Donald. 1984. "Thought and talk." In *Inquiries into Truth and Interpretation*. Oxford: Clarendon Press.

Davidson, Donald. 1985. "Rational animals." In *Actions and Events: Perspectives on the Philosophy of Donald Davidson*, edited by Ernest Le Pore and Brian McLaughlin. Oxford: Basil Blackwell.

Dennett, Daniel, ed. 1981. *Brainstorms: Philosophical Essays on Mind and Psychology*. Brighton: Harvester Press.

Dennett, Daniel C. 1984. *Elbow Room: The Varieties of Free Will Worth Wanting*. Oxford: New York: Clarendon Press.

Dennett, Daniel. 1987. *The Intentional Stance*. Cambridge, Mass: MIT Press.

Dennett, D. 1990. "True believers: the intentional strategy and why it works." In *Mind and Cognition: A Reader*, edited by Lycan, W. Oxford: Basil Blackwell.

Dennett, Daniel. 1991. *Consciousness Explained*. Auckland: Penguin Books.

Donaldson, M. 1979. *Children's Minds*. London: Fontana.

Donnellan, Keith, ed. 1977. *Reference and Definite Descriptions*, edited by Stephen Schwartz. London: Cornell University Press.

Dostoyevsky, Fyodor. 1971. *The Devils*: Penguin.

Dostoyevsky, Fyodor. 1981. *Crime and Punishment*. Toronto; New York: Bantam Books.

Dretske, Fred. 1995. *Naturalizing the Mind*. Cambridge, Massachusetts: Massachusetts Institute of Technology.

Dummett, Michael. 1981. *The Interpretation of Frege's Philosophy*. London: Duckworth.

Dupre, John. 1991. "Conversations with apes: reflections on the scientific study of language." In *Investigating Psychology: Sciences of the Mind After Wittgenstein*, edited by John Hyman. London: Routledge.

Edelman, Gerald. 1992. *Bright Air, Brilliant Fire: On the Matter of the Mind*. London: Allen Lane, The Penguin Press.

Evans, Gareth. 1982. *The Varieties of Reference*, edited by John McDowell. Oxford: Clarendon Press.

Fodor, Jerry. 1972. "Some reflections on L. S. Vygotsky's Thought and Language." *Cognition* 1.

Fodor, Jerry. 1987. *Psychosemantics*: MIT Press.

Fodor, Jerry. 1990. *A Theory of Content and Other Essays*. Cambridge: MIT.

Foucault, Michel. 1978. *The History of Sexuality*. Translated by Robert Hurley. New York: Pantheon.

Frege, Gottlob. 1977. *Logical Investigations*. Translated by P.T. Geach and R.H. Stoothoff. Oxford: Blackwell.

Friedman, Marilyn, and May, Larry, eds. 1996. *Mind and Morals: Essays on Cognitive Science and Ethics*. Cambridge, Mass: MIT Press.

Giddens, Anthony. 1993. *Sociology*. second ed. Cambridge: Polity Press.

Gillett, G. 1986. "Brain bisection and personal identity." *Mind* (1986).

Gillett. G. 1987. "Concepts, structures and meaning." *Inquiry* 30 (1987).

Gillett, G. 1988. "Learning to perceive." *Philosophical and Phenomenological Research*

XLVIII (1988): 601–19.

Gillett. G. 1991. "McGinn on ascriptions of content." *Inquiry* 34 (1991): 401–410.

Gillett, G. 1992. *Representation, Meaning and Thought*. Oxford: Clarendon.

Gillett, G. 1993. ""Ought" and well-being." *Inquiry* 36 (1993): p. 287–306.

Gillett, G. 1995. "Humpty Dumpty and the night of the triffids: Individualism and rule following." *Synthese* 105 (1995): 191–206.

Gillett, G. In press. "Dennett, Foucault and the memes." *Inquiry*.

Gillett, G. In press. "Wittgenstein and PVS." In *Wittgenstein and Bioethics*, edited by C. Elliott.

Grice, H.P. 1957. "Meaning." *Philosophical Review* 66: pp. 377–88.

Hacking, Ian. 1986. "Making up people." In *Reconstructing Individualism: Autonomy, Individuality and the Self in Western Thought*, edited by T C Heller, 222–236. Stanford: Stanford University Press.

Hacking, Ian. 1995. *Rewriting the Soul: Multiple Personality and the Sciences of Memory*. Princeton: Princeton University Press.

Haldane, J. 1989. "Brentano's problem." *Grazer Philosophische Studien* 35: 1–32.

Hammond, Howarth, and Keat. 1991. *Understanding Phenomenology*. Oxford: Blackwell.

Harré, Rom. 1983. *Personal Being*. Oxford: Blackwell.

Harré, Rom, and Gillett, Grant. 1994. *The Discursive Mind*. Thousand Oaks, Ca.: Sage.

Hume, D. [1739] 1969. *A Treatise of Human Nature*. Edited by Mossner. London: Penguin.

Husserl, Edmund. 1931. *Ideas: General Introduction to Pure Phenomenology*. Translated by Boyce Gibson: Unwin Brothers.

Husserl, Edmund. 1970. *Logical Investigations*. London: Routledge & Kegan Paul.

Husserl, Edmund. 1988. *Cartesian Meditations: An Introduction to Phenomenology*. Dordrecht; London: Kluwer Academic.

Jeffrey, Richard. 1985. "Animal Interpretation." In *Actions and Events: Perspectives on the Philosophy of Donald Davidson*, edited by Ernest Le Pore and Brian McLaughlin. Oxford: Basil Blackwell.

Jones, J. Garety, P. and Helmsley, D. 1987. "Measuring delusional experiences: a method and its application." *British Journal of Clinical Psychiatry* 26.

Kant, Immanuel. 1929. *Critique of Pure Reason*. Translated by Norman Kemp Smith. Hampshire: MacMillan Press Ltd.

Karmiloff-Smith, Annette. 1992. *Beyond Modularity: A Developmental Perspective on Cognitive Science*. Cambridge Massachusetts: MIT Press.

Keil, Frank C. 1989. *Concepts, Kinds and Cognitive Development*. Cambridge Massachusetts: MIT Press.

Kenny, Anthony. 1971. *Objects of Thought*. Oxford: Clarendon Press.

Kenny, Anthony. 1984. "Aquinas." In *Philosophy Through its Past*, edited by Ted Honderich. Harmondsworth: Penguin.

Kenny, Anthony. 1984. "Aquinas: Intentionality." In *Philosophy through its Past*, edited by T. Honderich. Harmondsworth: Penguin.

Kirchner, Wolfgang, and Dreller, Claudia. 1993. "Acoustical signals in the dance language of the giant honeybee, Apis Dorsata." *Behavioral Ecology and Sociobiology* 33, no. 2: 67–72.

Kripke, Saul. 1977. "Identity and necessity." In *Naming Necessity and Natural Kinds*, edited by Stephen Schwartz. London: Cornell University Press.

Kymlicka, Will. 1989. *Liberalism, Community and Culture*. New York: Oxford University Press.

Lakoff, George. 1987. *Women, Fire and Dangerous Things: What Categories Reveal About the Mind*. Chicago: University of Chicago Press.

Luria, A. 1973. *The Man with a Shattered World: A History of a Brain Wound*. London: Cape.

Luria. A. 1976. *Cognitive Development: Its Social and Cultural Foundations*. Cambridge Mass: Harvard University Press.

Macintyre, Alasdair. 1958. *The Unconscious: A Conceptual Analysis*. London: Routledge and Kegan Paul.

Marx, K. and Engels, F. 1969. *The German Ideology,* edited by C. J. Arthur. London: Collins.

Matsumoto, D. 1996. *Culture and Psychology*. Pacific Grove: Brooks/Cole.

McGinn, C. 1982. "Thought and object." In *Thought and Object: Essays on Intentionality*, edited by Woddfield. Oxford: Clarendon Press.

Millikan, R. 1991. "Perceptual content and the fregean myth." *Mind*.

Millikan, R. 1995. *White Queen Psychology and Other Essays for Alice*. Cambridge, Massachusetts: The MIT Press.

Nagel, T. 1971. "Brain bisection and the unity of consciousness." *Synthese* 22 (1971).

Nietzsche, Friedrich. 1967. *Thus spake Zarasthustra*. London, 1967.

Nola, Robert. 1994. "Post-Modernism, a French Cultural Chernobyl: Foucault on power/ knowledge." *Inquiry* 37: 3–43.

Parfit, Derek. 1984. *Reasons and Persons*. Oxford: Clarendon Press.

Parkin, A. 1996. *Explorations in Cognitive Neurospychology*. Oxford: Blackwell.

Peacocke, Chris. 1985. *Sense and Content*: Oxford University Press.

Peacocke, Chris. 1987. *Thoughts*. Oxford: Blackwell.

Pettit, Philip. 1993. *The Common Mind: An Essay on Psychology, Society, and Politics*. New York: Oxford University Press.

Pope, Paul VI. 1975. "Humanae Vitae." In *Philosophy and Sex*, edited by R. Baker and E. Elliston. New York: Prometheus Books.

Povinelli, D. 1996. "Chimpanzee theory of mind?: The long road to strong inference." In *Theories of Theories of Mind*, edited by Peter Carruthers and Peter Smith. New York: Cambridge University Press.

Premack, and Woodruff. 1978. "Does the chimpanzee have a theory of mind." *Behavioural and Brain Sciences* 4.

Putnam, Hilary. 1977. "Meaning and reference." In *Naming, Necessity and Natural Kinds*, edited by Stephen Schwartz. London: Cornell University Press.

Quinton, A. 1964. "The problem of perception." *Mind*: pp28–51.

Rangihau, John. 1992. "Being Maori" In *Te Ao Hurihuri,* edited by M. King. Auckland: Reed Books.

Reid, Thomas. 1983 [1785]. *Inquiry and Essays*, edited by R. Beanblossom and K. Lehrer. Indianapolis: Hackett.

Sajama, S., and Kampinnen, M. 1987. *A Historical Introduction to Phenomenology*. London: Croom Helm.

Salmon, W. 1993. "Scientific explanation and the causal structure of the world." In *Explanation*, edited by David Ruben. Oxford: Oxford University Press.

Sartre, J.P. 1948. *No Exit*. Translated by Stuart Gilbert. New York: Knopf.

Sartre, J.P. 1957. *Being and Nothingness: An Essay on Phenomenological Ontology*. Translated by Hazel E. Barnes. London: Methuen.

Sartre, J.P. 1968. *Search for a Method*. Translated by Hazel E. Barnes. New York: Vintage Books.

Sartre, J.P. 1976. *Critique of Dialectical Reason*. Translated by Alan Sheridan-Smith. London: NLB.

Scribner, S. 1979. "Modes of thinking and ways of speaking." In *New Directions in Discourse Processing*, edited by Freedle: Norwood: Able.

Searle, John. 1983. *Intentionality: An Essay in the Philosophy of Mind*. Cambridge: Cambridge University Press.

Seddon, G. 1972. "Logical possibility." *Mind* 31: 481–94.

Sherbourne, Donald. 1994. "Some reflections on Sartre's nothingness and Whitehead's perishing." *Review of Metaphysics* 48: 3–17.

Smith, Peter. 1996. "Language and the evolution of mind reading." In *Theories of Theories of Mind*, edited by Peter Carruthers and Peter Smith. Cambridge: Cambridge University Press.

Snowdon, Paul. 1981. "Perception, vision and causation." *Proceedings of the Aristotelian Society*.

Solomon, R. 1989. *From Hegel to Existentialism*. Oxford: Oxford University Press.

Sperry, R. 1979. "Brain bisection and the mechanisms of consciousness." In *The Brain and Conscious Behaviour*, edited by J.C.Eccles. New York: Springer.

Spitzer, M. 1990. "Kant on schizophrenia." In *Philosophy and Psychopathology,* edited by Spitzer and Maher. New York: Springer Verlag.

Spitzer, Robert L., Gibbon, Miriam, Skodol, Andrew E., Williams, Janet B. W., and First, Michael B. 1994. *DSM-IV Case Book: a Learning Companion to the Diagnostic an Statistical Manual of Mental Disorders*. Washington DC: American psychiatric press.

Strawson, P.F. 1959. *Individuals*. London: Methuen.

Strawson, P.F. 1966. *The Bounds of Sense*. London: Methuen.

Taylor, Charles. 1989. *Sources of the Self.* Cambridge: Cambridge University Press.

Teasdale, G., and Jennett, B. 1974. "Assessment of coma and impaired consciousness." *Lancet* 8, no. 2.

Trevarthen, C. 1979. "Communication and Cooperation in early Infancy: As Description of Primary Intersubjectivity." edited by M Bullowa: Cambridge University Press.

Vallacher, R. and Wegner, D. 1987. "What do people think they're doing? action identification and human behaviour." *American Psychological Association* 94, no. 1 (1987): 3–15.

von Frisch, F. , and M. Lindauer. 1965. "The language and orientation of the honey bee." In *Readings in Animal Behaviour*, edited by Thomas McGill. New York ; London: Holt, Rinehart and Winston.

Van Gulick, R. 1990. "Functionalism, information and content." In *Mind and Cognition,* edited by W.G.Lycan. Oxford: Blackwell.

Vygotsky, Lev. 1962. *Thought and Language*. Cambridge: MIT.

Vygotsky, Lev. 1978. *Mind in Society*. Translated by Michael Cole, Vera John-Steiner, Sylvia Scribner and Ellen Souberman. Cambridge, Massachusetts: Harvard University Press.

Walker, R. 1989. "Maori identity." In *Culture and Identity in New Zealand*, edited by Novitz D and B. Willmott. Christchurch: GP Books.

Walker, Alice. 1993. *Possessing the secret of Joy*. Auckland: Random House.

Weiskrantz, Lawrence. 1997. *Consciousness Lost and Found: A Neuropsychological Exploration*. Oxford: Oxford University Press.

Whiten, Andrew. 1996. "When does smart behaviour-reading become mind-reading?" In *Theories of Theories of Mind*, edited by Peter Carruthers and Peter Smith. Cambridge: Cambridge University.

Winch, Peter. 1958. *The Idea of a Social Science*. London: Routledge and Kegan Paul.

Wittgenstein, Ludwig. 1958. *The Blue and Brown Books*. Oxford: Basil Blackwell.

Wittgenstein, Ludwig. 1967. *Zettel*, edited by Anscombe and von Wright. Oxford: Blackwell.

Wittgenstein, Ludwig. 1969. *On Certainty*. Translated by D Paul, G Anscombe. Edited by G. Anscombe and G. von Wright. Oxford: Basil Blackwell.

Wittgenstein, Ludwig. 1974. *Philosophical Grammar*. Translated by A. Kenny. Oxford: Blackwells.

Wittgenstein, Ludwig. 1975. *Philosophical Remarks*. Oxford: Blackwell, 1975.

Wittgenstein, Ludwig. 1989. *Philosophical Investigations*. Translated by G. E. Anscombe. Worcester: Basil Blackwell.

Woodruff-Smith, David, and McIntyre, Ronald. 1982. *Husserl and Intentionality*. Dordrecht: Kluwer.

Index

In the series ADVANCES IN CONSCIOUSNESS RESEARCH (AiCR) the following titles have been published thus far or are scheduled for publication:

1. GLOBUS, Gordon G.: *The Postmodern Brain.* 1995.
2. ELLIS, Ralph D.: *Questioning Consciousness. The interplay of imagery, cognition, and emotion in the human brain.* 1995.
3. JIBU, Mari and Kunio YASUE: *Quantum Brain Dynamics and Consciousness. An introduction.* 1995.
4. HARDCASTLE, Valerie Gray: *Locating Consciousness.* 1995.
5. STUBENBERG, Leopold: *Consciousness and Qualia.* 1998.
6. GENNARO, Rocco J.: *Consciousness and Self-Consciousness. A defense of the higher-order thought theory of consciousness.* 1996.
7. MAC CORMAC, Earl and Maxim I. STAMENOV (eds): *Fractals of Brain, Fractals of Mind. In search of a symmetry bond.* 1996.
8. GROSSENBACHER, Peter G. (ed.): *Finding Consciousness in the Brain. A neurocognitive approach.* n.y.p.
9. Ó NUALLÁIN, Seán, Paul MC KEVITT and Eoghan MAC AOGÁIN (eds): *Two Sciences of Mind. Readings in cognitive science and consciousness.* 1997.
10. NEWTON, Natika: *Foundations of Understanding.* 1996.
11. PYLKKÖ, Pauli: *The Aconceptual Mind. Heideggerian themes in holistic naturalism.* 1998.
12. STAMENOV, Maxim I. (ed.): *Language Structure, Discourse and the Access to Consciousness.* 1997.
13. VELMANS, Max (ed.): *Investigating Phenomenal Consciousness. Methodologies and Maps.* 2000.
14. SHEETS-JOHNSTONE, Maxine: *The Primacy of Movement.* 1999.
15. CHALLIS, Bradford H. and Boris M. VELICHKOVSKY (eds.): *Stratification in Cognition and Consciousness.* 1999.
16. ELLIS, Ralph D. and Natika NEWTON (eds.): *The Caldron of Consciousness. Motivation, affect and self-organization – An anthology.* 2000.
17. HUTTO, Daniel D.: *The Presence of Mind.* 1999.
18. PALMER, Gary B. and Debra J. OCCHI (eds.): *Languages of Sentiment. Cultural constructions of emotional substrates.* 1999.
19. DAUTENHAHN, Kerstin (ed.): *Human Cognition and Social Agent Technology.* 2000.
20. KUNZENDORF, Robert G. and Benjamin WALLACE (eds.): *Individual Differences in Conscious Experience.* 2000.
21. HUTTO, Daniel D.: *Beyond Physicalism.* 2000.
22. ROSSETTI, Yves and Antti REVONSUO (eds.): *Beyond Dissociation. Interaction between dissociated implicit and explicit processing.* 2000.
23. ZAHAVI, Dan (ed.): *Exploring the Self. Philosophical and psychopathological perspectives on self-experience.* 2000.
24. ROVEE-COLLIER, Carolyn, Harlene HAYNE and Michael COLOMBO: *The Development of Implicit and Explicit Memory.* 2000.
25. BACHMANN, Talis: *Microgenetic Approach to the Conscious Mind.* 2000.
26. Ó NUALLÁIN, Seán (ed.): *Spatial Cognition. Selected papers from Mind III, Annual Conference of the Cognitive Science Society of Ireland, 1998.* 2000.

27. McMILLAN, John and Grant R. GILLETT: *Consciousness and Intentionality.* 2001.
28. ZACHAR, Peter: *Psychological Concepts and Biological Psychiatry. A philosophical analysis.* 2000.
29. VAN LOOCKE, Philip (ed.): *The Physical Nature of Consciousness.* n.y.p.
30. BROOK, Andrew and Richard C. DeVIDI (eds.): *Self-awareness and Self-reference.* n.y.p.
31. RAKOVER, Sam S. and Baruch CAHLON: *Face Recognition. Cognitive and computational processes.* n.y.p.